IET COMPUTING SERIES 46

Graphical Programming Using LabVIEW™

Other volumes in this series:

Graphical Programming Using LabVIEW^{TM}

Fundamentals and advanced techniques

Julio César Rodríguez-Quiñonez and Oscar Real-Moreno

The Institution of Engineering and Technology

Published by The Institution of Engineering and Technology, London, United Kingdom

The Institution of Engineering and Technology is registered as a Charity in England & Wales (no. 211014) and Scotland (no. SC038698).

The Institution of Engineering and Technology
Futures Place
Kings Way, Stevenage
Hertfordshire, SG1 2UA, United Kingdom

www.theiet.org

British Library Cataloguing in Publication Data
A catalogue record for this product is available from the British Library

ISBN 978-1-83953-460-7 (hardback)
ISBN 978-1-83953-461-4 (PDF)

Typeset in India by MPS Ltd
Printed in the UK by CPI Group (UK) Ltd, Croydon

To my wife Fernanda, my children Leonardo and Guillermo, and my parents José y Margarita, thank you for your support.
Julio C. Rodríguez-Quiñonez

To my parents Angelica and Oscar and to my siblings Priscila and Luis Angel.
Oscar Real-Moreno

The authors thank the Universidad Autónoma de Baja California, its affiliation institution, and CONACyT for their support.

Contents

About the authors

Julio César Rodríguez-Quiñonez is a professor/researcher in the Facultad de Ingeniería, Universidad Autónoma de Baja California, México. He is involved in the development of optical scanning prototype in the Applied Physics Department and a research leader in the development of a new stereo vision system prototype. His current research interests include automated metrology, stereo vision systems, control systems, robot navigation, and 3D laser scanners. He has edited 4 books and written over 30 journal papers, 35 conference papers, and several book chapters. He holds two patents on the dynamic triangulation method, and he has been a guest editor of *IEEE Sensors Journal, International Journal of Advanced Robotic Systems* and *Journal of Sensors*. He is a Senior Member of the IEEE. He holds a PhD from the Autonomous University of Baja California, Mexico.

Oscar Real-Moreno is teaching at the Technological University of San Luis Rio Colorado and studying to obtain his doctorate degree at the Facultad de Ingeniería, Universidad Autónoma de Baja California, México. His current research work is based on a new camera calibration method for active stereo vision systems by triangulation in real time and object detection. He received his Master of Engineering degree from the Autonomous University of Baja California, Mexico.

Introduction

LabVIEW^{TM} is a graphical programming language widely used in the industry for data acquisition, signal measurement, and automation tasks. Within the graphical programming languages, it is one of the best known and most complete for its number of functions and the hardware with which it can be connected. The most significant advantage of LabVIEW^{TM} is the speed with which programming solutions can be implemented once the development environment and programming logic are mastered. However, for programmers with experience in text programming languages, moving to a graphical programming language can bring some challenges such as mastery of data flow (the execution order of instructions) and concurrent programming. This book is intended to cover the learning of LabVIEW^{TM} from the basics to the implementation of sophisticated software solutions. This book starts with an explanation of the development environment, how to create simple programs using elementary functions (arithmetic and Boolean), and how to use debugging tools. New programmers need to read the first two chapters in detail, since the fundamentals are explained here. Data flow is how LabVIEW^{TM} runs and is a fundamental concept that needs to be mastered in order to use LabVIEW^{TM} properly. For programmers with experience in LabVIEW^{TM}, it is also recommended to read Chapter 1. Here are addressed concepts that will be used throughout the rest of the book and serve as a review for the concept of data flow, and the development environment. Chapter 2 is focused on code debugging techniques where the developer will learn methods that allow correcting unexpected behavior in the code.

The new developers who start in this programming language do so due to the speed with which sophisticated measurement, automation, or process control software can be developed; however, practice and dedication are required to reach this goal. Therefore, it is highly recommended to keep order in your studies, follow each chapter chronologically, and develop the examples presented in each chapter on your own.

In Chapter 3, the fundamental structures of LabVIEW^{TM} are explained, which are For loops, While loops, Cases, Sequences, and data feedback in loops using Shift Registers. In addition, this chapter introduces the concept of timing and ways of timing a VI. It is important for this chapter to study how data feedback occurs in loops since it is common for new developers to use local variables to send information from one iteration to another, which is a not recommended practice as it tends to cause race conditions. During the first four chapters, it will be seen that information flows between nodes using wires, including information that is sent between iterations, using wires and Shift Registers. The new developer (and experienced developers) must use wires for sending information whenever possible and keep this practice since the beginning of using LabVIEW^{TM} to generate good habits in this programming language. If you are not familiar with the concept of wires at this point, do not worry, keep it in mind as it is a concept that will be covered since Chapter 1.

In Chapter 4, the concept of modularity is introduced, which is analogous to functions in text-based programming language. LabVIEW^{TM} achieves modularity through SubVIs, and they are widely used to keep graphical code tidy (on the block diagram, which is where graphical code is developed).

In Chapter 5, arrays are introduced, a data type that handles collections of data of the same type, in addition, advanced configurations with structures and functions that allow optimizing the manipulation of arrays are presented. Reading this chapter is important for new and advanced developers because it explains features from structures and functions in LabVIEW^{TM} that allow efficient programming with arrays. In this chapter, the concept of local variables is introduced. Local variables will enable to send data without using wires; however, it is not recommended as it tends to cause race conditions, race conditions are a regular issue in concurrent programming that causes the loss of information, it is recommended to follow the recommendations of this chapter to avoid race conditions, additionally, in Chapter 15 are given approaches to avoid race conditions.

In Chapter 6, clusters are introduced, which is similar to structures that are handled in programming languages such as C++. Clusters are used in LabVIEW^{TM} to maintain the order in the block diagram, and reduce the number of connectors in a SubVI. This chapter also explains the Type Definitions. It is important to properly understand what Type Definitions are since they are used to maintain consistency between objects that are repeated in the program.

When starting to use LabVIEW^{TM}, the first thing that a new developer wants to perform is control instruments or use data acquisition systems. However, it is recommended that before starting to utilize hardware resources (instruments, acquisition systems, ports etc.) or software resources (files or folders), the new developer has practiced and understood the first five chapters. It can be considered that the first five chapters are the basics that are recommended to master before starting to use hardware or software resources.

In Chapter 7, the concept of resource is explained in a general way, and in a specific way it is explained software resources. It is common for automation applications or data acquisition tasks to require saving information from multiple sensors in a file. Therefore, the examples for reading and writing files in Chapter 7 are given using a file structure similar to the used by electrical testing machines. However, the same explained concepts can be used to read or write files with another kind of format.

In Chapter 8, the concept of hardware resources is explained. Different hardware resources, such as data acquisition systems, measurement instruments, and computer ports, can be used. This chapter describes how to use the NI MAX^{TM} application to see and test the hardware available on the computer. Subsequently, the use of the DAQmx library to communicate with National Instruments™ data acquisition systems is explained, providing practical examples for reading and writing analog and digital channels. In addition, an introduction to the VISA libraries is presented, which allow the computer to communicate through serial, USB, Ethernet, or GPIB ports with measurement instruments, microcontrollers, or other types of hardware that use these communication standards. For VISA communication, an example of communication between the computer and Arduino using USB serial communication is given. This practical example is recommended as a starting point to use the computer ports. Finally, the use of Instrument Drivers is explained, which allows the computer's rapid communication with a wide variety of measurement instruments from different manufacturers.

LabVIEW™ is a programming language used for automation, signal acquisition, and instrument control to which software engineering techniques can be applied. Although there are complete books of software engineering and courses, this book addresses some programming architectures (also known as design patterns) that allow the future scalability and maintainability of the developed programs. Therefore, in Chapter 9, the state machine architecture is introduced, which is used to create scalable solutions for electrical test machines, processes, or interfaces that respond to user actions. It is highly recommended that the new developer and experienced developers master this programming architecture, so Chapter 9 includes a complete example of an electrical test machine for coils using state machines.

Chapter 10 teaches programmatic control of object properties using property nodes and the use of invoke nodes to call different methods. The programmatic control of objects allows modifying properties at run time, such as enabling/disabling controls, color changes, emphasis, etc. This chapter is important to improve the usability of programs developed in LabVIEW™ by practicing the programmatic control of user interfaces.

Chapter 11 focuses on giving good practices for error and warning handling. In this chapter, the error cluster is studied in detail, and it is taught how to differentiate errors from warnings. In the same way, techniques for error management are provided, as well as tools to define own errors or warnings.

Chapter 12 shows the event programming paradigm. Event programming allows to reduce the program's resource consumption and run only when there is an event to respond to. These events can be generated in the user interface, or they can be generated programmatically. Regardless, event programming creates smooth user interfaces where no user action is lost.

Chapter 13 is a review project of the first 12 chapters. In Chapter 13, an ATM is programmed using event-driven state machines. It is recommended that new developers carry out this ATM as it implements most of the features and programming techniques have seen up to Chapter 12. In addition, this chapter explains new features that help to improve the interface and usability of a program. This project intends to implement the event-driven state machine architecture to create a scalable program with an interface that responds immediately to user actions. It is recommended to pay special attention to the organization and flow of the program.

The first 13 chapters provide the knowledge for creating interfaces that respond quickly to user actions, data acquisition systems, instrument control, the use of files, and the implementation of event-driven state machines. This knowledge helps develop electrical testing machines, which is a recurring task in the automation area. However, there are tasks such as acquiring high-speed signals where no information can be lost and need to be saved in a file as the use of variables or arrays can be surpassed by the amount of information. These tasks need high-speed DAQs and binary files to save the acquired data, which is why Chapters 14–17 show topics such as queuing, race conditions, advanced file usage, and real-time programming.

In Chapter 14, the use of queues is taught; queues allow information to be processed asynchronously; that is, the information can be generated continuously (for example, by a data acquisition system), and the processing is carried out at a different time. This allows not to interrupt the sampling process by processing a current measurement value. To do this, in Chapter 14, the Producer–Consumer design pattern is explained, and examples are provided. In addition, the Event-Driven Producer–Consumer pattern is also taught, which allows improving the response to the user interface actions of the Producer–Consumer pattern.

Chapter 15 shows race conditions. This condition is common in programs that use concurrent programming. Therefore, suggestions are given on avoiding such conditions and examples to detect and correct this situation.

Chapter 16 teaches advanced file handling. With this aim, binary files are explained, and examples are provided on how to write and read them, which is useful for working with data that is read from a measurement channel (for example, from a DAQ). This chapter also explains the use of relative paths, and new functions to work with files and folders are covered. The functions seen in this chapter are useful when creating or reading measurement log files or saving the results of a test machine.

Chapter 17 focuses on real-time programming using CompactRIO^{TM}, hardware from National Instruments^{TM} that uses FPGA boards as its base. This technology is shown due to its industrial application, versatility, and I/O connection capacity for different sensors. This chapter teaches both real-time operation and FPGA-level operation, which is preferred for high-speed and precise-timing tasks.

This book is suitable for undergraduate and graduate students, engineers, and researchers who want to learn methods and techniques to implement efficient and sophisticated solutions in data acquisition, signal measurement, or automation. It is recommended that the student know or have some basics of programming and electronics.

Part I

Fundamentals

Chapter 1
Introduction to LabVIEW™

This chapter gives an introduction to LabVIEW™, it will allow the reader to become familiar with the use of the software, it will explain the development environment, starting with the project explorer, how to properly structure projects and types of files in LabVIEW™, it will explain the definition of a virtual instrument and its parts, exposing the different functions available in the toolbars, the function and control palettes, an introduction to data types, how to build a virtual instrument and it will finish explaining about the inherent parallelism of LabVIEW™ and in what manner this graphical language executes a program by the concept of Data Flow.

1.1 What is LabVIEW™?

The name LabVIEW™ is formed by the words "laboratory virtual instrument engineering workbench" and it is a powerful graphic programing software designed for hardware systems and test, control, and design software. LabVIEW™ is a professional development system created by National Instruments™ in 1986; it is written in C, C++, and .NET and works with various operating systems like Windows, macOS, and Linux. It is used in many fields like research, control systems, industrial testing, education, etc. [1].

Contrary to text-based programming languages, LabVIEW™ uses a graphical programming environment based on block functions, structures, and data flow through cables between blocks and structures.

1.1.1 LabVIEW™ parallelism

One of the main advantages of the LabVIEW™ graphical programming language is its capability to work with parallel codes running simultaneously. For example, two different loop structures can be running simultaneously, and the execution speed of one loop would not affect the execution speed of the other loop regardless of its contents [2]. On the contrary, text-based languages can only execute one loop at a time. This is one of the many reasons why LabVIEW™ is a handy tool to develop applications because it lets the developer to focus on the problem to solve and not to lose time in finding complex ways to make the program work as intended.

Before learning how to program in this graphic language, knowing how the LabVIEW™ environment organized is essential. This is why the following sections of this chapter will focus on understanding some key elements like the project explorer, virtual instrument (which will be referred as VI for the rest of the book), data flow, and data types. After understanding these elements, there is a section to start programming with basic functions and another section for examples of these functions.

1.2   Project explorer

When opening LabVIEW^{TM}, it opens a window that asks if you want to create a project or open an existing project as shown in Figure 1.1. This is like the welcome window in other software. To understand how to create a new project and learn about the different kinds of projects, click the button "Create Project".

After clicking the button "Create Project", a new window appears as shown in Figure 1.2. This window gives the option to create a new blank project, but it also lets us open a new project with a predefined template, so you do not have to start a new project from scratch, you can use a template with some of the standard program design patterns in LabVIEW^{TM} like simple state machine (which is studied in more detail in Chapter 9), channeled message handler, queued message handler, etc. It also shows a few example projects that can be useful to understand new functions in the LabVIEW^{TM} programming environment.

To better understand the project explorer, how it works, and what tools can be used to organize our project, we are going to create a new blank project. To do it, make sure that "Blank Project" is selected by clicking on it; it should appear highlighted in yellow as in Figure 1.2, then click the "Finish" button.

After clicking the finish button, a new window pops up and this window is the project explorer as shown in Figure 1.3. The project explorer is normally used when

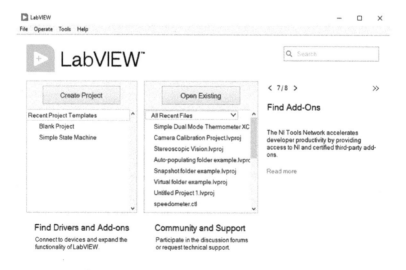

Figure 1.1   Opening LabVIEW^{TM} window

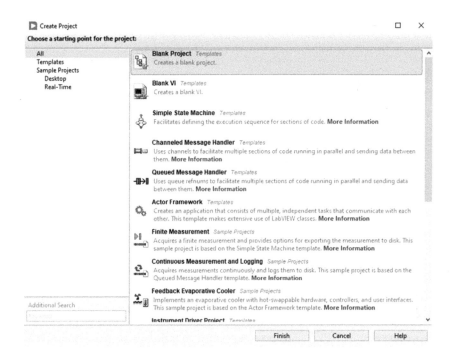

Figure 1.2   Create project window

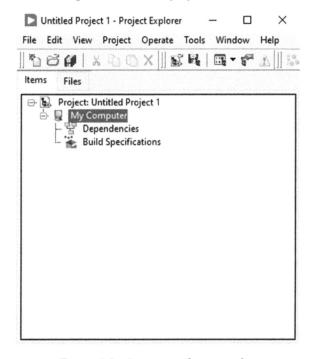

Figure 1.3   Project explorer window

the project requires several VIs, communicate the computer with hardware, or creates an executable file or a setup file. The use of the project explorer to communicate with hardware is explained in Chapter 8. Therefore, this section is going to be focused on the use of the project explorer for organization and its tools.

The project explorer window is divided by two tabs, the items tab and the files tab. The items tab organizes the project, and the files tab shows the path to all the files used in the project and it is usually used when we have a lot of files on our project.

One of the main advantages of using the items tab to organize the project is that it is possible to subdivide sections of it, for example, in Figure 1.3 can be seen that the sections 🔨 "Build Specifications" and 🖧 "Dependencies" are part of the section 🖥 "My Computer" and also this section is part of the main section 🗐 "Project: Untitled Project 1", which is the default name LabVIEW™ gives to the project before saving it with a different name. It is also possible to create more sections by adding other folders to help to organize the project.

1.2.1   Folders

There are different kinds of folders that you can use to organize the project, these are "normal" folders and virtual folders. Normal folders are divided in two types, snapshot and auto-populating folders and these work different than virtual folders and each of them can be helpful in different ways to organize our project.

1.2.1.1   Virtual folder

Virtual folders are the folders that only exist in the project explorer window, they do not create a new folder on disk or where the project is saved. To create a new virtual folder right click on the section where the virtual folder is wanted, in Figure 1.4, it is shown how to create a virtual folder in "My Computer", after right clicking the section, left click on "New" and then "Virtual Folder" and a virtual folder 📁

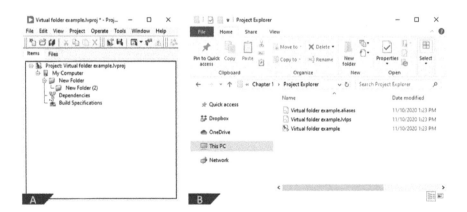

Figure 1.4   (A) Virtual folder creation and (B) project file location

appears with the name of "New Folder" which can be changed at that moment or later by right clicking the virtual folder and selecting the option "Rename".

Folders can be created inside other folders too, as shown in Figure 1.4, on the project explorer window, the virtual folder named "New Folder (2)" was created in the same way as the other folder with the only difference that instead of right clicking on "My Computer", the new wanted location for the new virtual folder was used, which in this case was the virtual folder named "New Folder". Also, at the right there is the location where the project is saved, and as can see, there are no files of the created folders, this is because virtual folders only exist on the items tab of the project explorer.

1.2.1.2   Folder (Snapshot)

As seen in the previous section, virtual folders only exist in the project explorer. Still, to use folders in the project file location, there are two options, the snapshot folders and the auto-populating folders.

To create a snapshot folder, create it first as a normal folder in the project file location. On the project explorer window, you need to right click on the section to create the snapshot folder, then go to add and click the option "Folder (Snapshot) …", a new window will appear. Then go to the desired folder location, open it, and click the "Current Folder" button. After that, the snapshot folder will appear on the project explorer.

In Figure 1.5 can be seen a new folder named "Snapshot folder example" in the project explorer window, and to the right, on the project file location, the folder created for this snapshot folder.

As can be seen, snapshot folders exist in the project location on disk and also on the project explorer window, but if a file is added to the snapshot folder, it will not be updated in the project explorer. A different kind of folder can be used to create a folder that updates every time a new file is added to the folder location, and this folder is the auto-population folder.

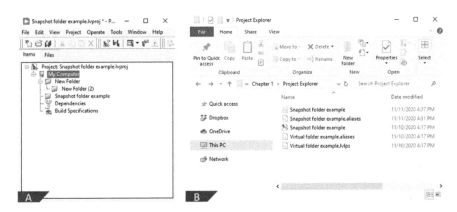

Figure 1.5   (A) Snapshot folder creation and (B) project file location

1.2.1.3   Folder (Auto-populating)

Auto-populating folders are used when the folder needs to be constantly updated with the files added to the project file location. Auto-populating folders are created the same way as snapshot folders. Still, instead of clicking on "Folder (Snapshot) ...", click on "Folder (Auto-populating) ..." and select the desired folder.

In Figure 1.6, in the project explorer window, a new folder called "Auto-populating folder example" 🗀 can be seen, which corresponds to the folder in the windows explorer. Also, a new text document is added to this folder and to the folder called "Snapshot folder example", and it can be seen that this file only appears on the auto-populating folder as expected. Suppose it is required that the new file added to the snapshot folder also appears on the project explorer. In that case, it can be added by right clicking on the folder, then add file and select it, or convert the snapshot folder to an auto-populating folder by clicking the option "Convert to Auto-populating Folder ...".

> • Tip #1: A folder on the project explorer can be deleted by right clicking on it and selecting "Remove from Project" or also by selecting the folder and pressing the delete key on the keyboard.

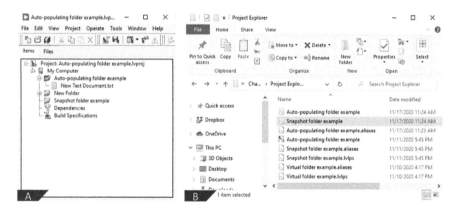

Figure 1.6   (A) Auto-populating folder creation and (B) project file location

1.3   Virtual instrument

The virtual instrument is the most important file of the LabVIEW^{TM} programming environment, and it is often referred as VI. This file is used to create the user interface and program the functionality [3]. There are different ways to create a new VI, it can be created from the project explorer by right clicking on the section (in the project explorer) to create it, then clicking new and finally on VI, and a new VI with the name of "untitled 1" 🖼, will appear as shown in Figure 1.7.

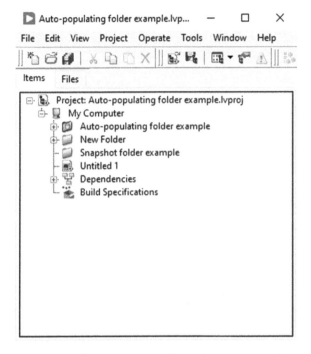

Figure 1.7   Creating a new VI on the project explorer

VIs can also be created from the first window that appears when we open LabVIEW^{TM} (Figure 1.1). To create a new VI, click on File at the top left of the window and then on New VI.

After opening a VI, two windows will appear as shown in Figure 1.8, the window with a gray background and a grid it is called front panel, which corresponds to the area to develop the user interface, and the window with a white background it is called block diagram, which is the area to code with the LabVIEW^{TM} graphical programming language.

> • Tip #2: VI windows can be arranged on screen by pressing Ctrl + T. They can also be arranged separately by selecting a window and pressing the windows key + left or right arrow.

1.3.1 Front panel

The front panel is the user interface, this is where the user is going to interact with the controls, indicators, messages, etc. It can be customized to fit the developer's preferences (for a better experience while developing), and it can also be modified

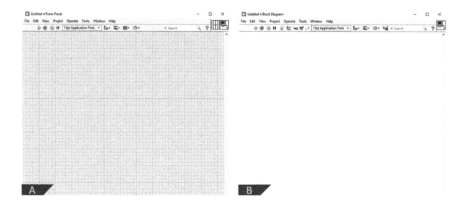

Figure 1.8   Virtual instrument: (A) front panel and (B) block diagram

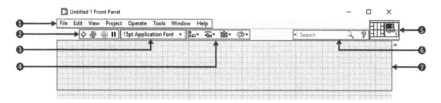

Figure 1.9   Front panel sections

to hide some sections. When a new VI is created, it will appear with some pre-determined sections as shown in Figure 1.9, which are explained below:

1. Menu. This section is composed of other subsections: File, Edit, View, Project, Operate, Tools, Window, and Help. Each subsection can help to accomplish different tasks such as saving the VI, undo or redo actions, creating a project, opening instrument drivers, arranging windows, and getting help on LabVIEW^{TM} topics. More options within Menu will be explored in further sections.

2. Program execution. There are four buttons in this section. The first one ⇨ (the arrow shape) will execute the code once. The second button ⟳ (2 arrows) will run the code continuously, which means that once it finishes an execution, it will run the code again and again until it is stopped. The third button, abort execution ⬤ (red circle), will stop the code immediately, regardless of what the program is doing. The fourth button is the pause button ‖ (two vertical bars) which function is to pause the execution of the code until it is pressed again.

3. Font properties. Change the font type, size, style and color, and other properties for text objects in the front panel.

4. Object organization. When making a program, it is really important that it is user friendly and well organized, this section provides four subsections with

their respective buttons that will help with align ⬚, distribute ⬚, resize ⬚, and reorder ⬚ objects. This section is explained in more detail in Chapter 6.

5. **VI icon and connector pane.** VIs can also be used as SubVIs (functions) on the block diagram of another VI. This section helps to define the input and/or output terminals in the connector pane of the VI and to create an Icon, this icon will be used to identify the SubVI in another VI. This topic is studied in more detail in Chapter 4.

6. **Help bar.** This section is divided in two, the first one is the search bar 🔍, to get help on a LabVIEW^{TM} topic by writing on it, and the second one is the button with the yellow question mark, this button opens a window called context help ❓ which gives information of an object in the front panel or the block diagram when put the mouse over the object.

7. **Workspace.** This section is used to create the user interface with objects such as buttons, indicators, etc. will be placed.

These sections are useful to properly create the user interface with controls and indicators, note that each control and indicator creates a terminal in the block diagram, a more deep explanation of them will be performed in other chapters of this book.

1.3.1.1   Tools palette

As you may have seen by now, the mouse cursor changes when moving it over some object in the front panel. LabVIEW^{TM} changes the cursor tools automatically based on its position and context, these tools may be used for resizing the object, modifying text, interacting with objects, etc. If more control over these tools is desired, the tools palette can be used. It can be opened by going to View>Tools Palette or by holding the shift key and right clicking on the workspace. As in the controls palette, depending on the method used to open the tools palette it will open as a window or in menu style as shown in Figure 1.10. By default, LabVIEW^{TM} has selected the automatic tool ▣, which is the one on the top with the green

Figure 1.10   (A) Tools palette window and (B) tools palette menu style

LED in a rectangle shape. The rest of the tools are explained below, numbered from one to ten, starting from top left.

1. Operation tool 🖑. This tool is used to interact with the object in the same way the user would do, like changing control values, moving sliders, clicking buttons, etc.
2. Positioning tool ▶. This tool is used to move or resize objects on the workspace.
3. Labeling tool **A**. It is used to add text to the workspace. After adding text, it can be moved or resized with the move tool.
4. Wiring tool ➤. This tool can only be used on the block diagram and it is used to wire nodes. This topic will be studied in detail in Section 1.3.2 "Block diagram".
5. Object shortcut menu tool �. This tool opens an object's menu when clicking on it. This menu can also be accessed with the automatic tool by right clicking on it.
6. Scrolling tool ✋. This tool is used to move through the workspace by maintaining the left click pressed over an empty space of the workspace and moving the cursor. To stop moving through the workspace just release the mouse click.
7. Breakpoint tool ●. This tool is only used on the block diagram, it is used to stop the program at a desired point on the block diagram. This topic will be studied in detail in Chapter 2.
8. Probe tool ➤(P). This tool is only used on the block diagram, it is used to monitor the value of a wire when running the program. This topic will be studied in detail in Chapter 2.
9. Get color tool 🖊. This tool is used to extract colors that can be later used with the coloring tool.
10. Coloring tool 🖌🖊. This tool is used to change the color of the background or objects on the workspace.

1.3.1.2   Controls palette

The controls palette is used to add controls and indicators in the workspace and it can be accessed by going to View>Controls Palette (from now on this notation will be used when a section from the menu needs to be used, this one means left click on View and then on Controls Palette) or by right clicking on the workspace. Depending on the method used to open the controls palette it will pop up a window control palette or a menu style control palette as shown in Figure 1.11.

The difference between these is that the menu style control palette will close if we click anywhere outside the controls palette and the window controls palette will stay open until we close it. The menu style controls palette can be changed to a window by clicking the pin at the top left at the controls palette.

The controls palette is also divided into subpalettes, most of them are for different styles of controls and indicators like Modern, NXG Style, Silver,

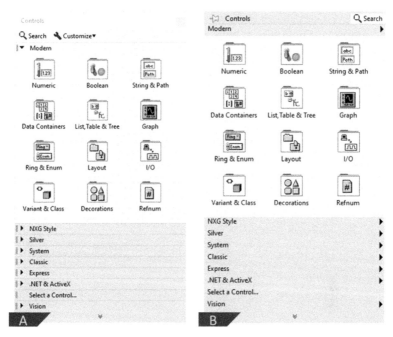

Figure 1.11   (A) Controls palette window and (B) controls palette menu style

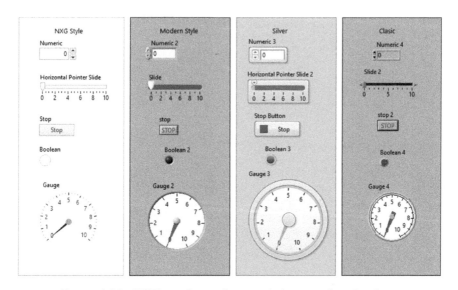

Figure 1.12   NXG, modern, silver, and classic style subpalettes

System, and Classic as shown in Figure 1.12. Other subpalettes like Express and .
NET and ActiveX include special types of controls and indicators.

Since the only difference between modern, NXG style, silver, system, and
classic subpalettes is that they have a different style, we will continue working with
modern subpalette, but everything should work with the other style palettes, except
in certain cases where some controls or indicators do not exist in some styles.

Controls are objects that can be to the workspace and the user can interact
with, like buttons, sliders, knobs, switches, scrollbars, etc., and Indicators are
objects that are used to show information to the user, like LEDs, progress bars,
numeric indicators, etc. The objects in the workspace of the front panel are represented by blocks on the block diagram and they give a certain type of information
depending on the control used. We can add objects to our workspace by selecting
them from the folders in the subpalettes. For example, in Figure 1.13 we created a
numeric control by going to Controls Palette>Numeric>Numeric Control, then
we can place the numeric control anywhere on the workspace. Note that when the
numeric control is added on the workspace, a numeric input terminal is also created
on the block diagram.

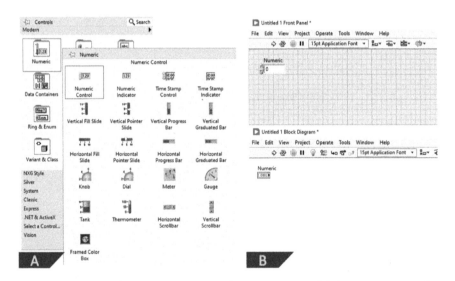

*Figure 1.13   (A) Adding numeric control instructions and (B) numeric control on
front panel workspace*

1.3.2 Block diagram

The block diagram is where all the functionality of the code is going to be programmed. This is where the terminals generated by the objects in the front panel
will be used in different ways depending on the application. The block diagram is

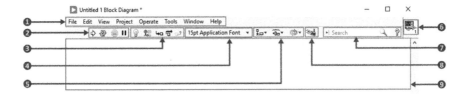

Figure 1.14   Block diagram sections

divided in various sections as shown in Figure 1.14, these sections are explained below:

1. Menu. This section is composed of other subsections: File, Edit, View, Project, Operate, Tools, Window, and Help. Each subsection can help accomplish different tasks such as saving the VI, undo or redo actions, creating a project, opening instrument drivers, arranging windows, and getting help on LabVIEW^{TM} topics. More options within Menu will be explored in further sections.

2. Program execution. There are four buttons in this section. The first one ⇨ (the arrow shape) will execute the code once. The second button (two arrows) will run the code continuously, which means that once it finishes an execution, it will run the code again and again until it is stopped. The third button, abort execution (red circle), will stop the code immediately, regardless of what the program is doing. The fourth button is the pause button ▌▌ (two vertical bars) which function is to pause the execution of the code until it is pressed again.

3. Debugging tools. This tools are used to correct unexpected behavior in the program. The button with the light bulb icon is called highlight execution and its function is to slow down the program execution and animate the data flow. The next button is retain wire values, it saves the wire values which can be seen by adding probes. The next three buttons are used to run the code step by step in different ways. Debugging tools is an effective way to fix problems in our code and it is studied in more detail in Chapter 2.

4. Font properties. Change the font type, size, style and color, and other properties for text objects in the Block Diagram.

5. Object organization. When making a program, it is really important that it is user friendly and well organized, this section provides four subsections with their respective buttons that will help with align, distribute, resize, and reorder objects. This section is explained in more detail in Chapter 6.

6. VI icon. This shows the icon of the VI or subVI and allows to modify it by double clicking on it. This topic is studied in more detail in Chapter 4.

7. Help bar. This section is divided in two, the first one is the search bar, where we can get help on a LabVIEW^{TM} topic by writing on it and the second one is the button with the yellow question mark, this button opens a window called context help which gives us information of an object in the front panel or the block diagram when we put the mouse over it.

8. Clean up diagram ⚙. This button reorganizes the code automatically and erases broken wires. Its use is recommended only for small block diagrams because larger block diagrams can be harder to read when rearranged automatically.

9. Workspace. This is the area where the wires and blocks such as nodes and subVIs are going to be placed. It can be resized to fit as many blocks as desired, but it is recommended to keep it as big as the screen or smaller.

As in the front panel, the functions palette can be opened in the same way on the block diagram, but the controls palette cannot be used here. Instead, the block diagram has the functions palette and can be opened by going to View>Functions Palette or by right clicking on the workspace. Depending on the method used to open the controls palette, it will pop up a window function palette or a menu style function palette as shown in Figure 1.15. It is important to note that each control or indicator created in the front panel will be a terminal in the block diagram.

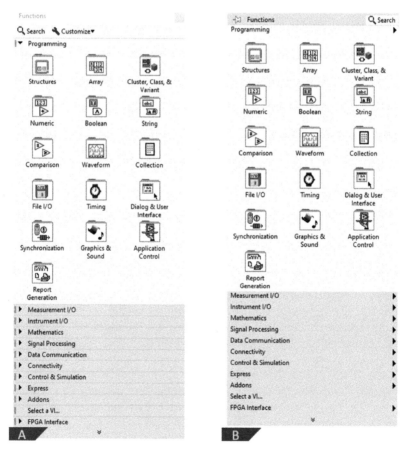

Figure 1.15   (A) Functions palette window and (B) functions palette menu style

The functions palette is used to add different kinds of blocks and structures to the workspace and it is divided in different sections like Programming, which contains the basic functions used in graphic language, Measurement I/O contains functions that can be used to take measurements with additional hardware, Instrument I/O contains functions that can be used to communicate with different devices, Mathematics contains from basic mathematic operations to advanced functions, etc. More sections can be added when installing more libraries to the LabVIEW^{TM} environment.

Each section is subdivided in folders that contain different blocks and structures organized by their functions. For example, the numeric functions folder contains different kinds of nodes to realize mathematic operations such as add, subtract, multiply, divide, etc., as shown in Figure 1.16(A). It also contains numeric constants, other functions and more subfolders which contain more specific functions.

To add functions to the workspace, just click on the desired function and drag it to the block diagram. Most block functions have inputs and outputs. For example, in Figure 1.16(B) an add function was created, then two numeric control inputs were connected to it and a numeric indicator as an output. After running the program, the result of this operation can be seen in the front panel. If the value of the controls is changed, it will not be shown on the numeric indicator until next time the program is executed. To execute the program multiple times you can use the button execute continuously.

• Tip #3: Constants, indicators or controls, can be created and automatically wired to the input/output by right clicking the input/output and then selecting create constant, indicator or control.

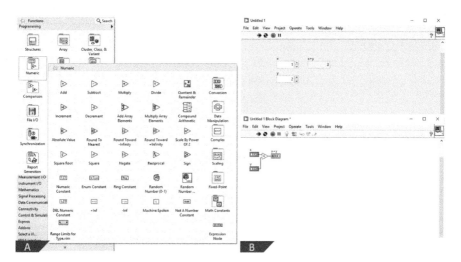

Figure 1.16   (A) Numeric functions and (B) numeric function on block diagram

1.4   Data flow and data types

Before learning about the functions that can be used on LabVIEW^{TM}, it is really important to understand the concepts of data flow and data types. Most students have trouble while programming in LabVIEW^{TM} due to their lack of understanding these concepts. As programs become more complex, the importance of mastering these key concepts increases. This is why it is recommended that the student does not start learning about other functions until these concepts are mastered.

1.4.1   Data flow

To understand how the code will be executed, first, it is important to know about wires and nodes. Wires are used to transfer information between nodes. The nodes are divided in three different kinds of nodes: Function nodes, which are the blocks used for basic functions. Structure nodes i.e., while loops, cases, events, etc. SubVI nodes, a special type of node, will be studied in more detail in Chapter 4.

Most nodes have inputs and outputs and information travels from one node to another [4]. So, there are two rules about data flow that needs to be understood to program properly in LabVIEW^{TM}:

Data flow rules

- A node will be executed only when all its inputs are available.
- A node only provides an output when it finishes execution.

For example, in Figure 1.17, there are two function nodes: add and subtract, three numeric controls: x, y, and z, and a numeric indicator that will show the result of the operation: $x + y - z$. In order for the numeric indicator to show this result, it needs to wait for the subtract node to do its operation and to do so, it needs all of its inputs to be available, the z input will be ready from the beginning, but the other input needs to wait for the add node to complete its operation. So the order of execution would be: the numeric controls x, y, and z are available since the beginning of the program and send the information to the inputs of the nodes they

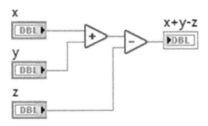

Figure 1.17   Function nodes

are wired to, then the add node will do its operation since all of its inputs are available, then the result will be sent to the subtract node which was waiting for this input, then it will do its operation and send the result to the numeric indicator. You can see this animated by activating the highlight execution button and executing the program. The subtract node will not send information through the output until it receives the necessary information on all of its inputs. This principle applies to all kinds of nodes and the programmer must take it into account on every step when coding. Most programmers struggle with graphic programming languages due to their lack of understanding of this fundamental principle. This becomes a real problem in the long term, making it harder to create complex programs.

Figure 1.18(A) shows a simple operation where the order of execution is as follows, the numeric constants 3 and 15 send their value to the functions they are connected, the next function to be executed is the divide function, since it has all of its input terminals available, then the divide function sends the result to the add function, which can now be executed because it was waiting for this terminal input value to be executed, finally the add function sends the value to the result indicator and the program stops. Figure 1.18(B) shows an example where it can be trickier to identify the order of execution, just by looking at block diagram, it may seem like the add function would be the first to be executed, but from the data flow rules, we know that the divide function cannot be executed first since it does not have all of its inputs available. The first function to be executed is the multiply function, which has available values of 4 and 5 at its terminals, then the subtract function is executed, then the divide function, and at the end the add function is executed. This is why it is important to understand the data flow basic rules, failing to understand them properly can lead to many errors while programming. Note that the objects from Figure 1.18 are improperly placed to accentuate the data flow problem, objects on the block diagram should be placed in a way that facilitates the data flow tracking.

1.4.2 Data types

As shown from comparing Figures 1.16 and 1.17, the numeric indicator, the controls, and the wires have different colors. This is because they are working with different data types [5], in this case, the diagram with the blue blocks and wires is working with data type I32 ▮▮▮, which is a long signed integer and this means that it can have positive

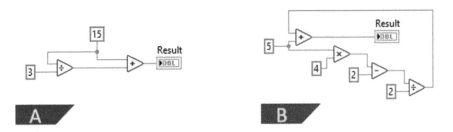

Figure 1.18 Data flow examples using numeric functions. (A) Divide and add and (B) add, multiply, subtract, and divide

and negative integer values. The diagram with the orange blocks and wires is working with a data type DBL [DBL], which is a double precision floating point and this means that it can have positive and negative floating values. Indicators and controls have different data types and they can be changed. The most common data types are listed in Table 1.1. Boolean data type [TF] can only store binary values true or false. String data type [abc] stores data as characters and can be used to create messages. Arrays [DBL] are used to store information on brackets of the same data type, for example, the one shown in Table 1.1 is an array that stores double-precision, floating-point integers and it can store numbers like [1.3, −5.3, 3, 1, 0, 100]. Arrays are studied in more detail in Chapter 5. The Enum data type [◁▷] is an enumerated type control and indicator that gives users a list of items to select. Waveform data type [∿] stores data, start time, and a time differential of a waveform, it is normally used to graph data over time. Error clusters [⊟] are used to pass the error information through the VI and they are used to detect where errors are occurring and send a message. There are more data types and they will be studied on different parts of this book as they are needed.

Some data types can be connected with other data type terminals even if they are not the same. For example, in Figure 1.19(A), all the terminal blocks are connected with different data types and as can be seen, some wires conserve the color of their terminal and other wires change to a dashed line with a symbol in the middle. These kinds of wires are called broken wires and they appear when trying to connect incompatible data types. When these kinds of wires exist on the block diagram, LabVIEW^TM will not allow the VI to be executed and will change the execute button icon for a gray broken arrow as in Figure 1.19(A), if the broken arrow button is clicked, LabVIEW^TM will show a message window where it will indicate the error of the code. This button does not only appears with broken wires, but it also will appear with different kinds of errors, for example, when a function node does not have all of its required inputs wired. On the other hand, going back to the wires that conserved their color, it can be observed that the terminals that are receiving the information have a red dot on the input, this dot is called coercion dot and it means that LabVIEW^TM is automatically converting from one data

Table 1.1   Basic data types

Data type	Block diagram representation	
Double-precision, floating-point integer	Numeric [DBL]	[DBL] Numeric 2
32-bit signed integer numeric	Numeric 3 [I32]	[I32] Numeric 4
Boolean	Boolean [TF]	[TF] Boolean 2
String	String [abc]	[abc] String 2
Numeric array	Array [DBL]	[DBL] Array 2
Enum	Enum [◁▷]	[◁▷] Enum 2
Waveform	Waveform [∿]	[∿] Waveform Graph
Error cluster	error in (no error) [⊟]	[⊟] error out

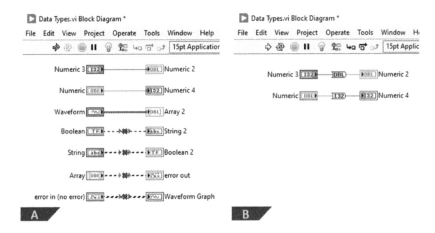

Figure 1.19   (A) Coercion dots and broken wires and (B) conversion functions

type from another. This does not mean an error, but it is recommended for better performance to convert the data before connecting it to a different node or terminal. For example, in Figure 1.19(B), the data from the indicator terminals are converted to the corresponding data type to which they are connected. These conversion functions can be added by going to **Functions Palette>Numeric>Conversion**.

• Tip #4: Broken wires can be erased by using the cleanup diagram button. If you do not want the block diagram to be reorganized you can erase the broken wires by pressing Ctrl + B on the keyboard.

1.5   Elementary functions, controls, and indicators

If you are reading this section it is because you fully understand the concepts of data flow and data types and you are ready to start learning about elementary functions, controls and indicators.

1.5.1   Elementary controls and indicators

As can be seen in the controls palette, there are different kinds of controls and indicators. This section explains the difference between the most common ones and how they can be used on the front panel and the block diagram.

1.5.1.1   Numeric controls and indicators

The numeric controls palette has a wide variety of controls and indicators, in Figure 1.20, the most common ones are shown. In general, there are three kinds of numeric controls: numeric control, slide control, and knob. Also, there are three numeric indicators: numeric indicator, slide indicator, and meter. As can be seen in Figure 1.20, the numeric controls and indicators look different on the front panel

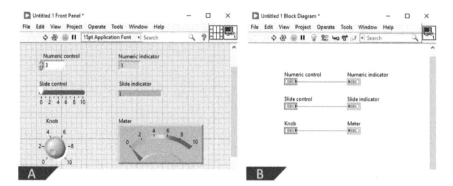

Figure 1.20   Elementary numeric controls and indicators on (A) front panel and (B) block diagram

but on the block diagram, all the controls and indicators are represented as terminals and look the same. It is because they are the same data type and they work in the same way on the block diagram, the only difference between them is how the information is shown to the user on the front panel.

The numeric control and numeric indicator are simple, the numeric controls lets the user change the value by clicking the arrows or by changing the number manually and the numeric indicator displays the number received in its terminal on the block diagram. The slide control lets the user change its value by moving a marker along a scale, the values of this scale can be changed by double clicking the minimum or maximum number or by going to **Object Menu>Scale>Properties**, this will pop-up an object properties window with the scale tab selected, this is where the minimum and maximum values of the scale can be modified. The slide indicator shows the received value in its terminal block in the form of a progress bar and its values can be changed in the same way as in the slide control. The knob lets the user change its value by turning its minimum and maximum values, can be changed in the same way as in the slider control. The meter indicator shows the received value on its terminal by pointing a needle to the corresponding value on the scale, which can be adjusted the same way as the slide control. The shown data types in Figure 1.20(B) are double-precision, but they can be changed as needed by going to **Object Menu>Representation** and selecting the desired data type.

1.5.1.2   Boolean controls and indicators

Boolean controls and indicators manage only one data type, which, as its name says it is Boolean, this means that it can only have true or false values. As in the numeric controls and indicators, the Boolean controls and indicators look different on the front panel, but on the block diagram look the same, because they are using the same data type as shown in Figure 1.21. The Boolean controls in Figure 1.21 work similarly but with a different appearance to represent the action being taken. For the Boolean indicators, the most common ones are the round led and the square led, which indicate the state received at their input terminal. Also, controls can be converted to indicators

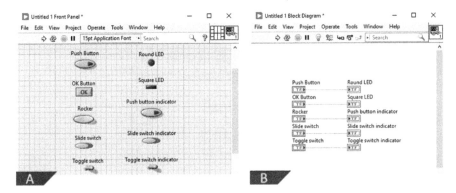

Figure 1.21 Elementary Boolean controls and indicators on (A) front panel and (B) block diagram

as shown in Figure 1.21(A) by going to Object Menu>Change to Indicator, but it is not recommended since it can confuse the user.

Boolean buttons have mechanical actions that are closely correlated with physical Boolean buttons. Physical real buttons have different mechanical actions, for example, some buttons conduct electricity when they are pressed, others do when they are released, and some buttons stay in the same state until they are pressed again. Well, virtual buttons on LabVIEW^{TM} are also programmed to have six different mechanical actions as listed below:

1. Switch when pressed. This mechanical action changes the state when pressed and stays in this new state until pressed again.
2. Switch when released. This mechanical action changes the state when the button is released and stays in this new state until pressed again.
3. Switch until released. This mechanical action changes the state when pressed and returns to its original state when released.
4. Latch when pressed. This mechanical action changes the state when the button is pressed and changes back to its original state immediately after sending the information of the state when pressed.
5. Latch when released. This mechanical action changes the state when the button is released and changes back to its original state immediately after sending the information of the state when released.
6. Latch until released. This mechanical action changes the state when the button is pressed and changes back to its original state after the button is released and the information of the state is sent.

Button mechanical actions can be changed by going to Object Menu> Mechanical Action and six different figures will appear as in Figure 1.22. Each figure represents a mechanical action with a diagram to represent the behavior of the button and the produced signal and hovering the mouse over a figure shows the name of the mechanical action at the top of the box. To have a better understanding of the mechanical actions it is recommended to create a VI with six buttons with

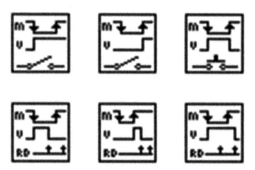

Figure 1.22   Mechanical actions

each mechanical action, an indicator for each one, and execute the VI with high-light execution enabled.

1.5.1.3   String controls and indicators

String controls and indicators are used to manage groups of characters and there are only two types of controls and one type of indicator, as shown in Figure 1.23. In this case, they look almost the same, with some subtle differences. Controls have with background, indicators have a gray background and the combo box control has an arrow button at the end of the control.

The string controls are boxes where the user can input text, for example, they can be used to fill a form where the user name is needed or some other information. The combo box is used when the programmer wants to give different options to the user. When the user clicks the arrow button, a drop-down list will appear with the items of that list. The item list can be modified by going to **Object Menu>Edit Items**, and a window with the edit items tab will appear. This window can be used to insert more items, delete items or reorder the items on the list.

1.5.2   Elementary functions

LabVIEW^{TM} functions palette has many subpalettes and each of them has many different functions. It is not viable to explain all of them in one book, but understanding the most common ones will help when trying to learn about other kinds of functions.

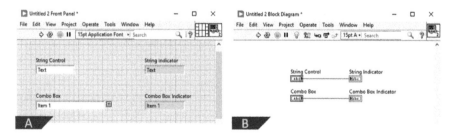

Figure 1.23   Elementary string controls and indicators on (A) front panel and (B) block diagram

1.5.2.1   Numeric functions

The numeric functions subpalette has a wide variety of functions and subfolders with more functions, as seen in Figure 1.24(A). The blocks with a yellow background are basic function nodes and they have symbols and a name to give the programmer an idea of what that function does, like add, subtract, multiply, divide, etc. But if the programmer needs more information about a certain function, the context help button comes handy. For example, in Figure 1.24(B) the context help window was opened by pressing the context help button (you can also press Ctrl + H top to open it) and it was used to get more information about the function Quotient & Remainder. The context help window shows the required inputs of the function and the expected output, it also gives a short description, the terminal data type and if more information is needed there is the detailed help option which will open a window with more information about the object.

The numeric functions palette also has some numeric constants that can be changed to a desired numeric value. Still, it also has some predetermined mathematical constants like π, Planck's constant, gravitational constant, etc. Explore the mathematics subpalette if you need more mathematical functions like trigonometric, exponential, algebraic, etc.

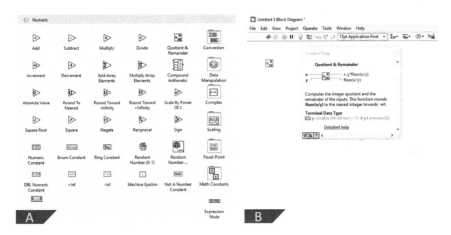

Figure 1.24   (A) Numeric functions subpalette and (B) context help on the block diagram

1.5.2.2   Boolean functions

The Boolean functions subpalette work similarly to the logic gates on digital circuits, as you can see in Figure 1.25, most of the functions have the same names as logic gates. For example, if the And function receive on its inputs a true and a false the output will be a false, if the Or function receives on its inputs a true and a false the output will be true, if the Not function receives a true input the output will be false, etc. If you do not know how these logic gates work, do not worry, you can always use the context help to learn how these functions work and the detailed help

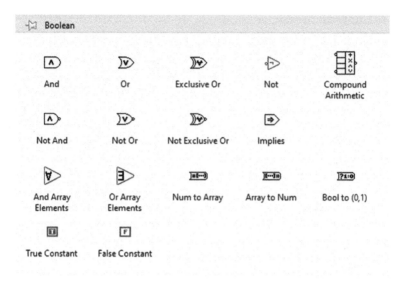

Figure 1.25   Boolean functions subpalette

even gives you the truth table, which is a table that shows the expected output for every combination of inputs.

1.5.2.3   Comparison functions

As its name says, the comparison functions subpalette shown in Figure 1.26 is used to compare values. Depending on the type of comparison functions, the

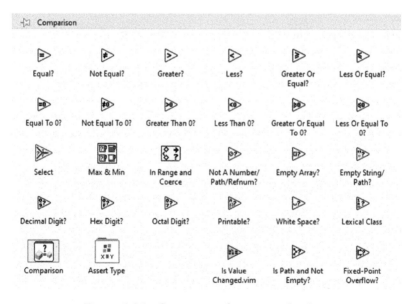

Figure 1.26   Comparison functions subpalette

output will be true if it meets the function comparison condition. For example, if the Equal? function receives on its inputs a one and a two the output value will be false, if the one and two are received by the Not Equal? function the output value will be true, if the one and two are received by the Greater? function the output value depends on how the inputs are connected, using the context help, it can be seen that there is an *x* input and a y input and the output will be true if the x input is greater than the *y* input. Comparison functions can work with different data types, for example, you can compare if two numbers are the same with the Equal? function even if they are not the same data type. These functions can also be used to compare strings, but they cannot be used to compare a number data type and a string, trying to connect them will result in broken wires, this property of accept different data types in the inputs is called Polymorphism and be explored in more detail in future chapters.

As can be seen, most elementary functions have special functions for array data type, arrays will be explained in more detail in Chapter 5 as arrays are data types that are most commonly used with loop structures.

1.6   Examples

This section will be divided into two: solved examples and examples to solve. This section aims to complement the learned topics in the chapter and give some ideas of how what is learned in the chapter can be used.

1.6.1   Solved examples

As its name says, this section gives three solved examples of programs and an explanation of how they were programmed. The first example is a program to find the area of a triangle given two variables, the second program is the sum of two dice, which is a program that generates two random numbers between one and six, and the third one is a price checker for different items on a list. All the programs use some of the elementary functions mentioned in this chapter and some new features.

1.6.1.1   Area of a triangle

Instructions: Create a program that calculates the area of a triangle, the user must have two numeric controls for the base and height and a numeric indicator where the result is displayed.

Solution: This is a simple program, it just needs two functions and a constant to realize the necessary calculations since the formula for the area of a triangle is base time height divided by two. This formula is applied on the block diagram as shown in Figure 1.27. Also, as you can see on the front panel, there are two numeric controls for the base and height, a numeric indicator for the area, and a triangle. This triangle is a decoration and can be added from the decorations subpalette.

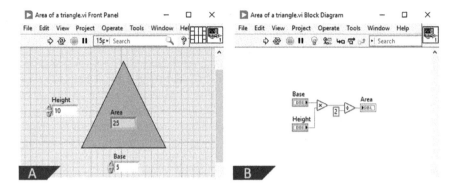

Figure 1.27   Area of a triangle: (A) front panel and (B) block diagram

1.6.1.2   Sum of two dice

Instructions: Create a program that generates two random numbers between one and six as in a die and the sum of these dices should be displayed on a numeric indicator.

Solution: The first problem on this program is to generate a random number between one and six, the numeric functions palette gives two options, using the subVI called Random Number (Range).vi or the node function Random Number (0–1). To understand the differences between them, the random number for **Dice 1** was obtained using the subVI called Random Number (Range).vi and for **Dice 2** the node function Random Number (0–1) was used as shown in Figure 1.28. The Random Number (Range).vi generates a random number from a specified range, the inputs for this subVI are the values of the range, in this case, one and six, then the output will be a random number (unsigned 64bit) which is connected to the numeric indicator called **Dice 1**. The node function Random Number (0–1) generates a random number between zero and one with data type double precision float, and then it is multiplied by six, rounded to the next highest integer and shown on the numeric indicator called **Dice 2**. Then the value of **Dice 1** is converted to

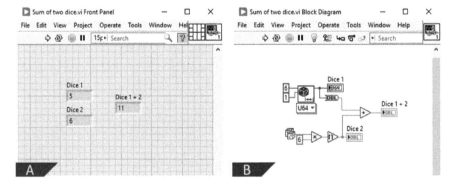

Figure 1.28   Sum of two dice: (A) front panel and (B) block diagram

double precision float, added with the value of Dice 2 and shown on the numeric indicator Dice 1 + 2.

1.6.1.3   Positive or negative?

Instructions: Create a program that tells the user if the result of $\frac{x}{2} - 10$ is "greater or equal to zero" or "less than zero". The x value is going to be given by the user on a numeric control and the result must be displayed on a string indicator.

Solution: The first step to create this program is to obtain the result of the equation as shown in Figure 1.29, then a comparison function was used to know if the result is equal or greater than zero, this function gives a Boolean output, which is used with the select function, this function has three inputs and one output, the middle input is a boolean selector and depending on its value the outcome of the output will be one of the other inputs, for the example in Figure 1.29 boolean input of the selector is true; therefore, the output will be "Result is greater or equal to zero", otherwise, the output of the selector will be "Result is less than zero".

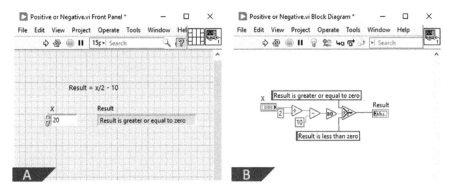

Figure 1.29   Positive or negative: (A) front panel and (B) block diagram

1.6.2   Examples to solve

This section gives three examples to solve, there is no explained solution in this book, but the solutions of the exercises can be achieved with the context of this chapter.

1.6.2.1   Quadratic equation calculator

Instructions: Create a program that provides the solutions to a quadratic equation. The program must have three numeric controls for constants a, b, and c, and two numeric indicators for each solution.

1.6.2.2   Square pyramid volume calculator

Instructions: Create a program that calculates the volume of a square pyramid. The program must have two numeric controls, one for the length of the base edge and one for the height of the pyramid. The result must be shown on a numeric indicator.

1.6.2.3   X in relation to Y

Instructions: Create a program that indicates if X is bigger than Y, smaller than Y or equal to Y. The program must have two numeric controls, one for X and one for Y, and a string indicator that shows the relation of X and Y.

Chapter 2

Debugging tools

This chapter explains the use of debugging tools to correct unexpected behavior in the program. The tools of "Highlight Execution", execution by "Steps", "Breakpoints" and "Probes" are studied. In addition, practical examples are presented to implement the conjunction use of these tools in debugging programming errors.

2.1 Debugging tools

If you already have experience programming in other languages, you must know that rarely a program will execute successfully the first time. This is a common problem when programming and almost every platform has its own tools to deal with this problem [6]. In LabVIEW^{TM}, these tools are highlight execution, execution by steps, breakpoints, and probes. These tools let the programmer analyze the code to find errors and correct them [7].

2.1.1 Highlight execution

The highlight execution 💡 is the button with a bulb in the debugging tools bar of the block diagram. When the program is executed and this button is pressed, the program's execution will be slower and the block diagram will show an animation of how the data is moving through the block diagram. For example, in Figure 2.1, the VI was executed with the highlight execution button active 💡. The figure represents the animation before the subtract function was executed and it shows the values of the constants flowing through the wires and the result from the divide function. Also, when the VI is being executed, the pause button ❚❚ can be used to analyze the code and the data values, and then the execution can be resumed by pressing the pause button again.

2.1.2 Execution by steps

Sometimes running the code with highlight execution is not enough to find errors in the code, and it is necessary to follow what the code is doing step by step to be able to find an error. This is where the executions by steps buttons come handy. These buttons are marked in Figure 2.2 inside a blue box and they are used to run the code step by step, which is also called single-stepping. It is recommended to use them with the highlight execution active. The first button is called Step Into ⤵ and it jumps into the next step of the code and pauses until it is pressed again, for

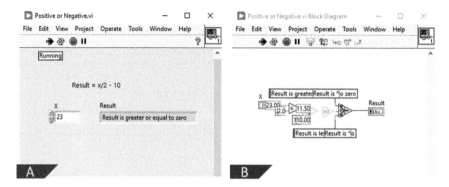

Figure 2.1   Program running with highlight execution active. (A) Front panel and (B) block diagram

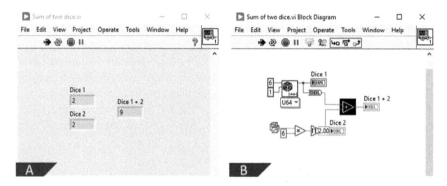

Figure 2.2   Execution by steps. (A) Front panel and (B) block diagram

example, in Figure 2.2, it is paused before the sum function is executed, if the **Step Into** button is pressed again, the result of the sum will be displayed on the numeric indicator called Dice 1 + 2. If there is a SubVI in the next step of execution, the Step Into button will open the SubVI and pause at the first step of code of this SubVI. If there is no need to open the SubVI and run through every step of it, the second button can be used, which is called **Step Over** ⌐⃗, this button works in the same way as in the Step Into button, the only difference is that this button does not opens SubVIs when single-stepping. The third button is called **Step Out** ⌐⃗ and it is used to finish the execution of the block diagram or to finish the code execution within a structure. When this button is pressed, the program will resume its execution until its task is finished, then the program will pause and disable the Step Into and Step Over buttons, the only button active will be the Step Out button. The Step Out button is mostly used to execute the code within a structure or when a SubVI is opened and single-stepping on this SubVI is not wanted, the Step Out button can be pressed to exit from this SubVI and continue single-stepping on the main VI.

• Tip #5: If you move the mouse over the Step Into or Step Over button, LabVIEW^{TM} will display a tip strip that describes the next step to be executed if you click that button.

2.1.3 Breakpoints

Execution by steps is really useful when we need control over the execution of the VI, but when the VI becomes more complex, it can take a lot of time to single-step the entire code, also, it can be frustrating when the part that needs to be analyzed requires a lot of steps to get there. To deal with this problem the breakpoint tool can be used. This tool can be placed on a VI, a node, or a wire and when the program is executed the VI will pause at that point. Then the VI can be resumed by pressing the pause button or it can be single-stepped using the execution by steps tools. The breakpoint tool can be accessed by going to View>Tools Palette or by pressing the shift key and right clicking on the workspace, then on the Tools Palette click on the button with the red circle which is the breakpoint symbol. For example, in Figure 2.3, the breakpoint tool was placed on the wire after the multiply function, then the program was executed and paused on the function where the wire is connected.

2.1.4 Probes

Sometimes it can be difficult to follow the animation to see the values move through the wires on the block diagram when the highlight execution is active, even if single-stepping is being used, the values disappear when the next step is executed. Probes can be placed to check the value flowing through a wire on the block diagram to deal with this problem.

Probes can be added to the block diagram by going to View>Tools Palette or by pressing the shift and right clicking on the workspace to open the Tools Palette, then selecting the probe tool which is the button with the letter P inside a yellow circle. Then with the probe tool selected, a probe can be added by clicking the desired

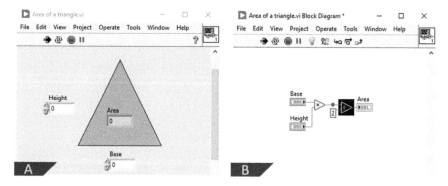

Figure 2.3   Use of breakpoint. (A) Front panel and (B) block diagram

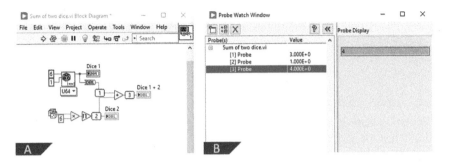

Figure 2.4   (A) Probes on block diagram and (B) Probe watch window

wire. For example, in Figure 2.4(A), three probes were added, they appear on the block diagram as a rounded box with a light yellow background and a number for each probe, in this case probe 1 is used to see the random number generated for Dice 1, probe 2 is used to see the random number generated for Dice 2, and probe 3 is used to see the sum of these two values. When the first probe is added to the block diagram, the Probe Watch Window will pop-up as shown in Figure 2.4(B), this window is divided into two, on the left side it shows a list of the probes that are being used divided by VIs in case there are more probes in different VIs at that moment and the right side shows a display of the value of the selected probe on the left side.

2.2   Debugging examples

This section presents different examples of how the debugging tools can be used to correct unexpected behavior. All the examples can be solved with any of the debugging tools, but each of them will be solved with a different debugging tool. Also, the examples used in this section are examples to solve from Section 1.6.2.

2.2.1   Quadratic equation calculator

Problem description: The VI shown in Figure 2.5 is a quadratic equation calculator, it is known that for the values of $a = 1$, $b = -2$ and $c = -3$, the results for X1

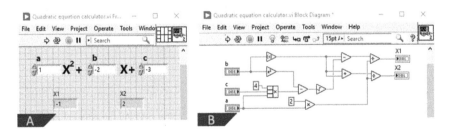

Figure 2.5   Quadratic equation calculator with error. (A) Front panel and (B) block diagram

and X2 should be −1 and 3. And as it can be seen, the value of X2 is not the expected result.

Solution: The problem with this VI can be an incorrectly wired function or a misplaced function, to verify this, the quadratic equation must be solved manually and then compare the results for every step of the VI, for example, one part of the quadratic equation formula is 4ac, which is also a step on the block diagram and running the VI step by step with highlight execution activated it can be seen that the value at that step is correct. To find the error on the VI, this process needs to be repeated until the value of a step does not match the expected value. The error for this block diagram was found on the wires connected to the sum function as shown in Figure 2.6(A), the expected value for that step was six and the step by step execution with highlight execution active showed the value was four, after checking the wires connected to the sum function it can be seen that one of the inputs was wrongly connected and it should be connected as shown on Figure 2.6(B). After making this change and executing the program again, the values for X1 and X2 are as expected.

2.2.2 Square pyramid volume calculator

Problem description: The VI shown in Figure 2.7 is a volume calculator for square pyramids. The formula used to calculate the volume of a square pyramid is

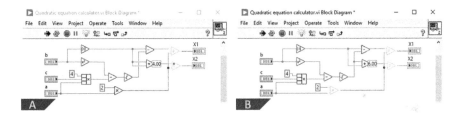

Figure 2.6 (A) Quadratic equation calculator with error and (B) quadratic equation calculator solved

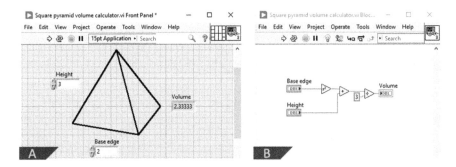

Figure 2.7 Square pyramid volume calculator. (A) Front panel and (B) block diagram

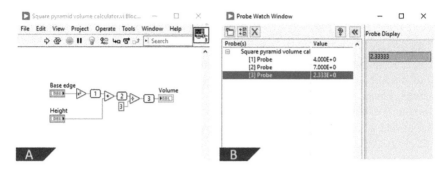

Figure 2.8   (A) Probes on square pyramid volume calculator and (B) probe watch window

$V = a^2 h/3$, where "a" is the base edge and "h" is the height of the pyramid. Then with a base of two units and a height of three units, the volume of the square pyramid should be four square units.

Solution: To find in which step the calculation error occurs, probes can be placed in different functions outputs as shown in Figure 2.8 and compare the results with the correct calculation done manually. Using the values from the problem description, in probe one, the expected result is "a" squared which is 4, the second probe is this result multiplied by "h" which should be 12, but the result of the probe shows that the result is 7. Checking the functions closely, it can be seen that it is not the multiply function, rather it is the sum function and it needs to be changed to the multiply function, this can be done by going to **Object Menu**>**Replace**>**Numeric Palette** and selecting the multiply function. After replacing the function for the correct one and executing the code, the value for the volume is as expected and the probes can be erased by closing the probe watch window.

2.2.3   X in relation to Y

Problem description: The VI shown in Figure 2.9 describes with text the relationship between the value of the X control and the Y control, this VI tells the user if X is bigger than Y, equal to Y or smaller than Y. The problem with the VI is that the results are not always as expected, only when X is smaller than Y.

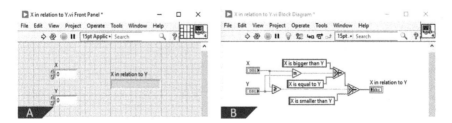

Figure 2.9   X in relation to Y. (A) Front panel and (B) block diagram

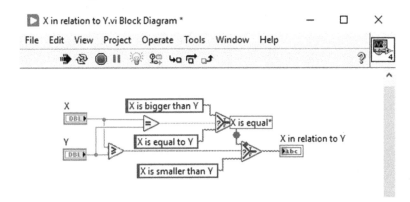

Figure 2.10   Breakpoint on the block diagram of X in relation to Y VI

Solution: As it is explained in the problem description, this VI is working as expected when the value of X is smaller than Y. Then the problem must be on the selector used for when the value of X is bigger or equal to Y, this is why a breakpoint is added after this function as shown in Figure 2.10. After placing the breakpoint and activating the highlight execution, the VI was executed with a value of three for the X control and one for the Y control, then the program stopped at the breakpoint and it can be seen that the highlight execution animation shows that the output value of the select function is "X is equal to Y" when it should be "X is bigger than Y" and this is error is due to the logic of how this VI was programmed, because before the selector there is the Equal? Function. Then this VI has two solutions, one is to replace the Equal? Function with the Greater? Function and the other solution is to invert the inputs of the selector and connect the constant "X is bigger than Y" on the false input and the constant "X is equal to Y" to the true input.

Chapter 3

Structures

Structures are nodes that execute the code that exists within them, just like any node, structures can have inputs and/or outputs. In order to execute a structure, it must have all its inputs available, in the same way, the structure will provide information through its output terminals until its execution ends. There are different types of structures such as for loops, while loops, cases, events, sequences, among others as shown in Figure 3.1. Structures can be used intuitively by developers who have experience in text-based programming; however, there are certain characteristics of the structures in LabVIEW^{TM} that you can take advantage to develop sophisticated applications avoiding being redundant in the code [8].

This chapter explains the use of basic structures such as: for loops, while loops, cases, and sequences. It also explains the feedback in loops using shift registers and feedback nodes, as well as the different data types that can be used in the selection terminal of case structure. Finally, different methods are studied for timing, giving the time to the processor to attend different tasks.

3.1   For loops

For loops allow iterative operations, a specific number of times in Figure 3.2 is shown a for loop in LabVIEW^{TM} that allows ten iterations, in the same way, the pseudocode of a text programming language that allows performing the same function can be appreciated.

To create a for loop, right click on the block diagram and open the functions palette, then select Programming>Structures>For Loop then create a box of the desired size on the block diagram to contain the for loop, see Figure 3.3.

In Figure 3.3(B), you can see the two main elements of a for loop: (1) Counting Terminal, which receives as input the number of times the for loop will iterate, (2) Iteration Terminal, which provides the current iteration number of the loop, it is important that you know that the iteration terminal is indexed to zero, so the first iteration of the for loop is iteration zero, the second iteration is iteration one, the third iteration is iteration two and so on.

By default, for loops create auto-indexed outputs in their output tunnels, this means that for each iteration, the value of the wired element to the auto-indexed output is saved in an array, which is sent to the next node or an output terminal when the execution of the for loop ends. In Figure 3.4(B), you can see the block

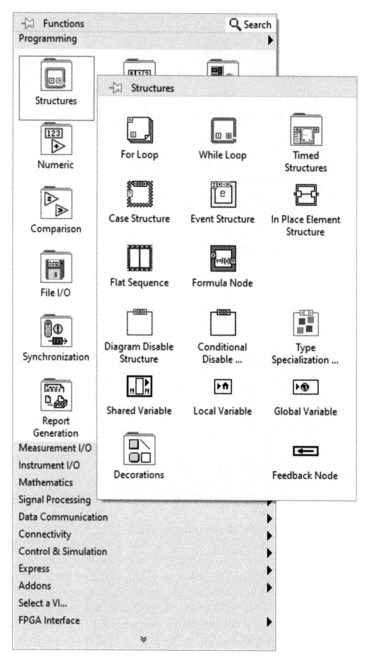

Figure 3.1   Different structures in the function's palette

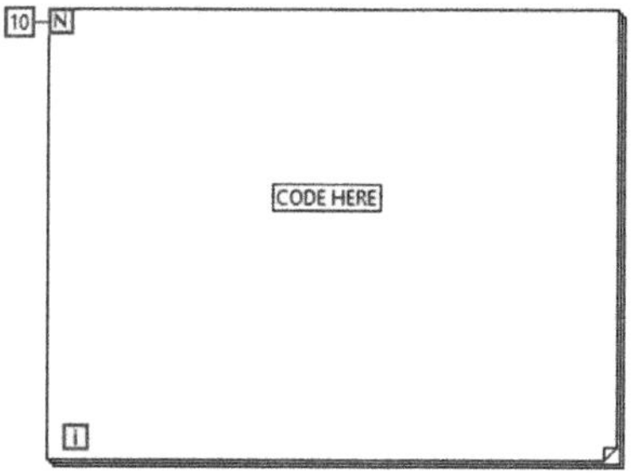

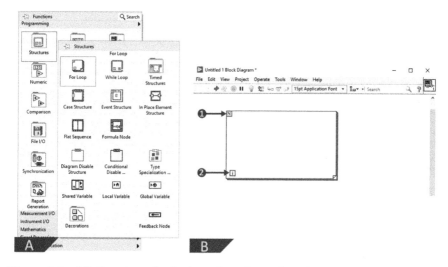

```
N=10;
for (i = 0; i < N; i++) {
    Code;
}
```

*Figure 3.2   Comparison of a for loop in LabVIEW^{TM} and a loop in text
programming language*

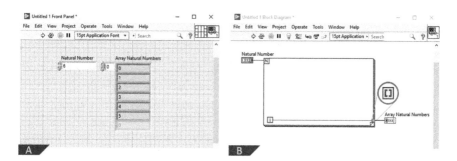

*Figure 3.3   (A) Creation of a for loop from the tools palette and (B) elements of a
for loop*

*Figure 3.4   (A) Front panel with Natural Number control, Array Natural Numbers
as indicator and (B) using a for loop to obtain natural numbers, these
are saved in the auto-indexed output, the auto-indexed is magnified
only for appreciation*

diagram of a for loop that generates the first "n" natural numbers indicated by the numerical control in the front panel seen in Figure 3.4(A) (note that this program considers the number zero as natural number, this is often know as "whole numbers"), the natural numbers are obtained through the iteration terminal and sent to the edge of the for loop, note that when you click on the edge to create the output tunnel, the auto-indexed output is automatically created which is identified by a white box containing two square brackets of the color data type.

It is important to know that auto-indexing can be used at the output or input of the for loop, to create an auto-indexed input you only must connect an array from outside the for loop; the auto-indexed input will take for each iteration of the for loop an array's element starting at index zero. You can also use the dimension of the array to indicate the number of iterations of the for loop. For example, if you connect an array of 20 elements to the auto-indexed input of a for loop, it is no longer necessary to connect the N terminal (of the for loop), since the for loop will iterate 20 times (as the array size), the implementation of this features are shown in Figure 3.5.

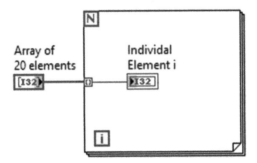

Figure 3.5   *Using the array size to indicate the number of iterations of a for loop and the auto-indexed input to obtain each element of the array*

3.2   While loops

While loops are programming structures that execute the code within them until a condition is met. While loops are created in the same way as for loops are created as shown in Figure 3.6. The two main elements in a while loop are (1) Iteration Terminal which provides the current number iteration of the loop and (2) Conditional Terminal which evaluates a boolean input to determine whether to stop or continue the while loop.

In Figure 3.7, you can see a while loop that stops when a boolean button is pressed, in the same way is presented the pseudocode in a text programming language that executes the routine until a similar condition is met.

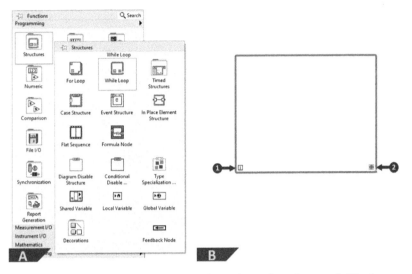

Figure 3.6   (A) Creation of a while loop from the tools palette and (B) elements of a while loop

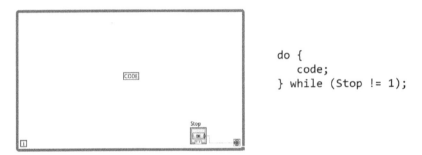

```
do {
    code;
} while (Stop != 1);
```

Figure 3.7   Comparison of a while loop in LabVIEW^TM and a loop in text programming language

• Tip #6: While loops in LabVIEW^{TM} always run at least once, otherwise, for loops can run zero times.

3.3   Cases

A case structure works in a similar way to "Case" statements in text programming languages, when a case structure has two boolean cases, then it works as an "if-then-else" statement. To create a case structure, right click on the block diagram and open the functions palette, then select Programming>Structures>Case Structure, see Figure 3.8(A), then create a box of the desired size on the block

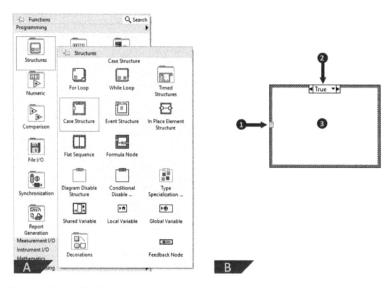

Figure 3.8   *(A) Steps to create a case structure and (B) elements in a case structure*

diagram to contain the case. The components of a case structure are (1) case selector, (2) selector label, and (3) the code that is executed in each of the cases (see Figure 3.8(B)).

The case structure by default accept a boolean data type in the case selector; however, the case structure can accept different data types, for example numeric, strings, enums, clusters, among others. Figure 3.9 shows the changes in the case selector as different data types are connected, in the same way the change in the selector label can also be seen.

Depending on the type of control that is connected to the case selector, it will be the type of cases that can be added in the selector label. For example, if a numeric control is connected to the case selector, then you can only have numeric cases in the selector label, if a string type control is connected to the

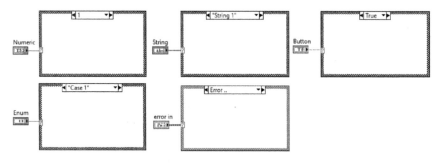

Figure 3.9   *Case selector with different data types as inputs*

case selector, then you can only have text cases in the selector label (this is appreciated in Figure 3.9) in the same way, if a Boolean control is connected to the case selector then you can only have Boolean cases (True, False) in the selector label.

Different operations can be performed on a case structure, these are accessed in the "shortcut menu" by right clicking on the edges of the structure. Among the options are "Add Case After", "Add Case Before", "Duplicate Case", "Delete this Case", and "Remove Empty Case", among others (see Figure 3.10). However, you should note that these operations change depending on the data type that is connected to the case selector, for example, if it is connected an enum control with multiple elements in the list, you could select "Add Caser For Every Value" to add a case for each element in the list, on the other hand, if a string type control is connected, you can select "Case Insensitive Match" so that the case is executed regardless of whether the string is written in uppercase or lowercase as shown in Figure 3.10.

To see all the cases that are inside a case structure, you must click on the down arrow on the selector label as shown in Figure 3.11. In the same way, you can use the arrows to the left and to the right to move between the available cases.

3.4   Sequences

To create a Flat Sequence structure, right click on the block diagram and open the functions palette, then select Programming>Structures>Flat Sequence, see Figure 3.12(A), then create a box of the desired size on the block diagram to

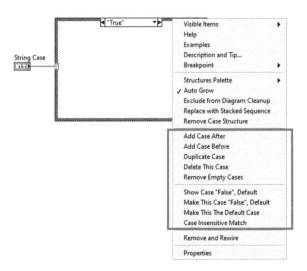

Figure 3.10   Accessing by the shortcut menu to the different operations that can be performed on a case structure

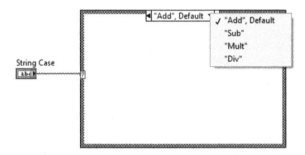

Figure 3.11   Using the drop-down arrow in the selector label to see all cases

contain the Sequence. To add frames to the sequence, go to the shortcut menu by right clicking on the edge of the sequence and select "Add Frame After", see Figure 3.12(B).

The sequence structure allows "forcing" the sequential execution of tasks in a program. As can be seen in Figure 3.13, the sequence structure has the appearance of a film (from old video films), the sequence begins by executing the code that is presented in the first frame, then it executes the code of the second frame and ends with the code of the third frame. In Figure 3.13, three dialog boxes are shown, one after other in each box of the sequence, when executing the code, you can see that dialog box 2 is displayed until you click OK in dialog box 1, as well as dialog box 3 is displayed until OK is pressed in dialog box 2, you can program the code in LabVIEW™ to check how it is executed, the function to display the messages is "One Button Dialog".

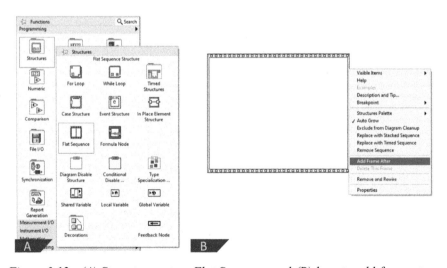

Figure 3.12   (A) Steps to create a Flat Sequence and (B) how to add frames to a sequence

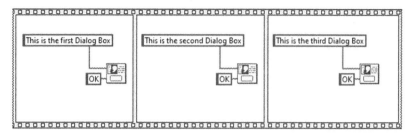

Figure 3.13   Flat sequence structure with three frames to display three dialog boxes

We recommend avoiding the use of the sequence structure, since it does not allow modifying the flow of the program at runtime, in addition, once the sequence has started it cannot be stopped until all the elements of the sequence have been executed. Use the data flow to organize the execution of your program. In the following chapters, you will be able to study the use of state machines, where advantages of this design pattern are shown over the use of sequential programming.

• Tip #7: You can change the appearance of the Flat Sequence to a Stacked Sequence in the Shortcut Menu to organize your code.

3.5   Timing

Timing is important to control the execution time of a program giving time to the processor to complete other tasks [9]. For example, a program that executes an addition type operation within a while loop and is not timed, would perform the addition millions of times per second and this is usually unnecessary. There are two widely used functions for timing applications, the first is "Wait" and the second is "Wait Until the Next ms Multiple", see Figure 3.14.

These two functions are similar but with subtle differences. The function Wait adds the number of milliseconds that is connected to its input to the time it takes a loop (or structure) to finish operations within it. On the other hand, the function Wait Until Next ms Multiple adds to the time it takes a loop to complete the execution of the code within it, the necessary milliseconds to reach the connected input of the Wait Until Next ms Multiple function, see Table 3.1.

Wait (ms)   Wait Until Next ms Multiple

Figure 3.14   Functions for timing in LabVIEW^{TM}

Table 3.1   Difference between different Wait functions

Code execution time within a loop	Function	Total time
100 ms	500 — ⌚ Wait (ms)	600 ms
100 ms	500 — 🎼 Wait Until Next ms Multiple	500 ms

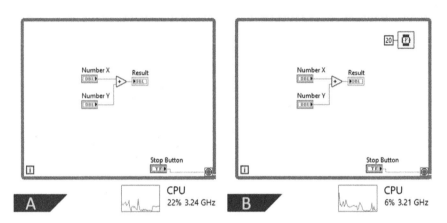

Figure 3.15   CPU resource use in (A) code without timing, CPU = 22%, (B) timed code, CPU = 6%

The following program executes the addition of two numbers. The code is executed first without timing (Figure 3.15(A)), then with timing (Figure 3.15(B)), for both executions the task manager is shown, and you can see that for a program without timing, the use of CPU resources is significantly higher.

Finally, it can be observed that the non-timing of a program can lead to overload the use of the CPU. From Figure 3.15, you can see that a simple operation (such as an addition) consumes a significant amount of CPU when a VI is not timed. In subsequent chapters, we will talk about alternative design patterns that allow you to run programs without timing, that do "not consume processor resources, and respond quickly to all user actions.

3.6   Feedback in loops

Typically, loops perform repetitive operations where the information from a previous iteration is required. To perform this, shift registers are the optimal way to send information from one iteration to another. Shift registers are created by right clicking on the edges of the loop>Add Shift Register, as in Figure 3.16(A), which will show two tunnels, one with a down arrow and the other with an up arrow in black color, which indicates the data type is undefined Figure 3.16(B). The right tunnel with the up arrow will send the information of the current iteration to the next iteration, the left tunnel with the down arrow receives the information of the previous iteration.

It is important that before executing a code with a shift register, the shift register(s) on the left is/are initialized, this is because the shift registers work as memory elements and maintain the value of the last execution of the program even when it has been ended. The values for the first run of a program that has uninitialized shift registers are given in Table 3.2.

In the Figure 3.17, you can see how a for loop where three units are added to the result of the previous iteration provides different results with initialized and uninitialized shift registers, in the same way, is shown how the result of the program will be affected in a second run when the shift register is uninitialized.

At this point, it is important to emphasize the importance of initializing the shift registers, this with the aim to maintain a stable program and avoid unexpected data or behaviors.

A second way to feedback data in loops is using "Feedback Nodes", which can be configured to provide data from one iteration to another in a loop, for this, the first step is to create the loop, then, place the "Feedback Node" from the functions

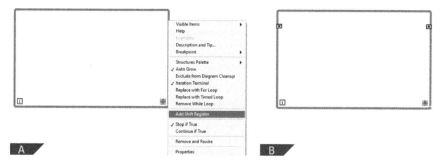

Figure 3.16 *(A) Creating a shift register in LabVIEW^{TM} and (B) the created shift register with undefined data type*

Table 3.2 Default values for
uninitialized shift registers

Data type	Uninitialized shift register value
Boolean	False
String	Empty
Numeric	Zero

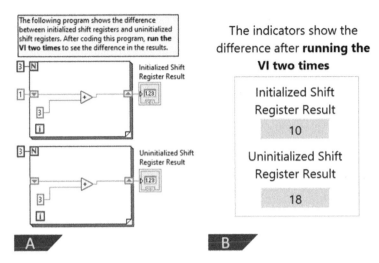

Figure 3.17   (A) Block diagram with two for loops, one with an initialized shift registers and the other with uninitialized shift registers. (B) Result after running the VI two times, note that the for loops with the uninitialized shift register provide a different result each time the VI is running

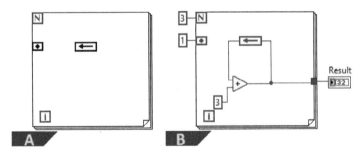

Figure 3.18   (A) Creation of a Feedback Node and (B) using Feedback Node initializer to initialize the loop every time the loop executes

palette in **Programming**> **Structures**> **Feedback Node** inside the loop, once the Feedback Node is created right clicking over the feedback node and select **Move Initializer One Loop Out** at this point the loop must have the appearance as shown in Figure 3.18(A), and can be modified as seen in Figure 3.18(B) in order to perform the same operation as the first loop in Figure 3.17.

3.7   Examples of VIs with structures

A common problem in science and engineering is the use of filters [10]. These are typically used to obtain signals that are within a noisy signal. In this sense, we can use low-pass filters to obtain signals that have low variations over time but are being affected by some external element. For example, the gravitational field occurs at low frequencies during accelerometer measurements [11]. You are asked to dynamically obtain the gravitational potential during each sampling moment (*i*) using the following low-pass filter formula for gravity extraction (3.1):

$$g_b = \lambda * g_{b(i-1)} + (1 - \lambda) * a_{b(i)} \tag{3.1}$$

where a_b is the accelerometer reading at time (*i*), lambda (λ) the filter cutoff coefficient, and g_b the filtered gravity value.

Coming up next, you will create a program that extracts the gravitational potential of a noisy accelerometer. Since you do not have a physical sensor connected, you will start by simulating the gravity readings obtained by an accelerometer with Gaussian white noise. To do this, in a blank VI open the block diagram and insert the Gaussian Noise function from the functions palette in Signal Processing> Sig Generation> Gaussian Noise, in the input samples connect a 200 as a numerical constant, and connect a double constant of 0.3 in the standard deviation input terminal, the output Gaussian Noise Pattern will be connected to an Add function where the array will be added with a double constant of value 9.81 (the value of gravity), later you will see that the Add function is polymorphic so accepts different data types as input, which allows to add an array with a constant. The output of the add will be connected to an indicator Waveform Graph (Silver), to do this, in the front panel from the controls palette, create the indicator from Silver> Graph> Waveform Graph (Silver), wire the output of the Add in the block diagram to the indicator Waveform Graph (Silver), in Figure 3.19 you can see the code that you must have created.

Next, modify the front panel to have the following appearance, the Lambda numerical control will be inserted to control the filter cutoff coefficient, remember that Lambda value is a double precision floating number with values between zero and one. It is possible to add more plots by resizing the upper right box where the identifier is located, in the same way you can change the name of the plots by

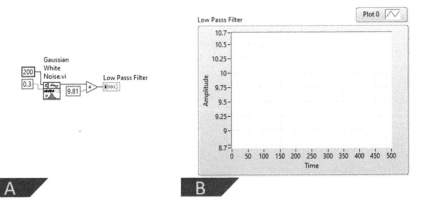

Figure 3.19   Creating a noisy gravity signal of 200 samples. (A) Block diagram and (B) front panel

double clicking on the names. The appearance of the front panel should look like the one shown in Figure 3.20.

• Tip #8: It is possible to modify the scale of the "y" axis from the properties of the graphical control so that it has values between 9 and 10.8. In the same way, in the properties of the numerical control Lambda, it is possible to define only inputs with values between zero and one, try to do so to familiarize yourself with the properties.

In the block diagram, a case structure will be inserted inside a for loop and you will use the Build Array function from **Programming> Array> Build Array** to create a two-dimensional array, in following chapters you will see in detail several functions to work with arrays. The first input of Build Array corresponds to the first row of the array and is connected to the gravity with Gaussian White Noise, the

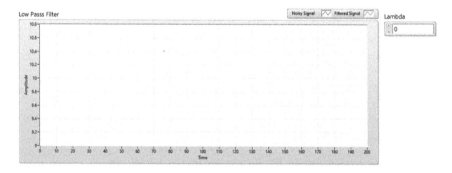

Figure 3.20   The front panel user interface

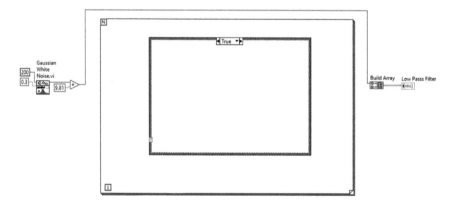

Figure 3.21   Inserting the for loop, case structure and Build Array function of the under-development filter

second row will remain for now unwire. The block diagram should look like Figure 3.21.

Thereafter, the gravity with Gaussian White Noise is connected to the for loop, note that connecting an array to the for loop by default creates an auto-indexed input which indicates that for each iteration of the for loop it will take an element of the array. Each element of the array is an input for the case structure, where for the first iteration propagates the first value of the array directly to the next iteration, therefore the case selector terminal enters to the **case true** only with iteration zero. On the other hand, a shift register is created to send the output value of the case structure to the next iteration, this output value is also saved in an array using the default auto-indexed output of the for loop, in Figure 3.22 you can see the block diagram to this point.

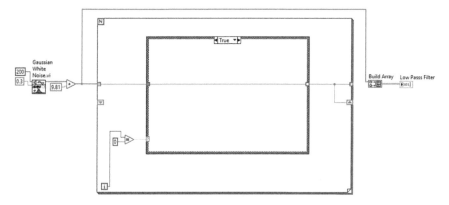

Figure 3.22   Obtaining each element of the array input by an auto-index input and sending the output of the case structure to next iteration by a shift register

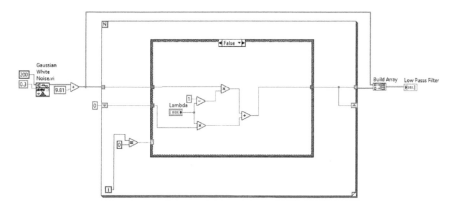

Figure 3.23   Graphic code of the false case (when i > 0) and final block diagram of the low-pass filter

Finally, inside the false case, (3.1) is programmed, where $g_{b(i-1)}$ corresponds to the output g_b of the previous iteration (which comes from the shift register) and is multiplied by Lamda, and $a_{b(i)}$ corresponds to the current value of the auto-indexed input, which is multiplied by $(1 - \lambda)$. The sum of both terms results in g_b which is connected to the auto-indexed output of the for loop, this array is connected as the second row of the Build Array, this way you have a two-dimensional array. The graph type indicator, Low Pass Filter, is a polymorphic indicator that accepts one or two-dimensional inputs, where if a two-dimensional input is connected, each row represents a different signal. Finally, it is important to initialize the shift register to zero. The block diagram for the false case can be seen in Figure 3.23.

Finally, you can perform some tests to check the performance of the developed filter, for example, test how is the performance of the filtered signal for Lambda values of $\lambda = 0.3, 0.5, 0.7,$ and 0.9. Next, in Figure 3.24, the performance of the filter for $\lambda = 0.7$ is presented.

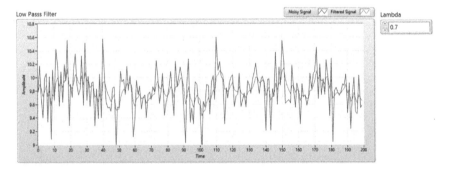

Figure 3.24   Filter performance for a cutoff frequency of $\lambda = 0.7$

Chapter 4

SubVIs

One of the main objectives of any program is scalability [12], this can be understood as the ability of a virtual instrument to implement new functionalities without significantly affecting the existing code. This scalability can be achieved by using modularity efficiently, which is performed in LabVIEW^{TM} using SubVIs. This chapter explains how to create SubVIs from existing code, create SubVIs from a VI, specify the type for connection in the connector pane, and create custom icons and some techniques and conventions to implement SubVIs efficiently.

4.1 Creating a subVI

There are two ways to create a new subVI, the first is to create a subVI from existing code on the main VI and the second is to convert a VI into a subVI. It does not matter which way is chosen to create a new subVI, at the end they will work the same way, the only difference is how they are created at the beginning.

4.1.1 SubVIs from existing code

Creating a subVI from existing code on the main VI is helpful when the VI is getting bigger and harder to read and organize. When this happens, it is recommended to analyze the code and determine which part is convenient to convert into a subVI. For example, in Figure 4.1, there is a VI that shows the user's average score over three rounds of a game and a message, this message changes depending on the average score.

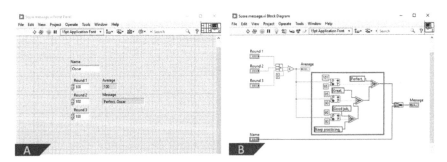

Figure 4.1   Score message VI. (A) Front panel and (B) block diagram

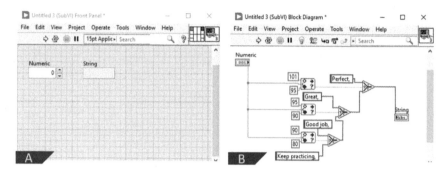

Figure 4.2   Message selector subVI. (A) Front panel and (B) block diagram

The block diagram inside the blue box is the part of the code that decides which message to select, this part can be converted into a subVI to simplify the code. The first step to convert this part of the code into a subVI is to select that part of the code, then on the block diagram window go to Edit>Create SubVI. After doing this, the selected code will disappear, and a new node with the VI icon will appear. This new node is the new subVI and it can be modified by double clicking on it, this will open a new front panel window for the subVI and by pressing Ctrl + E the block diagram for this new subVI will open as shown in Figure 4.2. Note that the VI opens as an untitled VI and needs to be saved as a new VI.

4.1.2   SubVIs from VI

If a part of the code is not programmed and it is known that it will be implemented with a subVI, there is no need to program it on the main VI and then convert that part into a subVI. This subVI can be created as a separate VI and then implemented into the main VI as a subVI. Using the example from Figure 4.2, this subVI can be created by opening a new VI and programming it in the same way. Then the inputs and outputs need to be indicated; when a subVI is created from existing code, they are created automatically, but when a subVI is created from a VI, the inputs and outputs need to be specified on the connector pane, this process is explained in Section 4.2. Then after indicating the inputs and outputs, a custom icon needs to be created to differentiate all the subVIs in the code, this process is explained in Section 4.3. When the subVI is finished, it can be dragged from the folder location to the block diagram of the main VI and connected to the corresponding inputs and outputs. It is important that the new subVI is saved in the same folder as the main VI and it is recommended to use the project explorer for better organization when working with subVIs.

4.2   Connector pane

At the top right in the front panel of every VI, there is the connector pane and the VI icon as shown in Figure 4.3. The block on the left is the connector pane, it has a pattern of divisions, which are used to indicate which terminal corresponds to the

Figure 4.3   Connector pane and VI icon

controls and indicators of the VI. This pattern can be changed to fulfill the needs of the subVI in case it needs more or fewer terminals to simplify the subVI. The pattern can be changed by right clicking on the connector pane and then going to patterns, this will show all the available patterns. Continuing with the example from the previous section, it only needs a pattern with one input and one output, so a simple pattern with two sections will fulfill these needs. Then it needs to be indicated which terminal corresponds to the numeric control and which terminal corresponds to the string indicator, this can be done by clicking one of the connector terminals and then the object on the workspace, after doing this, the section of the connector pane will change to the color of the objects data type. For example, the terminal connected to the numeric control will change to orange since it is a double precision data type, and the terminal connected to the string indicator will change to pink since the data type is a string.

4.3   Custom icons

When implementing a subVI the icon must give an idea of what this subVI does so that the main code can be easy to read, even for someone that has not programmed the main VI. The custom icon should represent with an image and/or text a simplification of the subVI.

To create a custom icon, double click on the subVI icon and then the Icon Editor window will appear as shown in Figure 4.4. At the right of the window, there is the preview of the icon, which is going to function as the workspace to modify the icon; then there are three boxes, the bottom one contains two smaller boxes, which are the line color and the fill color, the middle one contains buttons to mirror the icon horizontally and to rotate the icon 90 degrees clockwise and the top one is the editing tools box that includes the following tools:

> • Tip #9: When using an editing tool, if the left click is used the line color will be used as the specified color and if the right click is used, the use of line color and fill color will be inverted.

- Pencil: Draws individual pixels of the specified color.
- Line: Draws a line on the specified color.
- Dropper: Sets the line color of a pixel when the left click is pressed and the fill color when the right click is pressed.

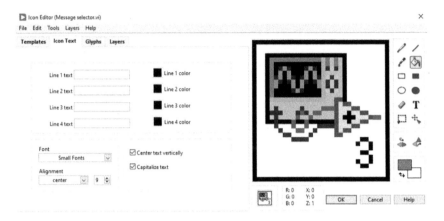

Figure 4.4   Icon editor window

- Fill: Fills all the connected pixels of the same color with the specified color.
- Rectangle: Draws a rectangle with the specified color. A double click on this icon will add a one-pixel border with the fill color to the entire icon.
- Filled rectangle: Draws a rectangle with a border in line color and filled with the fill color. A double click on this icon will add a one-pixel border pixel with the line color filled with the fill color.
- Ellipse: Draws an ellipse with the specified color.
- Filled ellipse: Draws an ellipse with a border in line color and filled with the fill color.
- Eraser: Converts individual pixels to transparent pixels.
- Text: Enters text at the specified location. Double clicking on this tool opens the Icon Editor Properties window, which can be used to modify the font, alignment, and font size.
- Select: Selects an area of the icon that can be cut, copied, or moved. Double clicking this icon selects the entire icon.
- Move: Moves all pixels on the layers.

There are four tabs on the left side of the Icon Editor window, as shown in Figure 4.5. The templates tab displays icon templates that can be used to customize the subVI, the selected template will appear on the layers tab. The Icon text tab is used to add text in different lines of the icon; the text color can be changed by line with the color boxes at the right of each line; and the font, alignment, and size can be changed with the options at the bottom left. If you add text Line 1 text, it will appear at the center of the icon; if you want the text to appear at their corresponding line, the Center text vertically must be unchecked. The glyphs tab displays glyphs sorted by category that can be used to customize the icon, to add a glyph to the icon just click on the desired glyph and when you move the mouse over the preview of the icon, the selected glyph will follow the mouse until the right click is pressed over the preview (or just drag the glyph over the preview of the icon). The layers

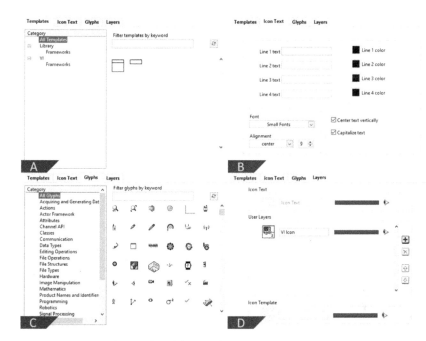

Figure 4.5   *Icon editor tabs. (A) Templates, (B) icon text, (C) glyphs, and (D) layers*

tab displays all layers for the icon separated by icon text, user layers, and icon template. Layers are useful to work in a non-destructive way, this means that the changes in one layer do not affect other layers. Also, the layers' opacity can be changed by moving the blue bar next to each layer to adjust it. To add more layers, click on the button with the blue plus sign, to delete a specific layer, select that layer and then click the delete button, which is the one with the red x, and to reorder the layers use the yellow arrow buttons.

Continuing with the example from Figure 4.2, the subVI custom icon can be created as shown in Figure 4.6, where the first step was to select the template and

Figure 4.6   *Custom icon creation. (A) Template and text, (B) background colors, and (C) glyphs*

add text as a header on a new layer, the second step was to create a new layer under the text layer and create the background and the last step was to add/create an image in a new layer that represents the function of the subVI, in this case it is an orange square representing the double-precision data type that is converted into a string which is represented in an orange square.

One of the most important things to remember when creating a subVI is that it must be used to make the code scalable and simpler. This can be achieved by efficient use of modularity when creating subVIs. When creating subVIs that have certain similarities or are applied for the same type of code, a good practice is to standardize the connector pane and custom icons by using headers of the same color.

4.4 SubVI documentation

When a subVI is created, it is important that it does not only have an image to give an idea of what the function of this subVI is. The input and output terminals should be named accordingly to their function and also its function must be documented in a short and accurate description. This documentation can be added by going to File>VI Properties, then on the properties window on Category> Documentation there is a section where the VI description can be written. This description will be shown on the Context Help window when used over the created subVI.

Continuing with the example from Figure 4.2, the score message VI code can be simplified as shown in Figure 4.7(A), where the part of the code that calculated the average of the three rounds was also converted into a subVI. Also, in Figure 4.7 (B), the context window for each subVI is shown with their terminal labeled accordingly and their corresponding documentation. As you can see from comparing the code from Figures 4.1(B) and 4.7(A), they work exactly in the same way. Still, the code from Figure 4.7(A) is easier to read and understand just by looking at it and using the context help window without having to analyze every step of the code in detail.

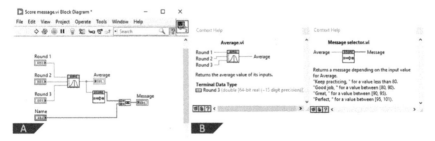

Figure 4.7   (A) Score message VI block diagram and (B) subVIs context help

• Tip #10: If a subVI is placed in multiple parts of the main VI and it happens that a copy is called at the same time that another copy of the same subVI, one will be executed and the other will wait until the first one finishes its execution.

4.5   SubVI creation examples

This section presents one example that can be divided into three exercises. This example is the VI shown in Figure 4.8, which is a VI that captures the name of a student and the grades over three tests, then after pressing the save button, the VI will display on the description string indicator the average of the student and if he approved the course depending on the average.

The VI also have a numeric indicator to show the average, a led that turns on if the student approved the course and an exit button that will display a message to the user to make sure that the user wants to exit the program.

The block diagram is as shown in Figure 4.9, it is a While Loop with a Flat Sequence inside, where the first sequence is a While Loop used to wait for the user to fill the necessary information. When the user presses the Exit or Save button, the While Loop will stop and the code will advance to the next sequence, this sequence has a Case Structure that will go to the false case if the Save button is pressed, and if the Exit button is pressed it will go to the true case. The false case is programmed to take the information of the previous state and calculate the average, check if it is greater than 80 and arrange the message for the description. The true case is used to display a dialog box where it asks the user "Are you sure you want to exit?" with two buttons, a Yes button to stop the program and a No button to continue with the program.

As you can see, the false case is the part of the code where more functions are used and it can be simplified by implementing three subVIs: one for the average, one to check if the student approved or not, and one to arrange the message used for

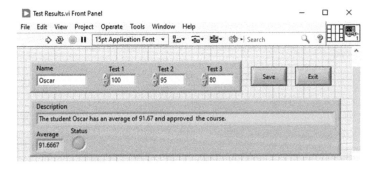

Figure 4.8   Test results front panel

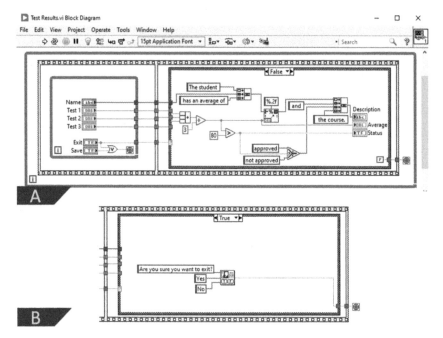

Figure 4.9   (A) Test results block diagram with false case and (B) test results block diagram with true case

the description. The creation of these three subVIs is explained in the following sections.

4.5.1   Average subVI

The average subVI is created by selecting the numeric constant, the compound arithmetic function, and the divide function as shown in Figure 4.10(A) inside the blue box, then by going to Edit>Create SubVI, the subVI is created. The next steps are to create a custom icon, change the numeric control name to Average, and write the VI documentation as shown in Figure 4.10(B).

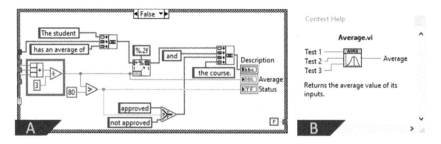

Figure 4.10   (A) Selection for average subVI and (B) average subVI context help

4.5.2   Approved SubVI

The approved subVI is created by selecting the Greater? Function, the Select function, and the string constants as shown in Figure 4.11(A) inside the blue box. It is important that the numeric constant is not selected because it will be used as an input in case that the pass value needs to be changed. After making the selection, the subVI can be created by going to Edit>Create subVI. Then the next steps are to create a custom icon, change the name of the controls and indicators to a more suitable one, and add the VI documentation as shown in Figure 4.11(B).

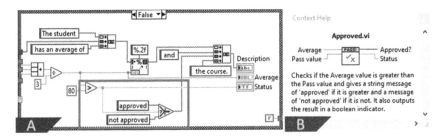

Figure 4.11   (A) Selection for approved subVI and (B) approved subVI context help

4.5.3   Arrange message subVI

The arrange message subVI is created by selecting the functions Concatenate Strings and Format to Strings, and the string constants as shown in Figure 4.12(A) inside the blue box. Note that the functions and constants were moved to the top part of the case to facilitate the selection. After making the selection, the subVI can be created by going to Edit>Create SubVI. The next steps are to create a custom icon and add the VI documentation as shown in Figure 4.12(B).

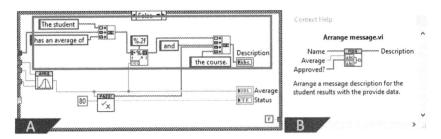

Figure 4.12   (A) Selection for arrange message subVI and (B) arrange message subVI context help

Chapter 5
Structures – LabVIEW™ features

One of the main applications of structures is working with arrays for iterative operations, ordering, and even searching information [13]. In this context, this chapter presents different approaches in which structures can be used to create and process arrays. In addition, with the aim to share data between parallel loops, the concept of variables is introduced. Finally, the concept of race conditions is explained to avoid some common problems using variables, and Formula Nodes are presented to have a structured way to implement mathematical formulas in text mode.

5.1 Arrays and loops

Arrays are collections of elements of the same data type [14]. These can be one-dimensional, two-dimensional, or multi-dimensional. Arrays are mainly used when working with repetitive operations and can be created from the front panel by placing an array control from the control palette **Silver>Data Containers>Array (Silver)** on the front panel. When the array container is created, it is observed that it is empty and without a defined data type. In order to define it, a control of the desired data type (Boolean, integer, string, etc.) is created and placed inside the array container, you can observe the change in appearance after doing that in Figure 5.1.

On the other hand, arrays can also be created from the block diagram, this from the function's palette in **Programming >> Array >> Array Constant**. When the constant is created, you will see the constant in black color, this indicates that the array does not yet have a defined data type. To define the constant array data type,

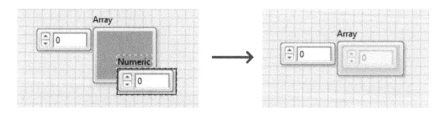

Figure 5.1   Creating a numeric array from an array data container

it is necessary to create a second constant of the desired data type (Boolean, integer, string, etc.) and place it inside the constant array, the creation process can be seen in Figure 5.2.

• Tip #11: The black color of a terminal in LabVIEW^{TM} indicates an undefined data type.

To create an array of two dimensions or more, right click on the Array Index >> Add Dimension, see Figure 5.3, this will allow you to add as many dimensions as necessary in the array.

To initialize an array, you can use the Initialize Array function from the function's palette in Programming >> Array >> Initialized Array, this creates

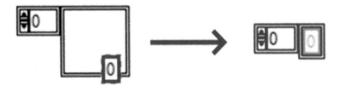

Figure 5.2   Creating an array constant in the block diagram

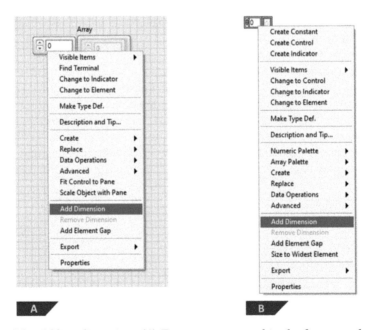

Figure 5.3   Adding dimension. (A) To an array control in the front panel and (B) to a constant array in the block diagram

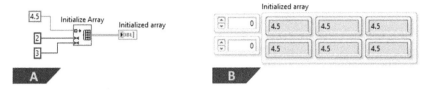

Figure 5.4   Using the Initialize Array function to create a two-dimensional array of two rows and three columns

an array with the number of elements specified in each of the dimensions, to add more dimensions, you just have to change the size of Initialize Array by clicking on the bottom edge of the function, drag and add the necessary dimensions. In Figure 5.4(A), you can see the initialization of an array of two rows and three columns, and in Figure 5.4(B), the control on the front panel is already initialized.

On the other hand, it is also possible to initialize arrays directly on a control array in the front panel or a constant array in the block diagram, for this it is necessary to click on the element within the array and write the data directly.

5.1.1   Functions and operations with arrays

Typically, arrays are used to perform repetitive operations. For example, in a digital signal with some amplitude, you may want to amplify it and for this you have to multiply the information of the signal (that is within an array) by a scalar. Another example is the sum of two digital signals where you would have to make the sum of elements found in the same instant of time in two independent signals, or you may want to perform a statistical analysis and need to determine which elements of an array are above or below a certain threshold. One approach to solving this type of problem is the use of loops where individual operations are performed with each of the elements of the array, however, LabVIEW^{TM} has arithmetic, comparison, and Boolean polymorphic functions which allow to simplify the code and perform operations that are normally performed through cycles. Polymorphism is the ability of a function to accept different data types as inputs. In Figure 5.5, different polymorphic operations and their output in the front panel are presented.

Polymorphic functions allow to simplify the code and are especially useful working with arrays, in Figure 5.5, you can see how an Add function can perform the addition of an array and a scalar or the addition of an array with another array, moreover, is shown how a Less? comparisons function can be used to Booleanly indicate which elements of an array meet a certain condition or the Round Toward +Infinity arithmetic functions that allow working with both arrays and scalars.

Although polymorphic functions serve to simplify the code when working with arrays, it is more common to manipulate the arrays directly through the different functions available to work with them, these functions can be accessed from Functions Palette in Programming >> Array. These functions are presented in Figure 5.6 and some examples of operating them are given.

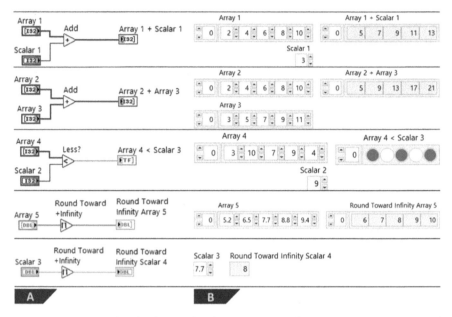

Figure 5.5   Example of polymorphic functions to perform typical operations with arrays, (A) Block diagram code and (B) Front Panel Controls and Indicators

5.1.2   Loop features

In Chapter 3, you learned how to create loops, auto indexing and how to work with shift registers or feedback nodes, however, there are additional settings or configurations to loops that can simplify the code.

5.1.2.1   Conditional auto-indexed output

For example, it is possible to create conditional auto-indexed outputs, which only save an element when a given condition is met. To create these outputs, do a right click over the **Auto-Indexed Output >> Tunnel Mode >> Conditional**, this will enable a Boolean conditional terminal with a question mark, this terminal must receive a True Boolean to save elements in the auto-indexed output array. Figure 5.7 shows a program to separate the odd numbers within an array, the function **Quotient & Remainder** is used to obtain the remainder when each element of the array is divided by two, and the **Not Equal?** Function is used to save only the elements with a remainder different than zero.

5.1.2.2   Stacked shift registers

Sometimes it is necessary to know the values of previous iterations, in Section 3.6, you studied how shift registers were created to send information from one iteration

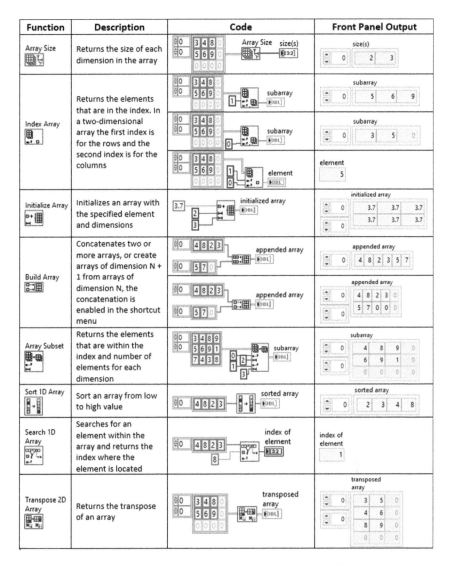

Figure 5.6   Some functions often used to work with arrays

to another; however, it is possible to create stacked shift registers to obtain the information from several previous outputs ($Y_{i-1}, Y_{i-2} \ldots Y_{i-n}$). Stacked shift registers are used in order to obtain the output value of previous iterations. To create stacked shift registers, create a shift register as described in Section 3.6, then go to the lower edge of the left shift register and using the vertical resize, add the necessary registers. Figure 5.8 shows the relationship between the position of the stacked shift register and the corresponding output value, where Y_i corresponds to the current output of the loop and $Y_{i-1}, Y_{i-2}, Y_{i-3}$ are the values of previous outputs.

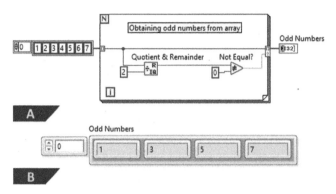

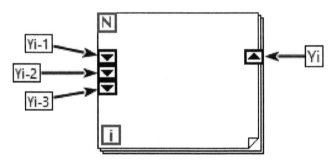

Figure 5.7   (A) Using a conditional terminal to save certain elements within auto-indexed output and (B) front panel output

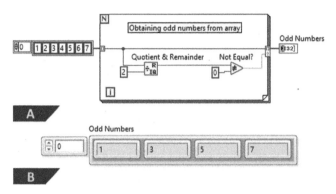

Figure 5.8   Relationship between the shift register output and the stacked shift register inputs

In the following example, you will observe a program that lets you calculate a Fibonacci number based on its position in a Fibonacci sequence. The Fibonacci sequence is a sequence where the current number is equal to the sum of the two previous numbers, the mathematical relationship of the Fibonacci sequence is

$$Y_i = Y_{i-1} + Y_{i-2}$$

Therefore, the first two numbers in the Fibonacci sequence are known values, these numbers are 0 and 1. In this way, the first 11 numbers in the Fibonacci series are 0, 1, 1, 2, 3, 5, 8, 13, 21, 34, 55 …

The program in Figure 5.9 uses the shift registers to calculate the numbers of the Fibonacci sequence by indicating the position of the number that you want to know.

As mentioned in Section 3.6 "Feedback in Loops", it is important that the input shift registers are initialized, this lets the program to be stable and work in the same way each time it is executed. In the same way, for the Figure 5.9 example, the initialization of the shift registers corresponds to the first two Fibonacci numbers that must be known to obtain the sequence.

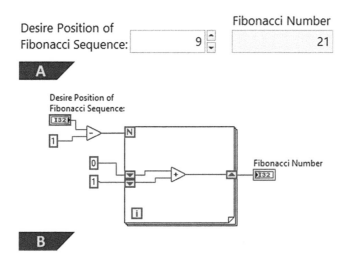

Figure 5.9   (A) Front panel of the Fibonacci program and (B) block diagram of the Fibonacci sequence program using shift registers

5.2   Data between parallel loops

Through the use of cables, information is transmitted from one node to another, and it is how the data flow is carried out. However, what happens when two processes in two loops running in parallel require sharing information? or what happens when two loops need to be stopped using the same Boolean control? There are situations where it is necessary to communicate information without the use of cables. One of the easiest approaches is the use of variables, where specifically for this section, we will address the use of Local Variables. Later in the book we will talk about other types of variables.

5.2.1   Local variables

The use of variables allows you to communicate information without using cables. These variables store the information in memory and can be consulted (or written) from different parts of the program. The location of the information depends on the type of variable; however, in this section we will be talking about local variables. A local variable is the one that has the information available within a VI.

   To see one of the most common applications in the use of local variables we can take back the asked question at the beginning of this section: What happens when it is necessary to stop two parallel loops using the same Boolean control? In Figure 5.10, there is an example of this course of action, if you run this code you will see that it is not possible to stop the loops since the control to stop them is outside the loops.

   Another possible method that you could possibly try is to place the Boolean control inside of one of the loops and send the information to a second loop. However, if you run Figure 5.11 program you will see that the first loop is

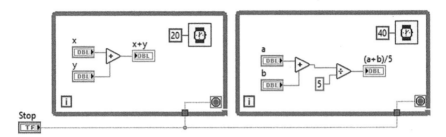

Figure 5.10   It is not possible to stop two parallel loops using controls from outside

executed correctly, but due to the data flow, the second loop will only be executed until the first loop has finished its execution. Also, you will notice that the second loop runs only once, because it receives a "True" on its input tunnel.

Therefore, from Figures 5.10 and 5.11 you can see that sometimes it is not possible to communicate all the information using only wires. For this, it is possible to use local variables. Local variables allow you to send information without the use of wires and are especially useful for communicating two parallel loops. To create a local variable, place over the Boolean control Stop, right click and select Shortcut Menu >> Create >> Local Variable, on the created variable right click on Shortcut Menu >> Change To Read. The new variable must be placed inside the second while loop and wired directly to the stop terminal, the program should look like the one in Figure 5.12. You should notice that the Run button will appear broken, this is because by default the Stop control is created as Latch and the Latch operations are incompatible with local variables. To correct this, place the cursor over the Stop button, right click and select Shortcut Menu >> Mechanical Action >> Switch When Released.

• Tip #12: The "Latch" mechanical action in a Boolean control is incompatible with local variables, change the mechanical action to "Switch" to create a local variable of a Boolean control.

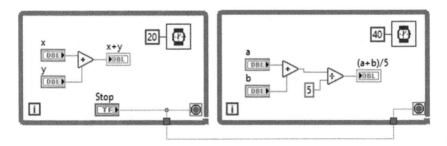

Figure 5.11   In this approach, the first loop can be stopped, but the second will iterate only once after the first loop is stopped

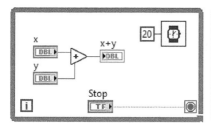 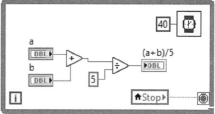

Figure 5.12   With this approach, it is possible to stop two while loops simultaneously using the same Boolean control

In the same way, it is possible to create local variables from other types of controls or indicators such as integers, strings, enums, etc. However, it is important to use wires to create your program and avoid the use of local variables as much as possible, since using local variables can cause race conditions and unexpected behaviors in your program. In the following sections, you will learn about what they are and how to avoid race conditions.

5.2.2   Race conditions

A race condition is a common problem in any program that works with multiple threads and exchange of information between them. A race condition occurs when the information of a variable is overwritten and who consults the information expects to read a different value (it could be some previous data or data that has not yet arrived). An example of a race condition is shown in Figure 5.13(A). This program performs the addition of one to the Result value. In a parallel loop, a one is subtracted from **Result** (as a local variable). A wait function is included for the temporization of both loops so that they are executed the same number of times. Under this logic, the Result value should be kept at zero, as the program adds and subtract one simultaneously. However, when running the program, it can be observed that a race condition occurs, where in some cases the **Result** value was overwritten, which caused the loss of some addition or subtraction. Observe the Front Panel in Figure 5.13(B), you can see that the number of iterations is the same in both loops, however, **Result** shows a different value than zero.

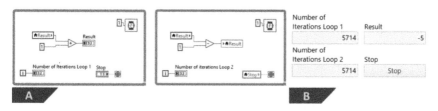

Figure 5.13   A race condition where writing a "Result" in two different parts of a program causes an unexpected output

In order to prevent race conditions, the use of local variables should be avoided, use wires instead to communicate data between the nodes' however, if it is imperative to use local variables, these should be used to consult the information and avoid the writing of a variable from two or more parts of the program.

> • Tip #13: Prevent race conditions by avoiding writing a variable in two or more parts of the program.

5.3   Formula nodes

LabVIEW^{TM} is an intuitive programming language where the operation of a program can be easy to interpret from the block diagram; however, there are some circumstances where you may want to implement a mathematical equation, and for many of these equations it is easier to see them as text code. In this sense, LabVIEW^{TM} has the Formula Node, a structure that allows the use of C++ syntax within a node. In Figure 5.14(A), there is an example of the equation for the uniformly accelerated rectilinear motion equation, in this case the program is simple;

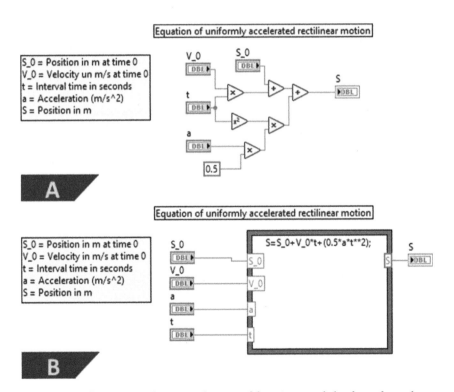

Figure 5.14   Comparison between the use of functions and the formula node to implement an equation

however, it is not intuitive to understand, a more familiar approach to implement such kind of equation can be seen in Figure 5.14(B), this approach using formula nodes.

To create a Formula Node from the Functions Palette, select Structures >> Formula Node, place the Formula Node in the block diagram at the desired size. To create the Inputs of the Formula Node, you must position the cursor on the edge of the Formula Node and Right Click >> Add Input; once the Input is created, write the name of the variable that will be used within the Formula Node, note that the variable name may have a different name than the element that is wired to that variable. To create an Output of the formula node, you must position the cursor over the edge of the formula node and Right Click >> Add Output. See Figure 5.14 in order to appreciate a Formula Node with different inputs, outputs, and the code within it.

• Tip #14: The Inputs and Outputs in a Formula Node may have different name than the element connected by wire to it.

Chapter 6

Organizing front panel and block diagram

During the code implantation in graphical programming languages, it is desirable to take care of the organization and cleanliness of the code, this is in order to increase its readability. In this sense, when there are multiple cables whose use is closely related, clusters are recommended [15]. This chapter explains how to create clusters to group data, it also explains how to create *.ctl files (control type files), this for the implementation of custom controls, type definitions, and strict type definitions, which allow the programmer to determine the appearance and functionality characteristics that want to be kept between custom controls.

6.1 Clusters

As you may have seen from Chapter 5, arrays are useful for group data elements of the same type. This makes data handling easier as only one wire is used to transfer the information. The disadvantage of arrays is that they can only manage one data type. To group data elements of mixed types, clusters can be used, the most common use of clusters is when the data elements to group are closely related. Figure 6.1 shows an example of a cluster control containing three data types, a numeric control, a Boolean control, and a string control, this cluster is connected to a cluster indicator with the same data types. The cluster control was created by going to **Controls Palette>Modern>Data Containers** and selecting cluster, when

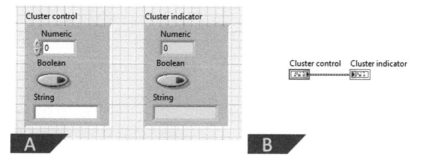

Figure 6.1 (A) Cluster control and indicator on front panel and (B) cluster control and indicator on the block diagram

the cluster is created, it appears as an empty box on the front panel, then different types of controls or indicators can be dragged into the cluster. The cluster indicator was created by right clicking on the terminal of the cluster control and then selecting create indicator. Note that when the cluster indicator is created, it automatically appears with the data types from the cluster control.

Constant clusters can also be created on the block diagram by going to Functions Palette>Programming>Cluster, Class, & Variant and then selecting cluster constant, when the cluster constant is created, a blank box will appear on the block diagram, then different types of constants can be dragged into the cluster constant.

Also, clusters can be created by bundling different data types on the block diagram using the Cluster, Class, & Variant subpalette functions as shown in Figure 6.2.

Unbundle by name, Bundle by name, Unbundle, and Bundle are the functions used to assemble new clusters or split clusters into their individual elements. Figure 6.3(A) shows the use of the Unbundle by name function, where a cluster is connected to the input terminal and the number of output terminals depends on the

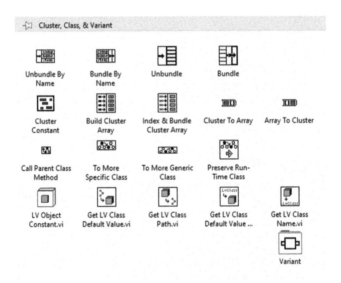

Figure 6.2   Cluster, Class, & Variant subpalette

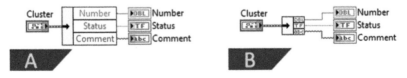

Figure 6.3   (A) Unbundle by name function and (B) unbundle

number of elements of the cluster, in this case the cluster had three elements and the unbundle by name function shows these three elements by name on its terminal outputs. The Unbundle function shown in Figure 6.3(B) works in the same way as the Unbundle by name function, with the only difference that the Unbundle function does not show the name of the elements of the cluster. Instead, it shows the data type of each element. The unbundle by name function is most commonly used as it will make the readability of the code an easier task. Use the unbundle by name function in order to keep the name of the elements visible.

The bundle by name function is used to create a cluster. If the cluster already exists, the bundle by name function can be used to update the information in one or more elements from a cluster as shown in Figure 6.4, where the value of the element called Number is updated by a numeric constant using the bundle name function. If another element instead of Number needs to be replaced, the element on the function can be changed by left clicking on the element's name to open a list of the elements of the cluster. This function can also be used to change multiple elements at a time by placing the mouse on the bottom edge of the function until the arrows appear then click and drag down to add more input terminals.

The Bundle function can be used the same way as the Bundle by name function, as shown in Figure 6.5(A). The difference of the Bundle function is that it will not show the name of every element, instead, the function will have an input terminal for every element of the cluster and only the wired terminals will be updated, the value of the rest of the elements will remain the same. Another application for the Bundle function is to assemble new clusters from individual elements, as shown in Figure 6.5(B).

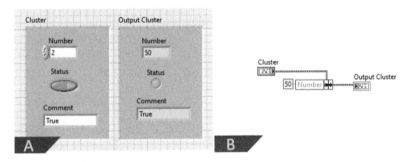

Figure 6.4   (A) Clusters on front panel and (B) Bundle by name function

Figure 6.5   (A) Replacing cluster element and (B) assembling new cluster

6.2   Control type files

As you may have seen, the number of controls and indicators to use on the front panel is limited. There are different subpalettes with the same controls and indicators in different styles and their size and color can be personalized to fit the needs of the user interface. But sometimes, this level of personalization is not enough to create programs, sometimes custom controls and indicators are needed. LabVIEW^{TM} has a feature that lets programmers to create their own custom controls and indicators, save them and use them in different subVIs.

Custom controls or indicators can be created by selecting the control or indicator on the block diagram and then going to Edit>Customize Control ... and this will open a new window as shown in Figure 6.6. This window looks like the front panel, but it is not, this is the control editor window and it cannot run the program. This window is used to customize the control, create a custom icon, and define the type of control that is being created. Also, this window can only be used to customize a single control or indicator, this means that it can only contain one control or indicator. Arrays or clusters that contain sub-controls or sub-indicators can also be customized since they count as a single control.

At the top left of the window, where the run button normally is on the front panel, there is a mode button used to switch between edit mode or customize mode. The edit mode is used to change the size and color of the control as it is done in the front panel. The customize mode is used to make even more changes to the control by allowing to modify individual parts of the control or indicator.

When the customize mode is active, the visualization of the control or indicator changes to show the individual parts that compose it as shown in Figure 6.7, where the individual parts are marked by a transparent rectangle with a white outline. The individual parts can also be viewed on the show parts window by going to Window>Show Parts Window. This window is used to see each part individually and edit the position and dimensions. In customize mode, each part can be moved with the positioning tool or rearranged with the align objects, distribute objects and reorder with the object organization tools.

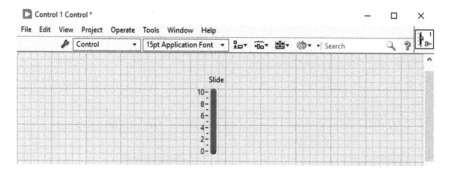

Figure 6.6   Custom control window, note at the top-right corner there is only an icon and no connector pane

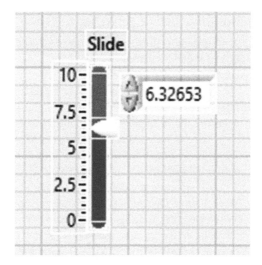

Figure 6.7 Customize mode on slider indicator

If you right click on a part of the control or indicator while the customize mode is active, a different menu will pop up depending on the type of part. For example, the digital display will open a menu that will let us change the visible items, replace the digital display, change the display format, create a cluster from selection, and change the part properties. Other parts, like the fill, allow replacing it with a graphic by using different options like import picture from clipboard, import file, etc. This option is really useful when more representation of a physical system is needed.

Also, multiple graphics can be used in one control that display at different times. For example, Figure 6.8(A) shows the true and false states of a normal Boolean control and Figure 6.8(B) shows the true and false states of a customized Boolean control, where the true and false graphics of the normal control were substituted for custom ones. Note that not all controls have this feature available, and the ones who do have this feature have an option on the shortcut menu called Picture Item which displays the graphics that belong to that item.

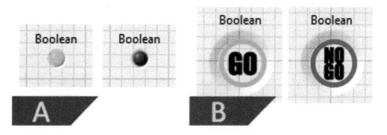

Figure 6.8 (A) Normal Boolean indicator and (B) customized Boolean indicator

6.2.1   Type definition and strict type definition

Once the custom control or indicator is finished and ready to be used on the front panel, it needs to be saved and then it can be placed over the front panel. It can be dragged from the windows folder where it was saved or it can be dragged from the project explorer. This new control can be placed as many times as needed on the front panel of the current VI or on different VIs. Note that if the file of the control is modified, it will not affect the controls placed on the front panel as each instance of the custom control is an independent copy. If you want the instances of the control to update when the file is modified, it needs to be saved as a type definition or strict type definition. A control can be created as a type definition or strict type definition by selecting its type before saving it. This can be done by selecting the control type at the drop down list to the right of the Customize Mode button. Depending on the chosen type for the control, the link between its instances used on VIs and the original file will be different.

Type definition controls create a link that updates that data type on the instances when the original control is modified. For example, suppose a slider control data type is changed from double to integer on the original file. In that case, all the instances linked to this control will automatically update to this new data type. On the other hand, if the changes made to the original file are cosmetic, the instances will not be updated to match the original. For example, if the color of the fill is changed or the range values of the slider are changed, this update will not be reflected in the instances of this control.

Strict type definition controls are used when all the changes made to the original control need to be updated to the instances, this includes data types, change on range values, cosmetic changes as color, size, etc. The only changes that do not update on the instances are the caption, label, description, tip strip, and default value. If you place an instance of a strict type definition control on a VI and you do not want that instance to automatically update anymore, you can remove the link to the original control by right clicking the instance and then selecting Disconnect from Type Def, this also applies to type definitions.

6.3   Examples of clusters and custom controls

This section has three examples: one for cluster implementation, one for custom indicator creation, and one as a combination of both, which is a custom cluster indicator.

6.3.1   Cluster implementation

Problem description: The VI shown in Figure 6.9 is the test results VI from Section 4.5. For this example, the VI will be used to move the Name, Test 1, Test 2, and Test 3 controls into a cluster control and the string, numeric, and Boolean indicators into a cluster indicator.

Solution: The first step before creating the clusters for this VI is to prepare the area for the clusters. In this case, the decorations on the back of the controls and

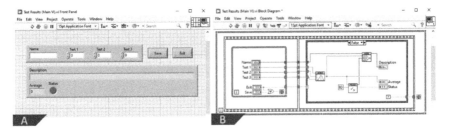

Figure 6.9 Test results VI. (A) Front panel and (B) block diagram

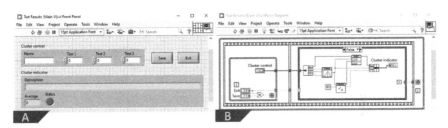

Figure 6.10 Test results VI with clusters. (A) Front panel and (B) block diagram

indicators need to be eliminated. Then a cluster can be created by going to Controls Palette>Data Containers and selecting the cluster. After placing the cluster on the front panel it needs to be resized to fit the controls Name, Test 1, Test 2, and Test 3, then these controls are selected and dragged into the cluster. The same steps apply for the cluster indicator with the Description, Average, and Status indicators. Now the front panel should look like Figure 6.10(A).

After creating the control and indicator clusters, the block diagram will appear with broken wires and the old controls and indicators will not appear anymore as now they are part of the new clusters. The new control and indicator clusters need to be wired so that the VI can continue to work in the same way as it did before the clusters. The first step is to clean up the broken wires, this is done by pressing Ctrl + B on the keyboard. Then the unbundle function is used with the control cluster on the case structure as shown in Figure 6.10(B), where the output terminals are connected to their corresponding subVIs depending on their data type as they did before the clusters were created. For the indicator cluster, the bundle function is used as shown in Figure 6.10(B), where the output terminals of the subVIs are connected to the bundle function and the output terminal of the bundle function is connected to the cluster indicator. As you can see, the application of these clusters simplifies the code, takes less space on the block diagram and if in the future it is needed to add more functionality to the program and more organization and cleanliness is needed, it can be easily done by creating a subVI on the case structure where the input terminal is the cluster control and the output is the cluster indicator, leaving the rest of the space on the block diagram to add more functionality to the program in a way that will be easier to read.

> • Tip #15: When working with PNG files, first modify the other items and then place the file with the other items. This is because you will not be able to select or edit the items behind PNG files.

6.3.2   Custom control creation

Problem description: Create a custom slider indicator for a production line that works with three kinds of beverages, green apple, strawberry, and orange. The slider indicator has to show the tank's liquid level of its corresponding flavor.

Solution: Most times, when making programs for industry applications, a graphical representation is needed to facilitate the measure visualization on the screen. For this case, a slider indicator in the shape of a tank with the fill color of each flavor is created as shown in Figure 6.11, where there are three slider indicators on the front panel. These sliders are copies from a custom type definition indicator as the same data type for each indicator needs to be preserved, but when the indicator is placed on the front panel, it needs to be modified to match the color of the beverage. This is why a strict type definition is not suitable for this application. The custom slider indicator was created by replacing the cosmetic item of the slider indicator with a PNG image of the tank, then the scale, housing, fill, digital display, and label were adjusted to fit the tank size and reordered to place the tank at the front, the fill at the middle, and the housing at the back. Then the custom indicator copies were placed on the front panel and the fill color was changed by going to **Object Menu>Properties>Appearance**. Note that the color tool could not be used because the PNG image is in front of the fill item from the indicator.

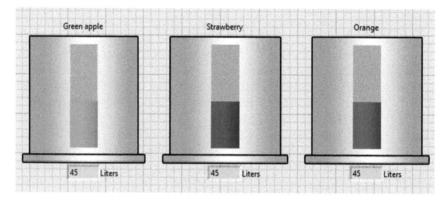

Figure 6.11   Custom slider indicators on front panel

6.3.3   Custom cluster indicator

Problem description: Create a custom cluster indicator to show the speed of a vehicle and the fuel level. The speed must be shown using a gauge and the fuel level a slide indicator. It is important that the indicators resemble the look of real car indicators.

   Solution: The first step to create this custom cluster indicator is to create a cluster on the custom control window and add the gauge and slider into the cluster as shown in Figure 6.12(A). Then a PNG image with the shape of a circle and a rectangle was added. Note that this image needs a transparent space for the fuel indicator. After the image is placed, the gauges colors are modified, the max value is changed, the Km/h label is added, and the slider indicator colors are changed and placed under the transparent part of the PNG file as shown in Figure 6.12(B).

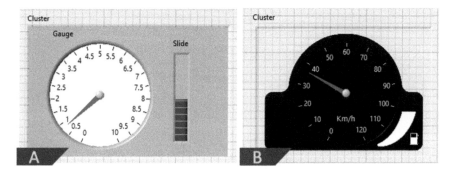

Figure 6.12   (A) Cluster indicator with gauge and slide and (B) customized cluster indicator

Chapter 7

Using software resources

This chapter explains the concept of resources and how they are accessed in LabVIEW^{TM}. As the access to resources is similar for software and hardware resources, this chapter will be focused on software resources, and hardware resources will be explained in the following chapters. The scope of this chapter is first to use software resources by high-level VIs and then to use them by low-level VIs; practical cases will be introduced, and several examples of the adequate use of each of them will be provided. In summary, this chapter introduces resources and presents practical cases and different approaches to solving them using files. Finally, structured forms to organize and present the information are taught.

7.1 Accessing resources

In LabVIEW^{TM}, a resource is any hardware or software element that can be accessed by a reference. The references point to a position in memory that is directly related to the resource that you want to access. Depending on the type of resource that to access, the type of reference also changes. For example, Table 7.1 illustrates some functions that allow to open or create a resource and their respective reference.

As can be seen in Table 7.1, there are different resources in LabVIEW^{TM}, however, it is important to know that for hardware resources such as DAQ, computer ports (ethernet, serial, USB, etc.) as well as electrical instruments (oscilloscopes, power supplies, multimeters, etc.) it is necessary that these are first recognized in the MAX (Measurement and Automation Explorer) before starting to work with them in LabVIEW^{TM}, you will learn more about it in Chapter 8. On the other hand, software resources such as files can be accessed directly in LabVIEW^{TM}.

The use of resources is like any other programming language; first, it is necessary to open or create the resource, then the resource can be used, and finally, the resource is closed. It is important to note that once the resource is opened, it cannot be used by any other program, therefore, in order to make the program available to other applications, it is necessary to properly close the resource after using it, in Figure 7.1 a flow diagram with these steps is presented.

This chapter will begin by learning about software resources, specifically files. In LabVIEW^{TM}, there are different ways to work with files. There are VIs that allow performing the three steps specified in Figure 7.1, in addition, there are

Table 7.1   Different kind of references from different resources

Type of resource	Creation of a reference		Type of reference
File	C:\Program Files (x86)\ National Instruments\ Demo.txt	Open/Create/ Replace File Refnum File	Refnum
	replace or create ▼		
DAQ	Digital Task	DAQmx Create Virtual Channel.vi task out	Task out
		Digital Input ▼	
VISA	VISA resource name	VISA Open Resource Out	Resource out

| Step 1: Open or Create the Resource | Step 2: Use the resource for as long as necessary | Step 3: Close the Resource |

Figure 7.1   Flow diagram of how to use resource

functions to work with each of the steps individually. The VIs that perform the three steps simultaneously are known as High-level File I/O VIs and the functions that perform the individual steps are known as Low-Level File I/O functions. To access different VIs or functions to work with files open from the function's palette Programming>>File I/O, in Table 7.2 the High-level File I/O and a brief description are shown.

On the other hand, Low-Level File I/O functions allow performing each step seen in Figure 7.1. Some of the most used functions to read and write ASCII Files are described in Table 7.3.

7.1.1   Using High-level File I/O VIs

Next, is presented the use of high-level File I/O VIs to write information such as spreadsheets, for that, it is necessary to create the front panel that is shown in Figure 7.2, note that it is necessary to create a 2D array and two Boolean buttons,

Table 7.2   Summary of High-level File I/O VIs

Function/VI	Description
Write Delimited Spreadsheet.vi	Convert Arrays into Strings and write the information into a delimited file (usual delimitations are tab and comma)
Read Delimited Spreadsheet.vi	Read a delimited file (as a *.csv file) and convert the strings into the specified data type (usual delimitations are tab and comma)
Write To Measurement File	VI express to save LVM, TDMS, TDMS, and xlsx Files
Read From Measurement File	VI express to read LVM, TDMS, TDMS, and generic text files, delimited by commas or Tab

Table 7.3   Summary of Low-Level File I/O Functions to work with ASCII Files

Function/VI	Description
Open/Create/ Replace File	Creates a new file from a specified path. As output, it provides the reference to the file (refnum)
Write to Text File	Writes a string inside a text file, as input requires the reference created from the function open/create/replace file or a path
Read from Text File	Reads a string inside a text file, as input requires the reference created from the function open/create/replace file or a path
Close File	Close the reference, this way the file can be accessed from other programs
Build Path	It allows creating paths from a base path and a name or relative path.
Application Directory.vi	Obtains the path of the application; if it is not an application, obtain the path of the project; if it is not a project, obtain the path of the main VI
Path Constant	Allows defining a hard drive address as a path constant

the text over the 2D array are free labels. The array is initialized directly in the front panel to have some information to write inside the File, so you can use the same information as in Figure 7.2.

After that, you will be going to create a block diagram program as in Figure 7.3 using a While Loop and a Case Structure, placing inside the Write Delimited Spreadsheet.vi, which is located in File I/O >> Write Delimited Spreadsheet.vi of the functions palette, in order to be able to appreciate all the inputs and outputs of the VI simultaneously, please select the option Shortcut Menu >> View as icon, then you will place the cursor at the bottom of the VI and resize it until we obtain the view that can be seen in Figure 7.3.

If you run this program and click over the save button, you will note that a file dialog is displayed to indicate the name of the file in which the information will be written, please write the filename as Demo.txt to see the information in a regular text editor (or choose a different name, only maintain the .txt extension in order to see the information from any text editor). If you open the created file, you will see the same information as in Figure 7.4.

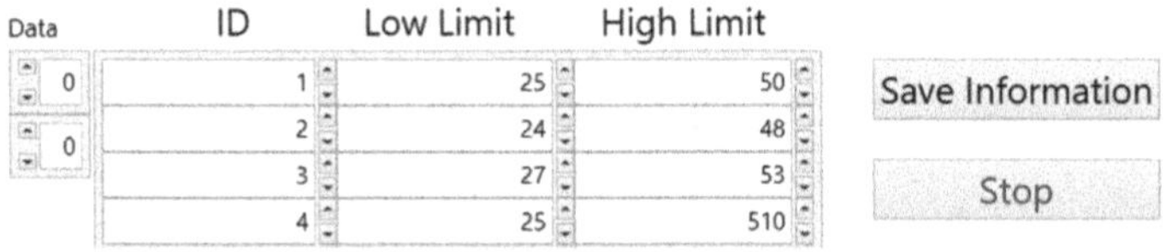

Figure 7.2   Front panel interface to save a spreadsheet in a file

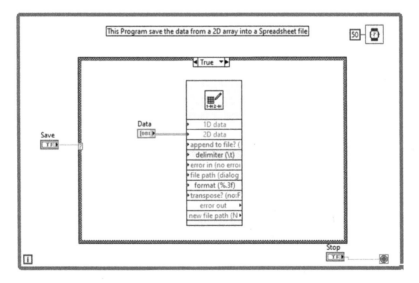

Figure 7.3   Block diagram code to use Write Delimited Spreadsheet.vi to write 2D data in a file

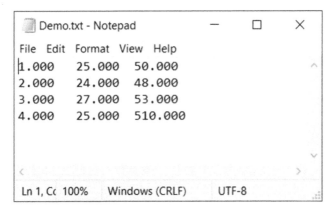

Figure 7.4   Image of the information inside the created delimited file

You can see that the structure is simple; however, it is possible to improve the way the information is written for formatting purposes, in such a way that the file can be automatically opened from a spreadsheet such as Excel. To do that, it is recommended to make some changes such as (1) changing the delimiter, (2) changing the number format to two digits of precision, and (3) programmatically creating the new file. To do this, it is necessary to modify the code as shown in Figure 7.5. Please note that the function Build Path is in Programming>> File I/O and the Application Directory.vi is in Programming>>File I/O>>File Constants.

• Tip #16: The *.csv files, are comma delimited file and is a common way to share information between different programs. The commas delimit the columns of a spreadsheet.

After running the code of Figure 7.5, you will notice that a csv file has been created, whose icon is an Excel file (if you have office installed). Double clicking on the file will open a spreadsheet as in Figure 7.6 with the file information.

It is recommended that once you have finished wiring the "Write Delimited Spreadsheet" subVI, change the view mode of the subVI to an icon to reduce the space in the block diagram.

7.1.2   Using Low-Level File I/O functions

The use of High-Level File I/O VIs for file reading or writing is useful when the data is read or written only once. However, for applications where it is necessary to constantly write/read the resource (file), the use of High-Level File I/O VIs becomes inefficient because the High-Level File I/O VIs perform three simultaneous operations: (1) open the resource, (2) write/read the resource, and (3) close the resource. For many applications, it is desirable to open the resource only once,

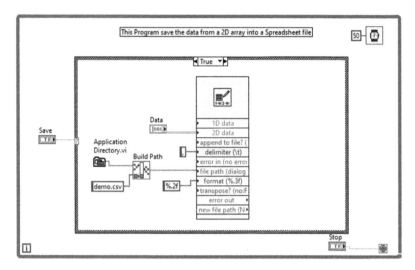

Figure 7.5   Block diagram code to save information in a csv file using relative path

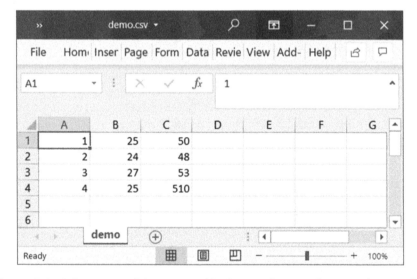

Figure 7.6   Information of the new csv file that can be open from excel or another spreadsheet software

then keep the resource in memory and write or read it as necessary; finally, when you finish using the resource, it is closed so that it is available to other applications. In this sense, when it is required to be able to perform each of these operations individually, the use of Low-Level File I/O functions is preferable.

In order to show the use of Low-Level File I/O functions, in Figure 7.7, a graphical user interface similar to the information obtained from an electrical test machine has been created in the front panel, where it is possible to capture information as "Date", "Test Name", "Result", "Operator Name". For demonstration purposes, all inputs in the "Test Cluster" are String control type. In addition, the user interface has three buttons: (1) Save: this allows you to save the captured information in "Test Cluster" in a text file, each time you click on "Save" the information is saved in a new line of the file, (2) read results history: allows you to read all the information that has been saved in the text file and (3) stop: it allows you to stop the program and close the text file.

Next, in Figure 7.8, the block diagram of Figure 7.7 is shown. You can see that the code can be divided into three parts: (1) initialization, where the text file is created or replaced, (2) functionality, a While loop with two cases, one case for the

Figure 7.7   Front panel to demonstrate the use of Low-Level File I/O functions to save data in a file and read the data of the file

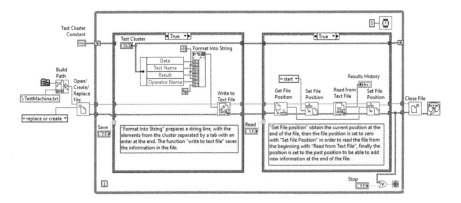

Figure 7.8   Block diagram implementing Low-Level File I/O Functions to write and read in a text file

save button and another case for the read button, and (3) close of the program, where the file is closed, and it is checked for errors. Similarly, it is important to mention that as soon as the program is inside the while loop, the file will be written or read as necessary.

First, the Open/Create/Replace File function replaces or creates the TestMachine.txt file, this file is created in the same directory as the VI (for more information see Table 7.3). After the creation of the file, it will remain in memory until the reference is closed, so it is not necessary to open the file each time you write or read it. Second, inside the while loop, the program has two cases, one for the Save button, where if it is true the data from the test cluster is passed to the Format Into String function to create a line, with the "Date", "Test Name", "Result", and "Operator Name" separated by a Tab and with an Entry value at the end of the line. This formatted data is passed to the Write to Text File Function to save the string into the file. If the user clicks the Save Button again, the new information will be written on the next line of the file. Otherwise, if the user clicks on the Read button, the program will use the Get File Position function to obtain the current position of the file (in Bytes), following the current logic, the actual position is at the end of the File, this position is used later. After getting the actual file position, you will use the Set File Position function to indicate a new position at the start of the file, this is in order to use the Read from Text File function to read the file from the beginning to the end of the text file. After reading the file, the file information is written in the Results History indicator, then the Set File Position is used to return the file position at the end of the file, this allows to use again the Write to Text File function and write the information at the end of the file. Note that in both cases (Save button and Read button), the program only passes the wires information for the False case (see Figure 7.9). Third, if the user clicks over the Stop button or if an error occurs, the program will exit the while loop and use the Close File function to properly close the file and finally report any error (if exists) using the simple error handler function. Using the Close File function will allow you to access the file from third-party applications.

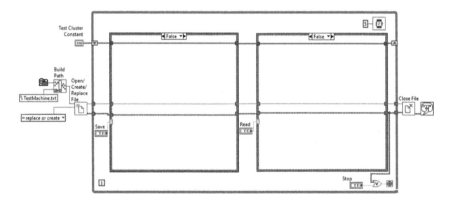

Figure 7.9   The false cases only pass the value of the wires

7.2 Formatting headers and working with multiple signals

The use of headers is a common practice in test machines. Headers help to organize information needed for further analysis or data processing, so it is important that the information in the headers are meaningful. In addition, it is necessary that the headers are organized in a way that simplifies further processing of the data. For example, compare the output information from two files that store the data of a flow sensor and a pressure sensor from a test machine. The Test Results indicator in Figure 7.10 shows the obtained information from a file with headers, while the Test Results 2 indicator from Figure 7.10 shows the same information but without headers, from this figure, it is observed that the use of headers provides relevant information for the subsequent analysis and interpretation of the data.

There are several ways to create headers within a text file; however, one of the most recommended is to use the function Format Into String to format each line of the text. For this, it is recommended that the function have (1) inputs for each of the columns that exist in the file, (2) an input for the character to delimit the space between columns, (3) an end of line input, and (4) an optional input with information from a previous string (Last String) that you want to concatenate. In Figure 7.11, you can see the Format Into String function with the inputs that will allow a string line with three columns separated by a delimiter (typically a comma for csv files or a tab).

The use of the Format Into String function is useful to create the text lines that will be written in a spreadsheet file with headers; however, it is desirable that the Format Into String is inside a SubVI, this will allow standardizing the format of the information, using the same delimiter between columns and organize the block diagram. In Figure 7.12 is shown the SubVI that contains the code corresponding to the Format Into String function of Figure 7.11. This SubVI will be used in further programs to create files with headers.

The program shown in Figure 7.13 allows creating a file with headers. In order to show this example, the information corresponding to "Operator Name", "Test", "Date" and "Serial Number" is captured directly in the front panel (Figure 7.14).

Test Results

	0	Operator Name	Michael Malone	
	0	Test	Valve Flow and Pressure	
	0	Date	10-06-21	
		Serial Number	APCK7895DS	
		Measurement	Flow in LPM	Preassure in PSI
		1	0.50	20.5
		2	0.51	20.5
		3	0.49	20.5
		4	0.50	20.5
		5	0.50	20.5
		6	0.51	20.4

Test Results 2

	0	1	0.50	20.5
	0	2	0.51	20.5
	0	3	0.49	20.5
		4	0.50	20.5
		5	0.50	20.5
		6	0.51	20.4

Figure 7.10   Obtained data from a file with headers and without headers; note that the contextual information is in the headers of the file

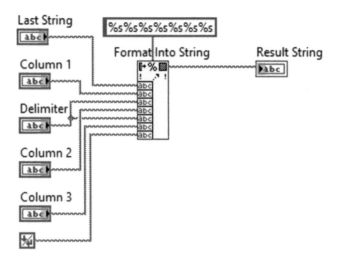

Figure 7.11   Creation of a single line of text, with three columns separated by a delimiter (comma or tab)

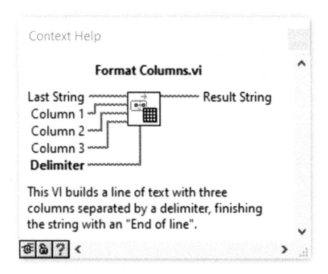

Figure 7.12   SubVI to format a spreadsheet line

You can see from Figure 7.13 that the Format Columns SubVI is used to format each of the lines of the csv file, the output of each of these SubVIs that are outside the for loop is connected to the following Format Columns SubVI, this to create all the headers that will be written to the file. Once the headers have been written, the new data generated for each of the channels can be recurrently written,

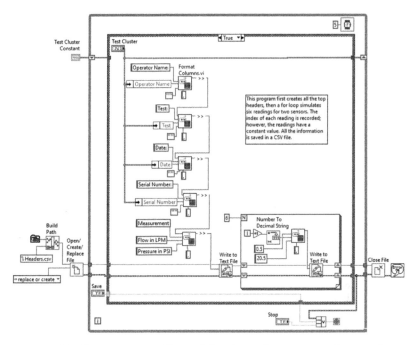

Figure 7.13   Creating a csv file with headers after pressing the save button

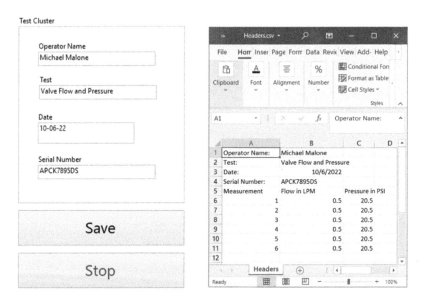

Figure 7.14   The front panel used to create a csv file with headers and the resulting csv file

in this case, the information from the "Flow in LPM" sensor and the "Pressure in PSI" sensor, this is performed within the for loop, where six readings are simulated, and this information is recorded within the Headers.csv file.

The front panel of the program, as well as the Headers.csv file with headers can be seen in Figure 7.14, it can be seen that the csv file can be opened from a spreadsheet.

7.3   Read and look information from a spreadsheet with headers

Just as it is common to export and save information from a spreadsheet with headings, it is also common to read and process the information that comes directly from a spreadsheet. To do this, it is possible to use high-level VIs that read the file completely and display it in a string array. To see this example, it is possible to take the Headers.csv file that was created in Section 7.2. Using the SubVI Read Delimited Spreadsheet.vi you can get all the data of the Headers.csv file in a 2D Array. Please see Figure 7.15 and the recommended inputs for this VI, first the Delimiter is a comma and second the Polimorfic VI Selector is a string, this kind of selection is recommended as you will work with an ASCII File with different kinds of data, so, it is desirable to first obtain the information in text, and then you can transform the data type using different conversions.

However, having the information in a 2D array only allows to present the information, but it is still necessary to have a way to search within the array. To do this, the use of the functions with arrays (seen in Section 5.1.1 "Functions and operations with arrays").

In order to present an example, first consider the following front panel from Figure 7.16. Where the indicator "Test Information" shows the data of the headers.csv file in a 2D Array (string datatype). "Specific information" is an enum controller and selects the property to look into "Test Information", "Channel" is an enum controller and selects the channel information to get.

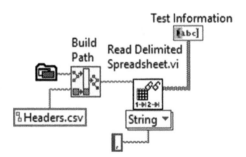

Figure 7.15   Using the Read Delimited Spreadsheet to obtain the data of Headers. csv in a 2D array

Test Information

▲ 0 ▼	Operator Name:	Michael Malone		
	Test:	Valve Flow and Pressure		
▲ 0 ▼	Date:	10-06-22		
	Serial Number:	APCK7895DS		
	Measurement	Flow in LPM	Pressure in PSI	
	1	0.5	20.5	
	2	0.5	20.5	
	3	0.5	20.5	
	4	0.5	20.5	
	5	0.5	20.5	
	6	0.5	20.5	

Channel

▲ ▼	Flow in LPM
▲ 0 ▼	0.5
	0.5
	0.5
	0.5
	0.5
	0.5

Specific Information

▲ ▼ Operator Name:	Michael Malone

Stop

Figure 7.16   A front panel to present the information from headers.cvs, the program looks for specific information of the test and the channel information

To be able to search within arrays, it is possible to use a SubVI Search Unsorted 1D Array, which is very useful to search for information in 1D arrays. To insert this SubVI, go to the function's palette and within Programming >> Array, select Search Unsorted 1D Array, where the SubVI inputs are those shown in Figure 7.17

In order to get the "Specific Information" several approaches can be considered; however, the following one is selected due to its simplicity. (1) First, get the first column (remember an array is indexed to zero) as a 1D Array, (2) Second, search the String of the Specific Information in the 1D Array and obtain the index, (3) Third, get the value of the obtained index position (of step 2) in the second column (remember the index is one as the array is indexed to zero) using the function Index Array. Figure 7.18 shows the code implementation to perform the mentioned steps.

To obtain the information of a Channel (for this example the two channels are Flow in LPM and Pressure in PSI) is very similar to getting the Specific Information, the main difference is that it is necessary to perform two searches. (1) is necessary to obtain the row index for the word Measurement in the first column,

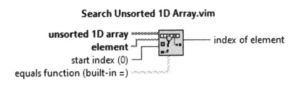

Figure 7.17   Map of connections for the Search Unsorted 1D Array SubVI

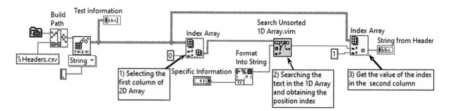

Figure 7.18   Performing the search of specific information into a 2D Array using Search Unsorted 1D Array

(2) obtain the elements of the row where the word Measurement was found, (3) search the element index of a specific Channel in the array of the step 2, (4) obtain all the elements of the column where the desired channel was found (using the index of step 3, (5) gets only the data of the Channel using the Array Subset function by starting the new array from the index position of measurement plus one. Figure 7.19 shows the code implementation to perform the mentioned steps.

In Figure 7.20, you will find the complete implementation of the program, which allows you to obtain the Specific information and data from a particular Channel. Some details that you will find when programming this code are in the Search Unsorted 1D Array function, which can have a broken cable when connecting the unsorted 1D array input, however this is corrected when wiring the element input, which must be of the same data type as the data within the array connected to unsorted 1D array (first input of the SubVI).

The block diagram in Figure 7.20 corresponds to the front panel of Figure 7.16. The program works continuously to search within an array in two dimensions. This program works for a single file, so this program can be optimized to work with different files at runtime. In Chapter 9, new approaches will be addressed to improve the scalability.

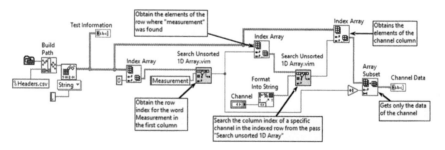

Figure 7.19   Looking for the information of a specific channel in a 2D array

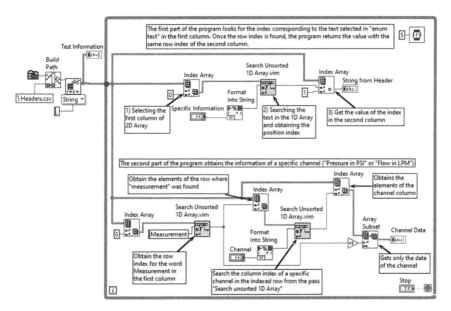

*Figure 7.20   Continuous implementation to obtain data from a file with headers,
the first part of the program looks for single items, and the second
part looks for the data in a specific channel*

Chapter 8

Using hardware resources

This chapter describes the use of hardware resources and their typical implementation. The chapter begins by explaining what NI MAX^{TM} is, an essential tool for hardware configuration and testing. Practical examples are provided for the use of data acquisition systems (using DAQs) and libraries to communicate with Arduino. In addition, communication through different computer ports using VISA libraries is addressed. Finally, instrument control through instrument drivers and VISA libraries is presented.

LabVIEW^{TM} facilitates the implementation of hardware through drivers using the communication protocols between the program being created and the hardware to use. The drivers used in this chapter are NI-VISA, NI-DAQmx, which installation is explained below, and the Arduino library, which installation will be presented in Section 8.4.

The installation of drivers in the newest versions of LabVIEW^{TM} is more straightforward than older versions; in older versions, it is necessary to download each driver separately. But in the new versions of LabVIEW^{TM} the drivers can be installed at the same time you are installing LabVIEW^{TM} as shown in Figure 8.1,

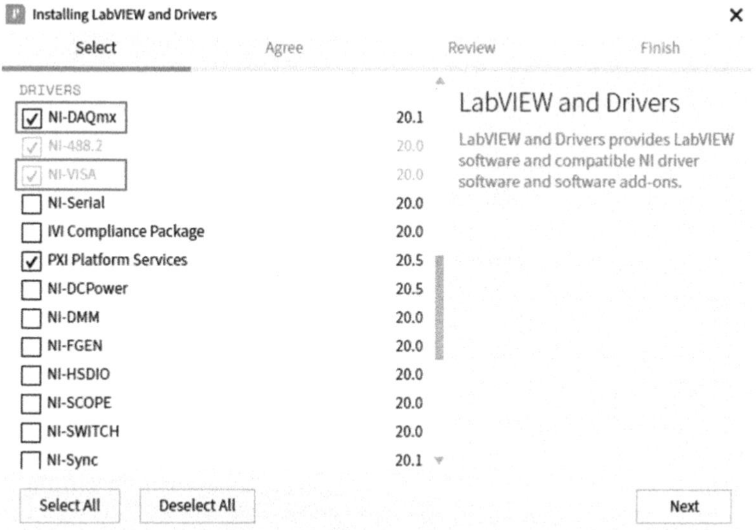

Figure 8.1 Installing NI-DAQmx and NI-VISA drivers

Figure 8.2   DAQmx and VISA libraries

make sure to select NI-DAQmx and NI-VISA on the drivers' section and follow the installation steps. If you already have LabVIEW^{TM} installed, but you did not install the drivers, you can use the same installation file to install the drivers.

After the driver installation is completed, the NI-DAQmx and NI-VISA libraries will be available for use on LabVIEW^{TM} as shown in Figure 8.2. The NI-DAQmx library is on Functions Palette>Measurement I/O and the VISA library is on Functions Palette>Instrument I/O.

8.1   NI MAX^{TM}

Before using hardware for programming on LabVIEW^{TM}, an essential tool is the NI MAX^{TM}, which is the National Instruments^{TM} Measurement & Automation Explorer. This tool provides access to the hardware. It can be used to prepare the hardware and software before programming in LabVIEW^{TM}. For example, NI MAX^{TM} can test the Digital Input/Outputs, send an analog output, or only see if the computer detects the hardware. It can also be used to create channels, tasks, interfaces, scales, virtual instruments, simulated devices, view devices or instruments connected to the system, etc.

Figure 8.3 shows the NI MAX^{TM} window. The icons on the left side are part of the configuration pane, and it is divided into two main sections: My System and Remote Systems. My System is also subdivided into four sections: Data Neighborhood, Devices and Interfaces, Scales, and Software. Data Neighborhood provides access to descriptively named shortcuts to configured physical channels in the system. Devices and Interfaces shows a list of installed and detected hardware. Scales provides access to all scales configured to perform operations on acquired data. Software allows the visualization, launching, and updating of the installed NI software. And Remote Systems is used to access a system not on the local subnet or if the firewall prevents MAX from discovering NI hardware.

As you may have seen, the subsections on My System can be subdivided into more subsections, for example, if you open the section Devices and Interfaces and if you have a webcam on your computer, it should appear in this section. When clicking on the webcam, the panel to the right will change to show the settings, acquisition attributes and camera attributes for the webcam. This will allow changing the acquisition rate, resolution, pixel format, etc. This panel will vary

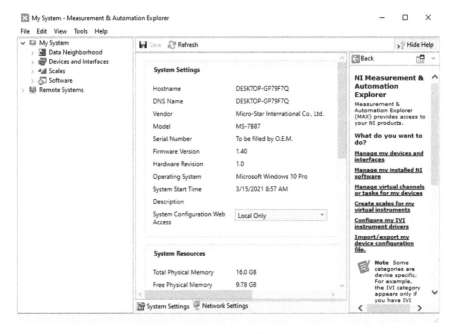

Figure 8.3 NI MAX^{TM} window

depending on the connected device and it allows us to prepare the hardware before using it on LabVIEW^{TM}.

8.2 Data acquisition systems

Data acquisition systems (usually known as DAQs), as its name says, are devices that acquire information from the real world to the computer or send different kinds of signals to the real world [16]. These devices are controlled by LabVIEW^{TM} and can perform different tasks, such as digital input/output, analog input/output, generating PWM signals, communication with other devices, etc. There is a wide variety of models for data acquisition systems, some of them have a limited number of inputs and outputs, like the NI myDAQ^{TM} as shown in Figure 8.4(B), which has eight digital inputs/outputs, two differential analog inputs, two analog outputs, a digital multimeter, etc. Other models of DAQs like the cDAQ-9174 shown in Figure 8.4(A), do not have a predefined number of inputs and outputs, instead, they have slots for modules with different applications. For example, the DAQ shown in Figure 8.4(A) has four slots for modules and three are being used. The first one is the module NI 9403, which is a configurable digital input/output module with 32 bidirectional channels, the second module is the NI 9263, which is a voltage output module with four channels and ±10 V, the third module is the NI 9219, which is an analog input module with four channels.

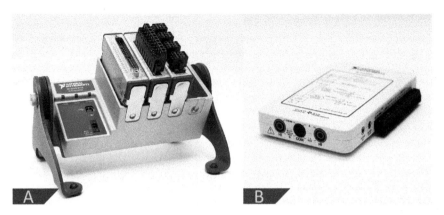

Figure 8.4   (A) NI cDAQ-9174 with three modules and (B) NI myDAQ^TM

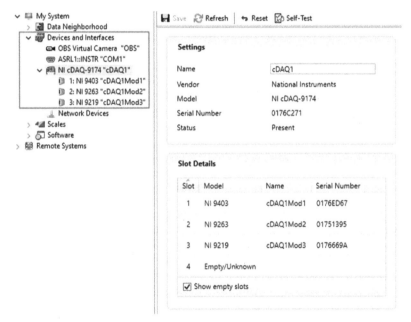

Figure 8.5   NI cDAQ-9174 on NI MAX^TM window

DAQs can be controlled with LabVIEW^TM using the NI DAQmx libraries, but before programming with them on LabVIEW^TM, it is important to check that the DAQ is properly installed, detected by the computer, and fully functional. This is done by opening the software NI MAX^TM, then on the Devices and Interfaces section, the DAQ connected to the computer should appear as shown in Figure 8.5, where the NI cDAQ-92174 appears as a new section with three modules inside of it. Successful communication verification between the computer and the DAQ can be done by clicking the Self-Test button; after clicking this button the message "The self test completed successfully" should appear.

The Self-Test can also be used with each module and the same message should appear after a successful test. But, another important feature of using the NI MAX^{TM} to test the hardware before using it on LabVIEW^{TM} is the test panel. To open a test panel select a module, then click the button Test Panel, which is at the right of the Self-Test button. Depending on the type of module, the test panel will be different. For example, Figure 8.6 shows the test panel for the digital input/ output module. It is divided into three sections: section one is for port selection, in this case the module only has one port, and this will be the only option; section two is used to select a direction line for the port and at the right you can define which bit will be input and which will be output; on section three the bits will appear as they were defined on section two, inputs will appear as LEDs and outputs will appear as switches. Note that one LED in Figure 8.6 is turned on, this is because it was physically connected to 5 V to check its functionality. This can be done with all the other inputs and it will take effect after pressing the start button.

Figure 8.7 shows the test panel for the analog output module, at the left of the window, the channel name, mode, transfer mechanism, and voltage limits and rate can be selected and at the right of the window, the output value of the channel can be selected with a numeric control or with a slide bar. To check that the value matches the selected voltage, measure the physical channel with a voltmeter after pressing the update button.

Figure 8.8 shows the test panel for the analog input module, at the left of the window, the channel name, rate, mode, samples to read, measurement type, input limits, units, terminal configuration, and coupling can be selected or modified and

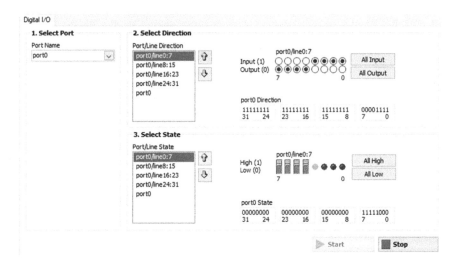

Figure 8.6   Module NI 9403 test panel

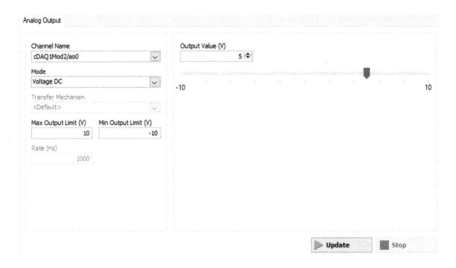

Figure 8.7   Module NI 9263 test panel

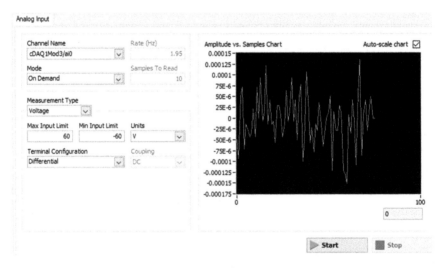

Figure 8.8   Module NI 9219 test panel

at the right of the window there is a chart of amplitude vs samples which will show the measured values of the selected channel after pressing the start button.

Once the correct operation of the DAQ is verified, it is ready to use in LabVIEW^{TM} using the NI DAQmx libraries shown in Figure 8.9. You can find them by going to **Functions palette>Measurement I/O>Ni DAQmx**. It is recommended to check all the blocks using the context help, in the following figures some of the most used DAQmx functions will be explained.

• Tip #17: To see the schematic of the device inputs and outputs click the Device Pinouts button.

The VI in Figure 8.10 is a VI used to read a digital signal from a DAQ. On the front panel, there is a control called lines, which is used to specify the digital port or line used from the DAQ to make the digital read, in this case, it is from the module one, port zero, line three. Also, on the front panel there is a LED called data which is used to display the digital read from line three, and a stop button to end the program. As can be seen in the block diagram, there are five functions from the DAQmx library. The first one is the Create Channel, this function is used to take the physical channel and converts it into a virtual channel. This physical channel is declared on the function's input by the lines control. As you can see at the bottom

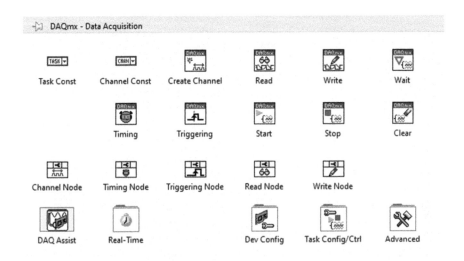

Figure 8.9   NI DAQmx library

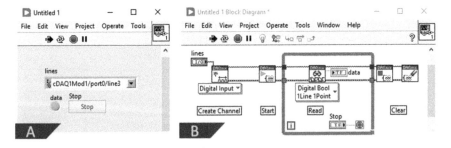

Figure 8.10   Digital input VI. (A) Front panel and (B) block Diagram

of the function, there is a drop-down list used to indicate the function of the channel being created, in this case, the channel is a digital input. The second function is the Start Task function, which is used to start the task on the indicated channel after finishing the configurations. Its inputs are the created task from the previous function and the error. The third function is the Read function, which is inside a while structure. This function also has a drop-down list, and it is used to indicate the kind of sample to be read, in this case it is Digital>Single Channel> Single Sample>Boolean (1 Line). This function will give the value read by the DAQ in the line indicated in the Create Channel function. Since this function is inside the while structure, the lecture from the DAQ will be continuously obtained and shown on the LED in the front panel. The last two functions are the Stop Task and Clear Task functions. The Stop function stops the task and returns it to the state before the Start function runs. The Clear function is used to clear the task and release any reserved resource.

The VI in Figure 8.11 is used to write a digital signal from the DAQ and it is similar to the VI in Figure 8.10, both of them have a while structure and the functions Create Channel, Start, Stop, and Clear. The main differences between these VIs are on the Create Channel function and that the Read function is substituted for the Write function. On the Create Channel function, the created channel is used for digital function, which means that the DAQ will write a true or false output on the declared line. As its name says, the Write function will write a Boolean value to the created channel. This value will depend on the value given on the data input of the function, and in order to write this Boolean value, it needs to be indicated on the drop-down list selecting Digital>Single Channel> Single Sample>Boolean (1 Line). As you can see on this VI, the same line was used from the previous VI, but it was declared as an output for this case.

The VI in Figure 8.12 is used to write an analog signal from the DAQ and it is also similar to the previous VIs. It also has a case structure and the functions Create Channel, Start, Stop, and Clear. The main differences are the Create Channel function, the Write function, and the selected line for the analog output. On the Create Channel function, the created channel is used for analog voltage output, which means that the DAQ will be able to output the indicated voltage on the physical channel, this physical channel is indicated on the line input of the function,

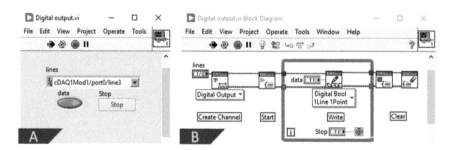

Figure 8.11   Digital output VI. (A) Front panel and (B) block diagram

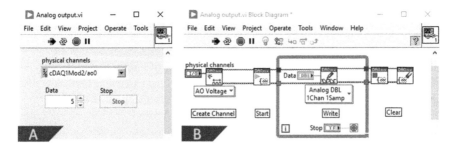

Figure 8.12   Analog output VI. (A) Front panel and (B) block diagram

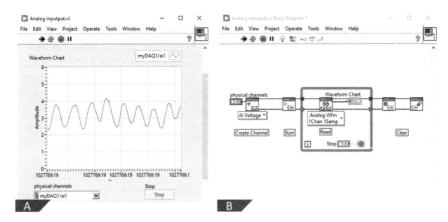

Figure 8.13   Analog input VI. (A) Front panel and (B) block diagram

in this case it is on the module two using the analog output zero. The Write function will output the voltage on the physical channel depending on the data input value. To write this double-precision value, it needs to be indicated on the drop-down list selecting Analog>Single Channel>Single Sample>DBL.

The VI in Figure 8.13 is used to read an analog signal from the DAQ and it uses the same functions as the digital input VI with some changes. The first difference is in the physical channel selected and the Create Channel function, in this case, it is set to Analog Input>Voltage as the channel will be used to take an analog voltage read. Finally, the second difference is on the Read function, in this case it is set to Analog>Single Channel>Single Sample>Waveform and as an output, the function gives a waveform data type that will be equal to the voltage read on the DAQ and shown on the front panel chart.

As you may have seen on the VIs shown in this section, they present a similar structure: create a channel, start a task, use a specific function for the task, and finally stop and clear the task (similar to software resources). This type of structure applies to most libraries, especially for instrument drivers.

8.3   VISA libraries and instrument control

In the previous section, the use of DAQs from National Instruments^{TM} was explained, and as DAQs, National Instruments^{TM} has a wide variety of instruments with their own library to use with LabVIEW^{TM}, but this does not mean that the hardware from National Instruments^{TM} is the only option. Communication with other devices is possible through the VISA libraries (see Figure 8.14). VISA stands for Virtual Instrument Software Architecture and it is an API, which means that it is an interface that allows communication between two devices. It provides a programming interface to control Ethernet/LXI, GPIB, serial, USB, PXI, and VXI instruments [17]. You can use the VISA libraries to communicate with instruments directly or download the instrument drivers for the device, which were created using the VISA libraries.

8.3.1   Control by VISA libraries

VISA libraries facilitate the communication with instruments, for example, Figure 8.15 shows a program that uses the VISA libraries to communicate with an Arduino, and this program is used to take a voltage measurement from the Arduino and show it on a waveform chart as shown on the front panel, where there is also the VISA resource name which is used to indicate the communication port where the Arduino is connected to the computer. On the block diagram, the first function used is the VISA Open, which opens a session to the device specified by the VISA resource name. Then there is a while structure, which is where the information sent by the Arduino is read and shown on the Waveform chart. This is done by using the VISA Read function, which reads the specified number of bytes sent by the Arduino and returns the data on the read buffer as string data type, then this data is converted to double-precision data type, and as the Arduino gives a value between 0 and 1024 for 0–5 voltage reads, the data read is converted to voltage value using mathematical functions. Finally, after the while structure, the VISA Close function closes the device session specified on the VISA resource name. In Figure 8.15(C), the code loaded into the Arduino is shown on the void

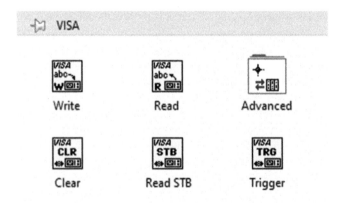

Figure 8.14   VISA libraries

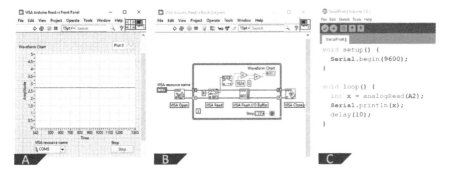

Figure 8.15   Communication with Arduino through VISA libraries. (A) Front panel, (B) block diagram, and (C) Arduino code

setup, the serial.begin() function is used to set the data rate for serial data transmission, and on the void loop, there is the main code, which takes the analog read and sends the data. The code on the Arduino and the code on the block diagram run simultaneously in order to be able to make the analog read and show it on the waveform chart.

8.3.2   Control by instrument drivers

As you may have seen, the use of VISA libraries requires knowledge about the communication protocols of the instrument to control. Sometimes it can be a hard and time-consuming task to program the communication between LabVIEW[TM] and the instrument; fortunately, there is a wide variety of instrument manufacturers that have their own drivers to use their equipment with LabVIEW[TM]. These instrument drivers are basically subVIs made using the VISA libraries to establish communication with the instrument. Instrument drivers are installed opening a new VI and going to Help>Find Instrument Drivers. This will open the NI instrument driver finder window as shown in Figure 8.16, select the manufacturer of the desired instrument on the drop-down list, type the model number on the Additional Keywords field, and then click the search button. This will open a search results window, at the left of the window the driver name will appear and at the right of the window information about the driver such as driver ADE, driver technology, required support software, driver revision, manufacturer, models supported, interfaces, operating systems and if NI supports it. To install this driver just click the install button and the installation window will appear with the message 'Installation successful' when it is done. After the successful installation click the Start using this driver button, if you go back to the instrument driver finder window you will see that you can explore the installed instrument driver and look at examples. Finally, you can see the installed instrument drivers on the block diagram by going to Functions palette>Instrument I/O>Instr Drivers.

If the instrument driver finder did not find a driver for your instrument, sometimes it can be downloaded from the manufacturer's web page, as it is in the case of the oscilloscope shown in Figure 8.17, which drivers do not appear on the

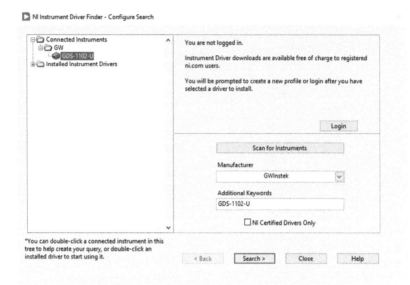

Figure 8.16   NI instrument driver finder window

Figure 8.17   GW Instek GDS-1102-U oscilloscope

instrument driver finder, the drivers for this oscilloscope can be installed manually following these steps: first, move the driver folder to the LabVIEW^{TM}/Instr.lib folder for which default location is C:\Program Files (x86)\National Instruments \LabVIEW 2020\instr.lib then on LabVIEW^{TM} on the block diagram or front panel window go to Tools>Advanced>Edit Palette Set. This will open three windows, Edit Controls and Functions Palette Set window, Functions window and Controls window. Then on the Functions palette go to Instrument I/O>Instr Drivers, right click in the palette window, and select Insert>Subpalette. This will open the Insert Subpalette window with five options to choose from. Select "Link to an existing palette file (.mnu)"; this will open a browse window to select the . mnu file, open the driver folder that you placed on LabVIEW™ 2020\instr.lib, open the Public folder, select the .mnu file and click OK. After doing these steps, the instrument drivers library will appear on the subpalette. Now just click Save Changes on the Edit Controls and Functions Palette Set window.

> • Tip #18: The easiest way to find the instrument drivers for your device when they do not appear on the Instrument Driver Finder is to search on the web the model of your instrument with the words "LabVIEW™ instrument driver" afterwards.

Note: Before manually installing the instrument drivers, ensure that the instrument drivers folder has the same name as it will appear on the subpalette as shown in Figure 8.18. Changing the name after installing the driver will not work.

After installing the subpalette for the instrument driver, you may notice a VI called VI Tree, which does not have inputs or outputs. This VI is used for documentation, if you open it and go to the block diagram (see Figure 8.19) you will find all the VIs for the instrument driver and the programming flow, which means that the VIs should be used in that order to build your code. It is recommended to check all of the VIs on the VI Tree using the context help before using them.

The VI in Figure 8.20 shows the use of the installed instrument drivers for the GDS-1102-U oscilloscope. As you can see, the structure of the functions used is similar to the structure shown on the VI tree. The first function is the initialize function, which establishes communication with the instrument indicated on the VISA resource name. The second function is for configuration, in this case it is the Autosetup function, which causes the oscilloscope to evaluate all input waveforms

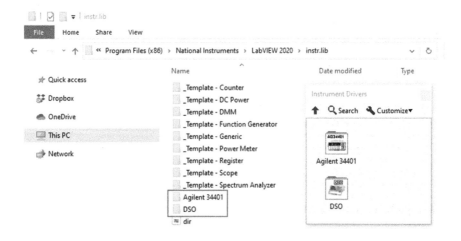

Figure 8.18   Instrument drivers folder

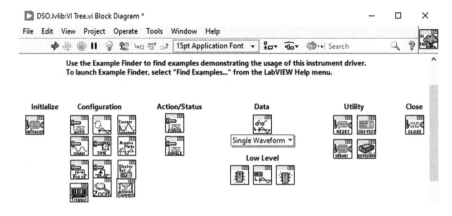

Figure 8.19   VI Tree block diagram

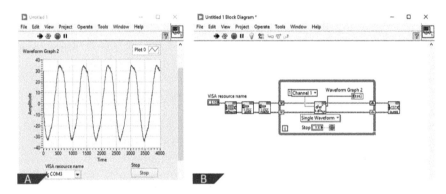

Figure 8.20   Voltage read using instrument drivers for GDS-1102-U oscilloscope

and find the optimum conditions for displaying the waveform. The third function is for Action/Status, in this case it is the Force function, which manually triggers the oscilloscope and displays the input signals. Then the fourth function is inside the while structure and it is the Read function, which initiates acquisition on channel 1 of the oscilloscope and displays it on Waveform Graph 2. Finally, the Close function performs an instrument error query and terminates the software connection to the instrument.

8.4   Arduino drivers

Arduino microcontrollers have been an important tool for people starting with programming and electronics, it is an open-source electronics platform based on easy to use hardware and software. It has many applications that can be found on the web, from beginner to advanced projects [18]. The Arduino microcontroller is programmed using a text-based language on the Arduino IDE and it can communicate with LabVIEW^{TM} using the VISA libraries as shown in Figure 8.15, in this example, the code is used to send information from the Arduino platform to be read on the computer using LabVIEW^{TM}, but if more functionality is needed, the code from the Arduino and from the block diagram will become more complex just to establish the communication for all the functionalities needed. Fortunately, Arduino has its drivers for LabVIEW^{TM} [19].

The Arduino drivers are installed using the VI Package Manager (VIPM), you can open it from the front panel or the block diagram window by going to Tools>VI Package Manage. This will load the VIPM in a new window as shown in Figure 8.21, then on the search bar, write "Arduino", then select LabVIEW^{TM} Interface for Arduino and click the Install button at the top right of the window. After the installation is complete, a new window will appear with the results, action installed and status no errors, to end the installation click the Finish button.

After the installation is complete, the Arduino library will appear on the functions palette as shown in Figure 8.22. The Arduino library includes various subpalettes, the low level subpalette is used for basic functions as digital write, digital read, analog write, analog read, etc. The Sensors subpalette is used to facilitate the instrumentation of different sensors and actuators such as thermistors, photoresistors, IR sensors, RGB LEDs, seven-segment displays, thumbsticks, servo motors, stepper motors, LCDs, etc. The Utility subpalette has different subVIs for packing data, send and receive data, calculate update frequency, record timing data, etc.

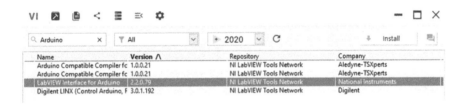

Figure 8.21   VI Package Manager window

Figure 8.22   Arduino library

Finally, the examples palette includes the use of subVIs from the other palettes, these examples include VIs for analog read, thermistor read, servo motor, stepper motor and more.

Before start using the Arduino library to communicate with the Arduino board, it is important to upload a code to the Arduino board from the Arduino IDE, you will find this code after installing the Arduino library on the installation folder, the default location is: C:\Program Files (x86)\National Instruments\LabVIEW 2020\vi.lib\LabVIEW Interface for Arduino\Firmware. In this folder you will find the LIFA_Base file, which is the code to upload on the Arduino board as shown in Figure 8.23. This code provides a basic Arduino sketch for interfacing with LabVIEW^{TM}. Note: sometimes, when the code is uploaded with a newer version of the Arduino IDE, the communication between LabVIEW^{TM} and the Arduino board will cause an error, this error can be solved by uploading the code from an older version of the Arduino IDE like Arduino 1.8.2.

Once the LIFA base code is uploaded to the Arduino board, the Arduino library can be used to control the Arduino board from LabVIEW^{TM}. Figure 8.24 shows an example of a Digital Input/Output VI using the Arduino board. The first

Figure 8.23   LIFA base code. (A) File location and (B) Arduino IDE

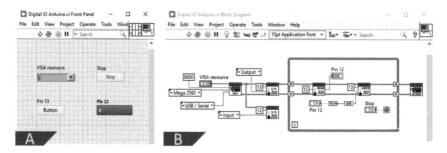

Figure 8.24   Digital Input/Output VI using the Arduino library and the Arduino board. (A) Front panel and (B) block diagram

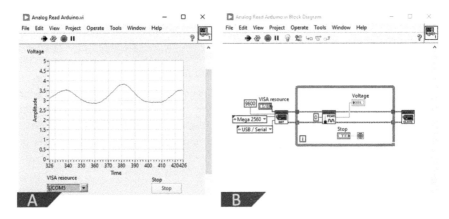

Figure 8.25   Analog read VI using the Arduino library and the Arduino board. (A)
Front panel and (B) block diagram

block is the Init function, which initializes a connection to the indicate Arduino board on the VISA resource running the LIFA Base code loaded in the Arduino board. On this function, the corresponding baud rate to the Arduino board being used, the board type used, and the connection type needs to be indicated correctly in order to create the communication between the Arduino board and LabVIEW™. The next two functions are the Set Digital Pin Mode and they are used to set pin 13 as an output and pin 12 as an input. Then on the while loop there is the Digital Read Pin function, this function reads the digital value of the pin 12, which was previously declared as an input. The other function on the while loop is the Digital Write Pin function, this function writes the specified value on pin 13, which was previously declared as an output. As you can see, the functions inside the while loop work with 8-bit unsigned integer data type, this is why the pin 13 button is converted to integer and then to 8-bit integer. Finally, at the end of the block diagram, the Close function closes the active connection to the Arduino board.

Figure 8.25 shows an analog read VI using the Arduino library and the Arduino board. As you can see, this VI also uses the Init function with the same inputs in its terminals as in the VI from Figure 8.24, since the same Arduino board is being used. The Analog Read Pin function within the while structure reads the analog voltage on pin A0 on the Arduino board and displays it on the Voltage waveform chart. Finally, at the end of the block diagram, the Close function ends the active connection with the Arduino board.

8.5   Examples of VIs using hardware

This section presents two examples of hardware applications to be solved with DAQ and Arduino. The first example is for stepper motor control and the second example is an automatic light switch.

8.5.1   Examples description

8.5.1.1   Stepper motor control

Problem description: Use a DAQ or Arduino to control a stepper motor. The stepper motor is connected to a driver with three inputs: pul, dir, and en. The pul input will force the motor to take a step each time it receives a pulse, the dir input will cause the motor to turn clockwise if the input is high (True) or counter-clockwise if the input is low (False), finally, the en input will energize the driver when the input is high. Create a program that enables the motor and controls the velocity and direction.

8.5.1.2   Automatic light switch

Problem description: Use a DAQ or Arduino to turn on an outdoor light bulb at night. The light bulb is connected to a relay, and a photoresistor on series with a resistor to create a voltage divider will be used to know when it gets dark. The light bulb must turn on at night, but the program needs to have an option to turn it off if needed.

8.5.2   Examples with DAQs

This section presents the solution to the stepper motor control and the automatic light switch VIs using the DAQmx library and the myDAQ^{TM}.

8.5.2.1   Stepper motor control using DAQmx library

Solution: The VI in Figure 8.26 is used to generate the required signals by the driver for the stepper motor control using the DAQmx library. On the front panel, there are three buttons, a pointer slider control and three line controls. The mechanical action of Enable and Direction buttons is set to switch when pressed, so

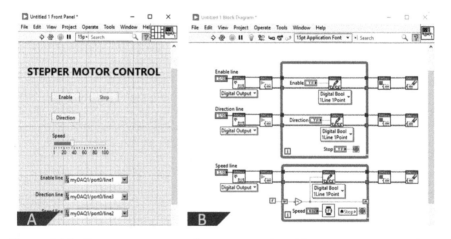

Figure 8.26   Stepper motor control VI using DAQmx library. (A) Front panel and (B) block diagram

that the button stays in the new state when pressed and the user can continue using other controls on the program. The Stop button mechanical action is set to switch until released so that when it is pressed, it returns to the previous state after stopping the program. The Speed slider control is used to change the rotation speed of the motor, the numbers on the slider are the milliseconds that the program will wait to give a pulse to the driver and generate a step. Finally, the line controls are used to set the enable, direction and speed line on the myDAQ^{TM}. The block diagram is divided in two parts with a while loop structure each one. The top part is where the Enable and the Direction signals are generated and sent to the corresponding lines using the Write function. First, the corresponding lines are set as digital outputs, the tasks are transitioned to the running state, then on the while loop the Enable and Direction states are sent to the myDAQ^{TM} using the write function. The bottom part is used for speed control. It is in a different while structure so that the timing used for the pulse generation does not affect the Enable and Direction controls and that the speed generation is not affected by the other functions. First, the speed line is set as a digital output, the task is transitioned to the running state, then the while loop is being executed at the speed set on the speed slider control, each time the while structure is executed, the value on the input terminal of the write function will change between true and false due to the not function connected to a shift register on the while loop, this will generate a pulse train at the selected speed which will be sent to the pul input of the stepper motor driver to generate the rotation steps on the stepper motor.

8.5.2.2   Automatic light switch using DAQmx library

Solution: The VI in Figure 8.27 is used to send a signal to the relay when the light must be turned on or off depending on the light intensity. On the left side of the block diagram, there are two Create Channel functions, the first one is used to create the analog input voltage task, which is going to be used to read the voltage value from the voltage divider. The second Create Channel function is set as digital

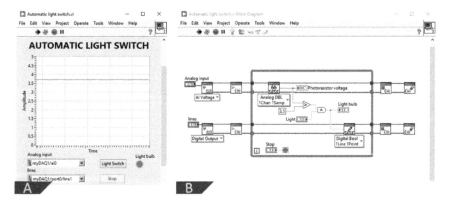

Figure 8.27   Automatic light switch VI using DAQmx library. (A) Front panel and (B) block diagram

output, which is going to be used to turn on or off the light bulb by sending the signal to the relay. On the while loop structure, the first function is the Read function, which gives the voltage value from the photoresistor voltage divider, this voltage value is compared with a reference value of 3.5 with the Greater? Function, if the voltage value is greater than 3.5, the light bulb should be turned on, but before connecting the output terminal of the Greater? Function to the Write function, it is connected to an And function in order to be able to turn off the light if needed. Finally, the output terminal of the And function is connected to the Write function to be able to control the light bulb using the relay.

8.5.3   Examples with Arduino

8.5.3.1   Stepper motor control using Arduino library

Solution: As you can see, the stepper motor control VI shown in Figure 8.28 using the Arduino library is pretty similar to the VI in Figure 8.26, especially on the front panel. It has the same controls for enable, direction, stop and speed, the only controls that do not appear are the controls used to indicate the physical channel being used for each task. Instead, there is the VISA resource control, which indicates the port where the Arduino is connected to the computer. The block diagram has a similar structure, first, the Arduino is initialized, then the necessary pins are declared as outputs, then there are two while structures, one for the enable and direction controls and one for the speed control. Finally, the Close function ends the active connection with the Arduino board.

8.5.3.2   Automatic light switch using Arduino library

Solution: The automatic light switch VI shown in Figure 8.29 using the Arduino library is pretty similar to its version for the DAQmx library (see Figure 8.27). On the front panel, there is the chart for the Photoresistor voltage, the light switch and stop buttons and the light bulb indicator LED, the only difference is that in this case, there are no controls for the physical channel, instead there is the VISA resource for the port where the Arduino board is connected. The block diagram has

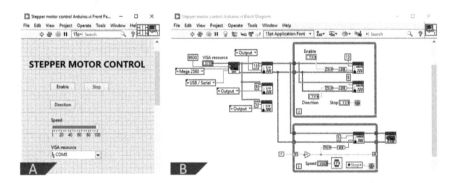

Figure 8.28   Stepper motor control VI using Arduino library. (A) Front panel and (B) block diagram

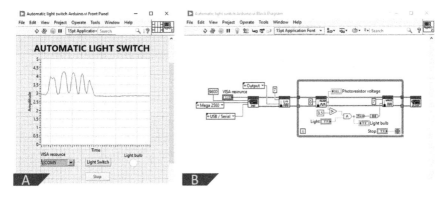

Figure 8.29   Automatic light switch using Arduino library. (A) Front panel and (B) block diagram

a similar structure, first, the Arduino is initialized and pin 7 is declared as an output, then, within the while structure, the photoresistor voltage is read using the analog read pin function, this voltage is compared with the reference value of 3.5, which is the value where the light must be turned on. If the photoresistor voltage read is greater than 3.5 and the light button is on, the light bulb will turn on using the digital write pin function. Finally, after the while loop stops, the close function ends the communication with the Arduino board.

Chapter 9

Implementing test machines with a basic architecture

The efficient programming of a test machine depends on the scalability of the code, and the use of an architecture that different programmers can understand. In these cases, the use of state machine design pattern is a widely accepted implementation by the programmer community, allowing flexibility to program different kinds of tests and configurations on a single machine [20]. This design pattern is explained in detail and practical examples of its implementation are presented.

9.1 Code scalability and design patterns

Code scalability refers to the capability to add new features to a VI in such a way that they have a minimal impact on the surrounding code, allowing a flowed expansion of the application. For this aim, programmers have taken multiple efforts to standardize different design patterns that allow the scalability of the code. A design pattern is an implementation of code that has proven helpful through the efforts of multiple developers. These code implementations present a "general framework" that facilitates the readability and scalability of the code for a team of developers, to share code implementations and/or for future new features in a program. There are different kinds of design patterns, some of them designed for test machines, others for a flow user interface, others to read information from digital acquisition systems avoiding losing information, among others. For the aim of this chapter, the State machine design pattern is introduced.

9.2 State transition diagram

State machines solve problems that present sequential programming, where the elements of a sequence cannot be repeated or where the order in the execution in the elements within the sequence cannot be changed. State machine programming is familiar to computer engineers or electronics engineers who have experience with Mealy and Moore machines, however, this chapter will explain the state machine from its fundamentals and how it can be implemented in LabVIEW^{TM}. For this, the following concepts will be introduced.

• State: It is a case that performs a function.
•Transition: Action that sends a program from one state to another

States and transitions are highly correlated, usually, the result of a function inside of a state is used to determine the next transition; however, there are cases (states) where the transition is direct, and one state only can go to another state.

There are different applications for a state machine, one of them is in the implementation of test machines, where each of the states refers to a different part of the test. Another possible application is in the development of user interfaces, where each state is related to the different actions that the user can have.

However, for any of the possible applications, it is always desirable to make a state transition diagram before starting with the programming. In Figure 9.1, you can see a state transition diagram for an electrical test machine. This is a machine to test coils with two possible tests, "Resistance Test" and "Hipot Test". The number of tests will depend on whether it is the abbreviated test or not.

From Figure 9.1 it is possible to identify each of the possible states by the circles and each of the possible transitions with the arrows. For this diagram it is observed that each state has two possible transitions (except for the states "Discard Coil" or "Successful Coil Test" which is where the program ends); however, it is possible to design state transition diagrams with more transitions or even direct transitions from one state to another. Another thing to keep in mind is that this type of diagram is not completely sequential, for example, the Start state can go into two possible states depending on whether the test is an abbreviated test or not. Also, the Resistance test and the Hipot test states can reach the discard coil state if the test fails.

State transition diagrams are useful for visualizing how all states interact and it is desirable to have them before beginning with the programming and implementation of a state machine.

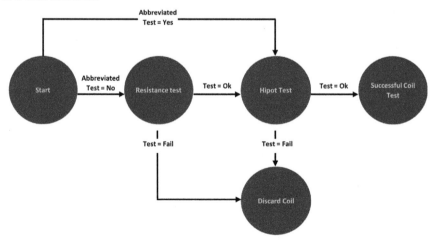

Figure 9.1   Example of a state transition diagram for coil test machine

9.3   State machine design pattern

The state machine design pattern allows you to implement a state transition diagram. The elements that make up this design pattern are (1) constant enum type definition, (2) a while loop, (3) shift register, and (4) case structure. The framework of a state machine can be seen in Figure 9.2.

The while loop allows the cyclical execution of the state machine. The case structure contains a case for each possible state. The constant enum type definition is a list with the names of all the possible states to which the state machine can be directed, and the shift register is how the state transition occurs between iterations. The states to be included within a state machine depend on the type of application being developed; however, it is always desirable to create an initialization state, which will allow to restart variables, as well as to set the initial properties of your program (programmatic control of properties and methods will be looked at in Chapter 10). In addition, it is desirable to create a start state and a stop state, the stop case is used to close resources before stopping the program.

> • Why a enum type definition? The enum type definition is used to ensure the scalability of the state machine. Having a type definition allows updating the list of new states from a single place, on the other hand, if multiple enums (non-type definitions) were used with different elements in the lists, this would cause coercion points, so it would not be possible to identify the name of the states in the selector label of the case structure.

Next, an example of a state machine will be shown where the state transition diagram of Figure 1.1 will be implemented. The program is a simulation, so the values of resistance and hipot and the operating limits will be defined directly on the front panel before starting the test.

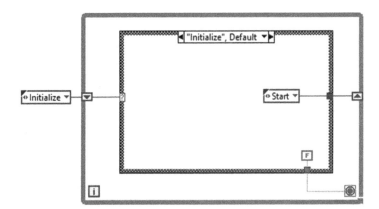

Figure 9.2   Framework of a state machine

9.4 State machine design examples

To start, the state machine is desirable to create a blank project to have the main VI and the enum type definition organized. The following user interface in Figure 9.3 has been created inside the main VI to implement the state transition diagram of Figure 9.1. First, the test parameters can be identified (as a cluster), which are the Resistance Upper Limit (double), Resistance Lower Limit (double), the Hipot Test voltage (double), and the Abbreviated Test (Boolean) control to indicate whether the test is abbreviated or not. Also, since this program is a simulation, you must include the Coil Resistance (double) and whether or not the coil passed the hipot test in the control Pass Hipot Test (Boolean). In a real test environment, both, coil resistance and if the coil passes the hipot test can be obtained by digital acquisition systems. Finally, there are the Start Test control (Boolean), the Result indicator (String), and a control to stop the program (Boolean). You can design the user interface and do subsequent programming directly from the example below.

To start with the program, you need to create an enum type definition with the following State: Initialize, Start, Resistance Test, Hipot Test, Discard Coil, Successful Coil, and Stop as shown in Figure 9.4, save the enum in a *.ctl file.

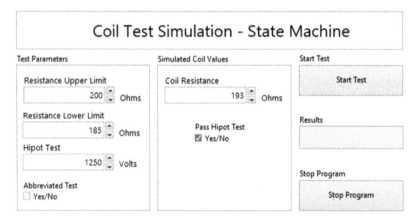

Figure 9.3   Front panel of the coil test simulation – state machine

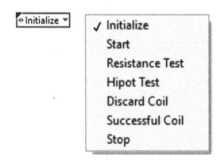

Figure 9.4   List of states inside of the enum type definition

The next step is to create the state machine. For this, as seen in Section 9.3, you need to create a while loop, a case structure, and a shift register (enum type definition data type) for the transition between states. It is important that after connecting the enum type definition to the selection terminal of the case structure, place the mouse pointer at the edge of the case structure and select Right click>>Add a Case for Every Value. After that, go to the Initialize case, this will be the first case to program, add the transition code (the two selectors to choose between different possible states), create a shift register to send the information of test parameters cluster to the next state and initialize the shift register outside the while loop with a cluster constant. Finally, add a wait function inside the while loop with an input of 5 milliseconds. Develop the program to look like Figure 9.5.

In the Start State, the program unbundles the input cluster to read the Abbreviated Test Boolean control, If the test is abbreviated, the next state is Hipot Test, if the test is not abbreviated, the next state is Resistance Test. Develop the Start state to look like Figure 9.6.

In the Resistance Test state, the program checks if the Coil Resistance is within the upper and lower limits given in the Test Parameters. For this aim, the In Range and Coerce function is used. To add this function from the Functions Palette, go to Programming>>Comparison>>In Range and Coerce. If the coil resistance is within the range, the next state is Hipot Test, if not, the next state is Discard Coil, and an error message is displayed. Develop the Resistance Test state to look like Figure 9.7.

The next state is Hipot Test, since the program is a simulation, the Pass Hipot Test boolean check box is used to determine if the hipot test passed. On a test machine, this Boolean check box can be replaced with a digital input from an external hipot testing machine, or with the appropriate hardware you can implement your own Hipot Test Machine. Note that if the Hipot Test fails, an error message dialog will appear and the state machine goes to the Discard Coil state, if

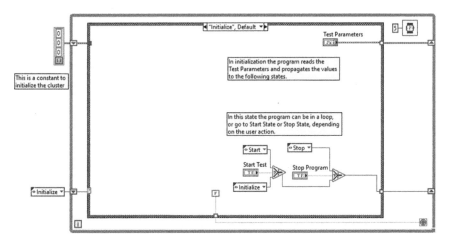

Figure 9.5   Functional code and transition of the initialize state

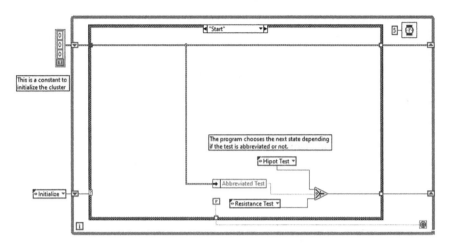

Figure 9.6   Start State transition to Hipot Test or Resistance Test

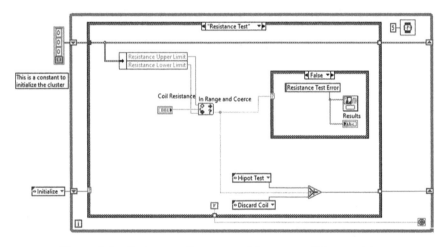

Figure 9.7   Resistance Test state with two possible transitions

not, the next state is Successful Coil. Develop the Hipot Test state to look like Figure 9.8.

The state Discard Coil shows the "Failed Coil Test" message in the Results indicator, this state waits 3,000 ms and then performs a direct transition to the Initialize state. Note that the information of the Test Parameters cluster is propagated, to does not lose information. Develop the Discard Coil state to look like Figure 9.9.

The Successful Coil state shows the "Successful Coil Test" message in the Results indicator, this state waits 3,000 ms and then performs a direct transition to the Initialize state. Note that the information of the Test Parameters cluster is

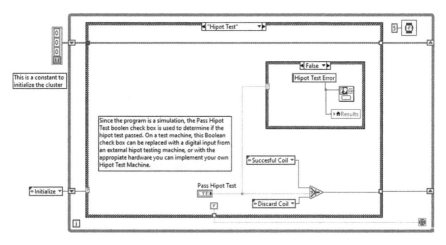

Figure 9.8   Hipot Test state with two possible transitions and error message if the test fails

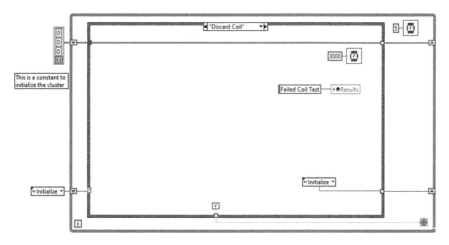

Figure 9.9   Discard Coil state with a direct transition to the Initialize state

propagated, to not to lose information. Develop the Successful Coil state to look like Figure 9.10.

Finally, the Stop state finishes the program. To reach this state, click on stop before starting the test. To maintain the code consistency, the transition from this state is to the same state (Stop State), the information in the Test Parameters cluster is propagated and the constant to the conditional terminal of the while loop is True. Develop the Stop state to look like Figure 9.11. Note that all the tunnels of the case structure must be fully colored.

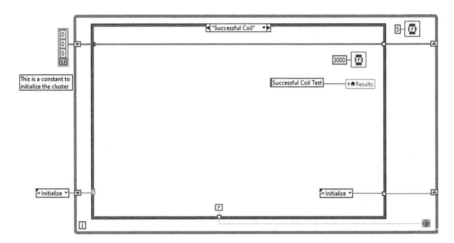

Figure 9.10   Successful Coil state with a direct transition to Initialize state

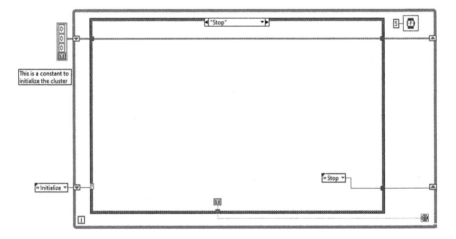

Figure 9.11   Stop state with a direct transition to the same state

9.5   State machine recommendations

1. Begin with a state transition diagram before starting with a state machine.
2. Identify all the possible functions that the program can perform as a state.
3. Use an enum type definition to define all the possible states.
4. Avoid naming two states with similar or equivalent names.
5. At the end of the code, check that all states are reachable.
6. You can add an error cluster to direct the program to a safe ending state and display the error using a Simple Error Handler.

Part II

Advanced techniques

Chapter 10

Controlling the user interface

The convenience of a software is tightly related to the feedback that the program can provide, this through different signals or visual changes in the interface. In the same way, it is expected that the program can execute specific methods that are transversal and common among similar programs [21]. This chapter explains how to modify different properties of objects and how to call different types of methods at runtime. In addition, it will be explained what they are and how to create control references that allow calling properties and methods from SubVIs.

10.1 Property nodes

As you may have seen from Chapter 1, the objects on the front panel have different properties and methods that can be modified, such as size, label, color, position, value, etc. As shown in Chapter 1, these properties and methods can be modified when the program is being edited, but they can also be changed when the program is being executed. Property nodes perform the change of properties in execution time. This section explains how to use property nodes and their most common applications.

The property nodes allow the block diagram to change the properties of a control or indicator on the front panel. To create a property node go to Object Menu>Create>Property node, here you will see the context menu to select one of the properties for the selected object. The list on this context menu will change depending on the selected object.

One of the most common use of the property nodes is to disable and grayed out a control (for example, to prevent the user from entering data). It is done by using the Disabled property node, which has three states. Table 10.1 shows the states for the Disabled property node, how the control will look on the front panel, how it is used on the block diagram, and a description of how they function. Note: When creating a property node it will appear as read, to change it just right click on it and select Change all to write.

Another common application of the property nodes is to initialize the value of controls and indicators when the program starts running. As you may have seen, when you execute a program, then stop it and execute it again, the values on the controls and indicators will remain with the values of the last execution. One way of initializing the value of the controls to a default value is using the property node

Table 10.1   Enable property node states

Front panel	Block diagram	Description
Numeric 0	Numeric / ‹›Enabled ▼ – ›Disabled	The enabled state is to leave the control in their normal state and it will work as usual
Numeric 0	Numeric / ‹›Disabled ▼ – ›Disabled	The Disabled state will not let the user interact with the control and/or change its value
Numeric 0	Numeric / ‹›Disabled and Grayed Out ▼ – ›Disabled	This state works as the Disabled state and it will also change the appearance of the control

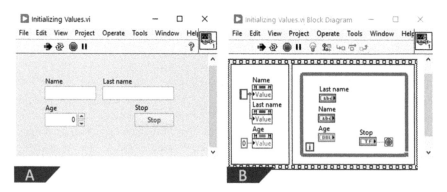

Figure 10.1   Initializing values VI. (A) Front panel and (B) block diagram

Value. For example, the VI in Figure 10.1 shows a VI that normally, when executed a second time, would appear with the values of the previous execution. Still, as it has the Value property node for each control, they appear with the input values, in this case a blank string for the string controls and a zero for the numeric control. Note that the property nodes are in the first sequence, so they will be executed when the program starts running.

Sometimes when some action occurs in the program, you will want the user to focus their attention on a particular control to know what should be their next action. This can be done using the Blinking property node or the Key Focus property node as shown in Figure 10.2, where the Blinking property node is linked to Button 1 and the Key Focus property node is linked to Button 2. Both of these property nodes highlight the controls in different ways.

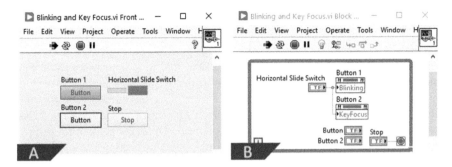

Figure 10.2   Blinking and Key Focus property nodes. (A) Front panel and (B) block diagram

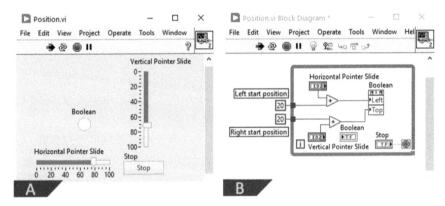

Figure 10.3   Left and top property node. (A) Front panel and (B) block diagram

The position is a property for every object on the front panel and it can also be changed using the property nodes. For example, the VI in Figure 10.3 modifies the position of the Boolean LED indicator using the Left and Top property nodes, you can find them by going to **Object Menu>Create>Property Node>Position**. This property node has two elements, they can be added by placing the mouse at the bottom of the property node and expanding it, then just select the desired property. Another way to modify the left and top positions is by selecting the All Elements option when creating the property node. This will create a property node with just one element called position, and this element receives the top and left position as a cluster. The VI starts with two numeric constants that are used for the default left and top positions, then on the while loop the value of the default positions is added with the value of the pointer sliders to modify the position of the Boolean LED indicator using the property node. When the user moves the Vertical Pointer Slide, the Boolean LED indicator will move on the vertical axis, the same applies for the Horizontal Pointer Slide, which will move the Boolean LED indicator on the horizontal axis.

Captions and labels of objects on the front panel are helpful tools to give the user a glance about what objects will be used. But sometimes, this is not enough, the user will want/need more information about the object. To give the user more information about the objects on the front panel, the tip strips can be used. For example, on the VI in Figure 10.4, a tip strip that says "This box only accepts positive integers" appears when the mouse hovers over the numeric control, and when the mouse hovers over the Stop button, a tip strip with the message "This button will end the program execution" will appear. Tip strips are helpful to give more information to the user about the controls without affecting the style of the user interface since tip strips appear when the mouse hovers over the objects and disappear after the mouse moves over. Note that tip strips can be placed before a while loop and the message will still appear.

The default color for numeric indicators on the NXG Style palette is a gray background and black text, but sometimes you may need to change them depending on the indicator's value for a more intuitive user interface. For example, on the VI in Figure 10.5, the numeric indicator called Number changes the background and

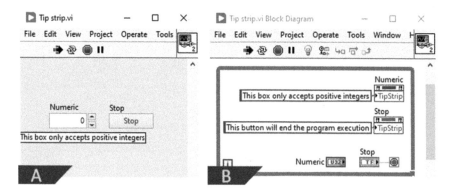

Figure 10.4   Tip strip property node. (A) Front panel and (B) block diagram

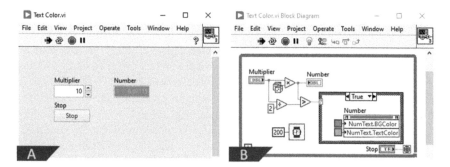

Figure 10.5   Numeric indicator background and text color. (A) Front panel and (B) block diagram

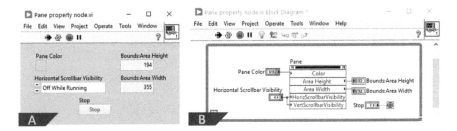

Figure 10.6   Pane property node. (A) Front panel and (B) block diagram

text color depending on its value. If its value is higher than half the value of the control called Multiplier, the Number indicator background will turn dark green and the text light green. If the Number indicator value is lower or equal than half the value of the control called Multiplier, the Number indicator background will turn dark red and the text light red. To do this, a property node with two elements was used on the true case and another property node with the same two elements on the false case. These two elements for the property nodes are found by going to Object Menu>Create>Property Node>Numeric Text>Text Colors and here BG Color and Text Color were used. To indicate the color to be used with each element, just right click the element and select create constant, this will create a color constant which can be changed by clicking on it and selecting the desired color.

The use of property nodes is not only limited to the objects on the front panel, but they can also be used to modify properties of the front panel. For example, the VI in Figure 10.6 shows the use of a property node linked to the pane to modify various properties. This property node was created using the Quick Drop window (Ctrl + space), searching "Property node" and selecting the option Property Node. When the property node is placed, it needs to be linked to the pane, this is done by right clicking on the property node and then going to Link to>Pane>Pane, and it is ready to use with the different methods and properties of the pane. As you can see in Figure 10.6, the background color is modified with a color control, the bound area height and width of the window are shown on the indicators and the scrollbars visibility is off while the program is running. Note that some properties can only be set to read, as it is the case for the area height and area width.

10.2   Invoke nodes

Another type of node is the invoke node, which is used to execute specific methods that are transversal among similar programs. This section explains how to call different types of methods at run-time. Invoke nodes are added to the block diagram by going to Functions pallete>Programming>Application control

Figure 10.7   Invoke node

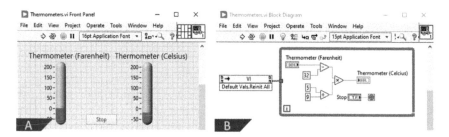

Figure 10.8   VI class invoke node used to reinitialize all values to default. (A) Front panel and (B) block diagram

and selecting Invoke Node. This will create the function shown in Figure 10.7, which is the invoke node. This function invokes a method or action on a reference, in this case, the reference is the application class and the method is selected by clicking on Method; this will show a list of all the available methods for the current reference.

Figure 10.8 shows a VI that contains two thermometers: one of them is a control with units on Fahrenheit, and the other thermometer is an indicator that displays the converted value from the Fahrenheit thermometer to Celsius. In this example, an invoke node is being used to reinitialize the values of all controls and indicators to their default value. This is done by placing an invoke node and changing its class to VI. To change the class of an invoke node, right click on it and then go to Select Class>VI Server>VI and select VI. After the class is selected, the next step is to select the method by clicking on Method on the invoke node and going to Default Values and selecting Reinitialize All to Default, this will change the text on the invoke node to Default Vals.Reinit All as shown on the block diagram. Also, note that the invoke node is connected to the while loop through an error cluster to ensure that the values are reinitialized to default before the while loop when the program starts executing.

The VI in Figure 10.9 is the same VI from the previous example but with a few modifications to obtain a screenshot of the front panel by using an invoke node with the get image method on the VI class. This method is selected by clicking on method, going to Front Panel and selecting Get Image, this will change the text on the invoke node to FP.Get image and will create two input terminals and one output terminal on the invoke node. The Visible Area Only terminal as a Boolean input terminal, if the value is True, the image generated will include just the objects

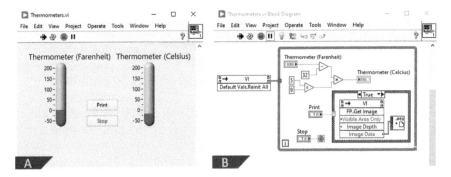

Figure 10.9   *Invoke node used to get image from the front panel. (A) Front panel and (B) block diagram*

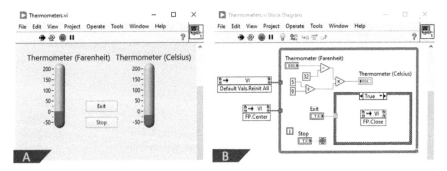

Figure 10.10   *Center front panel and close front panel. (A) Front panel and (B) block diagram*

of the visible area, and if it is False, the image will include all the front panel objects, if the terminal is unwired the default value is True. The Image Depth terminal modifies the color depth or number of supported colors, if it is unwired the default value is eight, which is for 8-bit image of 256 colors. Finally, the Image Data output terminal provides information about the image in a cluster, this information includes image type, image depth, image, mask, colors, and rectangle. The invoke node with the Get image method in this example is placed inside a case structure on the True case, when the Print button is pressed, the invoke node will be executed, and the image data is sent to the Write JPEG File function which will open a window to save the image file on JPEG format.

Figure 10.10 uses the same example of the thermometers, but in this case two new invoke nodes were added, and the get image invoke node was eliminated. The first of the new invoke nodes added is below the invoke node used to reinitialize the default values. This new invoke node is used to center the front panel window on the screen, this method is placed by clicking on method, then Front Panel and selecting Center. The other invoke node is placed inside the case structure, it is used to close the VI when the Exit button is pressed. This method is placed by clicking on method, then Front Panel and selecting Close. When the exit button is pressed, the VI will be closed, but LabVIEW^{TM} will remain open, if the programmer wants LabVIEW^{TM} also to be closed, there is the function Quit LabVIEW^{TM} and can be found on Functions Palette>Programming>Application control.

The close method may seem impractical while programming because it closes the VI while the code is being modified, needing to open it again. Nevertheless, it can be useful in subVIs when they are used as a pop-up window as shown in the example from Figure 10.11. This example is used to simulate a loading bar, and it consists of two Vis: the main VI is just a while loop with a Start button; if it is pressed, it executes a subVI that opens a window simulating a loading bar and closes when it finished loading. Figure 10.11(A) shows the front panel of the main VI, which contains the Start button and a Stop button to stop the program. Figure 10.11(B) is the block diagram of the main VI, it contains a while loop with a case structure inside of it, the False case of this structure is empty, and the True case contains the subVI that simulates a loading bar when the Start button is pressed. Figure 10.11(C) shows the front panel of the loading bar subVI, which includes a horizontal progress bar that is used to display the loading bar simulation.

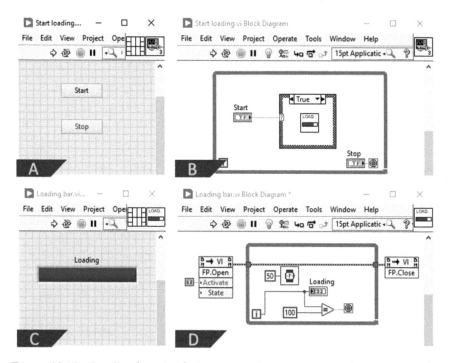

Figure 10.11   Loading bar simulation generating a pop-up window using invoke nodes. (A) Main VI front panel, (B) main VI block diagram, (C) pop-up window front panel, (D) pop-up window block diagram

Figure 10.11(C) is the block diagram of the loading bar subVI, it contains two invoke nodes and a while loop that generates the values for the loading bar using the loop iteration each 50 milliseconds and stopping the while loop once the iterations reach 100 milliseconds. The first invoke node is connected to the while loop through the error cluster to force the order execution, the class of this invoke node is VI from Object Menu>Select Class>Vi Server>VI and the selected method is the Open method from Method>Front Panel. This invoke node opens the front panel window and it contains two terminals. The Activate terminal opens the front panel window if the input value is True, if it is False, the front panel window will not open; the default value if unwired is False. The State terminal sets a state in which the front panel window will be opened, it is an enum data type with six values ranging from zero to six, where the default value is one or standard which opens the front panel window without minimizing, maximizing, or hiding the window, if one of this actions is needed, they can be used in other values of the enum which can be found on the context help of this invoke node. Finally, the second invoke node is after the while loop, and it is also connected to the while loop through an error cluster to force the execution of this function after the while loop finishes its execution, this invoke node uses the Close method from the VI class from Object Menu>Select Class>Vi Server>VI. In this sense, when the main VI is executed and the Start button is pressed, the front panel of the subVI will open and the loading bar simulation will start, once the progress bar finishes loading, the front panel window of the subVI will close and the program execution on the main VI will continue until the Stop button is pressed.

10.3   Control references

In the examples of Section 10.1 all the property nodes are directly linked to the objects on the front panel or the pane, this is an implicitly linked property node, but this is not the only way of linking an object to a property node, there are also explicitly linked property nodes. These property nodes are linked to the object using control references of the object which are connected to the property node. Figure 10.12(A) shows an example of an implicitly linked property node and Figure 10.12(B) shows its equivalent in an explicitly linked property node. These property nodes need a reference to indicate the link between the property node and the object. In this case, the control reference of the numeric control was created by right clicking the object and going to Create>Reference.

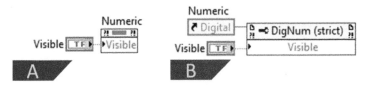

Figure 10.12   (A) Implicit property node and (B) explicit property node

The VI in Figure 10.13 shows an example of a property node being used with two different control references. This property node is used to modify the disabled property of an object on the front panel, the object which property will be changed depends on the position of the Horizontal Slide Switch, when the switch is on the true state, the select function will return the value of the control reference for the Boolean indicator, and when the switch is on the false state, the select function will return the value of the control reference for the Numeric indicator. Finally, the Disabled property is modified using the Disabled control. This VI uses only one property node and one control to modify the Disabled property of two objects on the front panel, this VI could also be programmed with the use of implicitly linked property nodes, but the implementation would require more space on the block diagram and it would be a little more complex.

The use of explicit property nodes allows different ways of programming for modifying properties of the objects on the front panel. For example, the VI in Figure 10.14 shows three control references used to build an array, then it is connected to a For loop with an auto-indexed tunnel, this will let modifying the Colors property of one object per iteration. This is useful when too many controls or indicators need to be initialized without using one property node for each object.

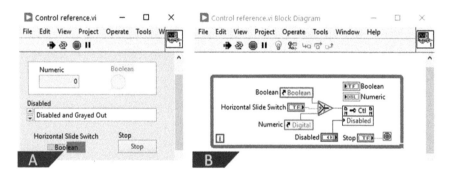

Figure 10.13   Control reference. (A) Front panel and (B) block diagram

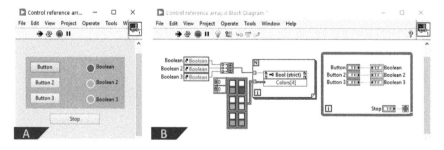

Figure 10.14   Control reference array. (A) Front panel and (B) block diagram

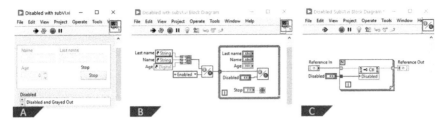

Figure 10.15   Using an explicit property node on a subVI. (A) Main VI front panel,
(B) main VI block diagram, and (C) subVI block diagram

Another use for the explicit property nodes is that they can be implemented on
SubVIs. This is something that cannot be done with implicit property nodes as they
are directly linked to an object on the VI. When you create a subVI from selection
with an implicit property node, it will be automatically converted into an explicit
property node on the subVI. The VI in Figure 10.15 shows an example of an explicit
property node being used in a sub VI. This subVI is being used to change the
Disabled property of the objects that it receives in an array of control references. The
VI uses the start of the program to initialize the objects as enabled, and it is used
again on the While loop to modify the disabled property with the Disabled control.

10.4   User interface control example

This section presents an example of how the property nodes can be implemented in
a program to create a functional user interface with common methods among
similar programs. In Figure 10.16, the front panel of the Test Simulation VI is
shown. This VI simulates a test machine for an equipment, this test is performed by

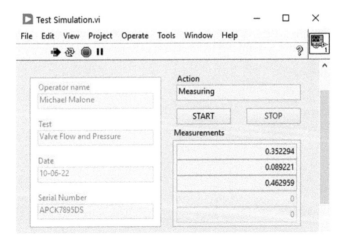

Figure 10.16   Test simulation VI front panel

taking five measurements and then stores the acquired data along with the information introduced by the user on the form on the left.

This VI simulates the data acquisition part and the saving data on file part to focus on the use of the property nodes. This program consists of three main steps: the first one is to wait for the user information, the second one is the data acquisition simulation, and the final step is the simulation of data saving on file as shown in Figure 10.17. All the code for the program is inside a while loop structure which will stop when the Stop control is pressed, this control is inside another while loop structure, on this structure the string "Waiting for user information" is shown on the Action indicator and the program is waiting for the user to fill the form and press the Start button. This button is connected to an or function that also has connected the Stop button, both of these buttons will stop the while loop structure but the Stop button will end the program and when the start button is pressed the program will not stop and the case structure will enter into the False case, here there are two structures and a subVI which is used to disable and gray out the controls that the user must fill, so that, he cannot modify them while the system is taking measurements as shown in Figure 10.16, then the first structure to be executed is the for loop structure, this structure is used to simulate the data acquisition using a random number generator and a timer. Also, on this structure, the message shown on the Action indicator is changed to "Measuring". The last structure to be executed inside the false case is a sequence structure, which is used to simulate the saving of the form filled by the user and the measurements on a file. The simulation only shows the message "Saving" on the Action indicator and a wait function so that the message can be read. After the sequence structure finishes its execution, the main while loop structure starts again and the two subVIs are used to clear the form and enable the controls used in that form, and also there is a property node to initialize the Measurements indicator.

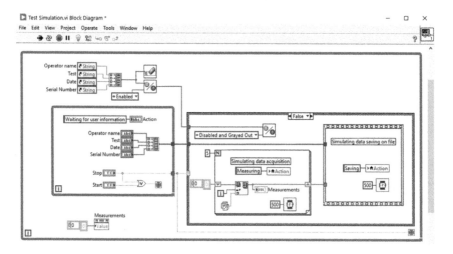

Figure 10.17   Test simulation VI block diagram

Figure 10.18(A) shows the subVI used to modify the Disabled property of the controls that the user must fill, it has two inputs (Reference In and Disabled controls) and one output (Reference Out indicator). And Figure 10.18(B) shows the subVI used to initialize the string controls of the form, it has one input (Reference In) and one output (Reference out). This subVI will modify the Value property of the string controls to a blank space.

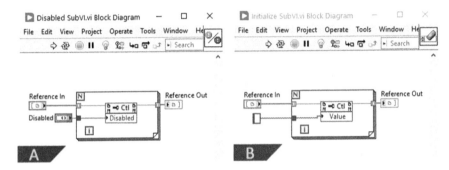

Figure 10.18   Explicit property node subVIs. (A) Disabled subVI and (B) initialize subVI

Chapter 11

Error handling

Error handling is a fundamental feature in an application, without a mechanism to notify the user that an error has occurred and the cause of it, the program would simply stop working. It is for this reason that this chapter explains how to manage errors properly, it begins by defining errors and warnings, custom errors will be created and appropriate ways to stop a program and display errors will be explained.

11.1   Errors and warnings

Errors and warnings on LabVIEW^{TM} are used to detect why and where errors occur in a VI. In LabVIEW^{TM} errors have their own data type, they are called error clusters, which is a special cluster data type that includes a Boolean indicator for the status, a numeric indicator for the code, and a string indicator for the source as shown in Figure 11.1.

To have a better understanding of the errors let us use the VI from Figure 11.2 as an example. The VI works in the following way: when this VI is executed, it will open a window to select a text file that will be shown on the "Text" string indicator on the front panel.

The VI shown in Figure 11.2 works properly when the user opens the text file, but when the user presses the cancel button instead, the VI will pause, and an error window will appear as shown in Figure 11.3(A) where the window tells that an error occurred at the function Open/Create/Replace File, and it is due to the operation being canceled by the user. If the stop button is pressed on that window the VI will stop its execution, but if the continue button is pressed, the VI will continue its execution to Read from Text File where another error window will appear, as shown in Figure 11.3(B), this error was generated as the previous function did not provide a valid path to use in the Read from Text File function. If the continue button is pressed again, the VI will continue its execution to the Close File function, where a third error window will pop-up as shown in Figure 11.3(C), this is because the previous function also did not provide a valid path to be used with the Close File function generating the same error. This is called automatic error handling and it can be better observed by executing the VI with highlight execution and/or step by step execution.

These error windows are helpful in development mode to detect errors and correct them, it is important to mention that the errors message from the automatic

Figure 11.1   Error cluster indicator

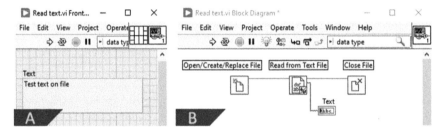

Figure 11.2   Read text VI. (A) Front panel and (B) block diagram

Figure 11.3   (A) Error on Open/Create/Replace File, (B) error on Read from Text File and (C) error on Close File

error handler are not available in runtime mode (to the end user of the program) and does not stop the VI execution. The last part is crucial when handling errors on VIs as sudden stops of the program can be dangerous depending on the application of the VI, instead of letting the VI stop, special actions should be taken to handle the errors generated. This can be done by using manual error handling as shown in Figure 11.4(A), where the error cluster is spread by the functions using the error in and error out of each function. In order to appreciate the change, the VI was

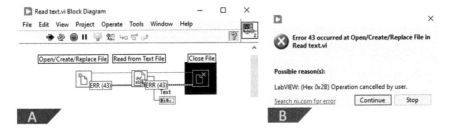

Figure 11.4   Manual error handling. (A) Block diagram and (B) error window

executed using highlight execution and the button cancel was pressed at the moment of selecting the text file to generate the same error as before. As you can see, this time the VI did not stop at the Open/Create/Replace File function; instead, the error passed through the error cluster to the Read from Text File, and since it received an error, the function did not get executed as usual and it just passed the error to the Close File function, which is the last function connected to the error cluster and this is where the VI stopped and showed the error window as shown in Figure 11.4(B).

To see the contents of the error cluster, an indicator can be used as shown in Figure 11.5, where a cluster indicator is placed after the Close File function. In this case, the error window does not appear since the error passes through the Close File function. The error out indicator shows the status, which indicates that an error occurred, the code tells what error was, and the source indicates where the error occurred, in this case, it was on the Open/Create/Replace File Function on the Read text VI.

The values of the error cluster can be manipulated separately to perform an action in case of an error. For example, in Figure 11.6, the Unbundle by Name function is used to connect the error code to a case structure where a dialog box

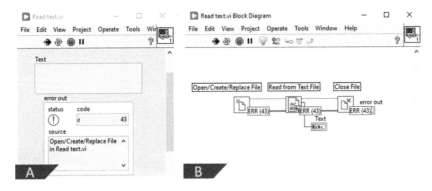

Figure 11.5   Manual error handling with cluster indicator. (A) Front panel and (B) block diagram

with the message "Please select a file" is shown to the user when the error 43 appears, which is the error that occurs when the user does not select a file.

The case structure's polymorphic property can also be used with the error cluster instead of using the Unbundle by Name function. In Figure 11.7, the error cluster is connected directly to the case structure and automatically creates the "No Error" and "Error .." cases with a green frame for the "No Error" case and a red frame for the "Error .." case. This approach is useful when an action needs to be taken without considering the error code.

• Tip #19: When the value of the status in the error cluster is True it means that an error occurred and when it is False it means that no error occurred.

If a specific action to certain error codes needs to be performed, the dots on the "Error .." case can be changed for the error code and a case must be selected as Default as shown in Figure 11.8, where the "No Error" case stays the same, the "Error .." case was changed to "Error 1", and turned into the Default case, and finally a new case was created for the error code 43.

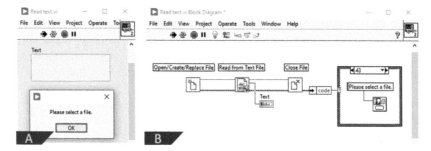

Figure 11.6   Error code 43 – Please select a file message dialog box. (A) Front panel and (B) block diagram

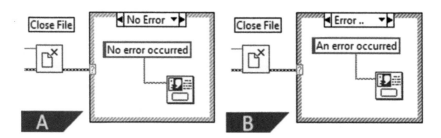

Figure 11.7   Case structure polymorphic property. (A) No Error and (B) Error

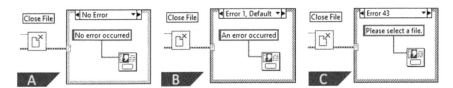

Figure 11.8   Case structure. (A) No Error, (B) Error 1, Default and (C) Error 43

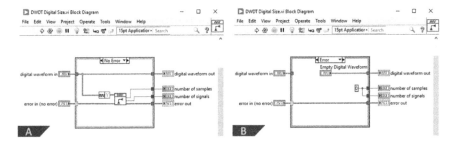

Figure 11.9   Digital Size function. (A) No Error case and (B) Error case

As mentioned before, when a function receives an error through the "error in" the VI does not execute as usual; instead, most functions just pass the error information through the error out to the next function. To have a graphic representation of this, let us take a look at the function from **Functions palette>Waveform> Digital Wfm>Digital Size**, this function is a subVI and it can be opened by placing it on the block diagram and double clicking on it to open the subVI and pressing "**Ctrl + E**" to open the block diagram. This VI has an error in a cluster connected to a case structure as shown in Figure 11.9, where the "No Error" case executes the VI as usual and the "Error" case returns an empty digital waveform, zeros on the other outputs and passes the error through the case to the error out. As you can see, this VI has the same functioning principle when receiving an error as the VIs mentioned before. When an error occurs, the function passes the error information through the error out terminal.

As in the function Digital Size, the error clusters connected to a case structure can also be implemented in your own subVIs. For example, the subVIs of the VI created in Figure 4.7 can be modified as shown in Figure 11.10 to include the error in an error out terminals on the subVIs, where a case structure was added, leaving the terminals outside of it and the error cluster control was connected to the case selector which also passed through the "No error" and "Error" case to get connected to an error out cluster indicator outside the case structure. In the "Error" case, the unwired tunnels were connected to an empty constant for the "Message selector" subVI and a numeric constant with value zero for the "Average" subVI.

The error clusters can also be used to control the execution order of the functions. To have a better understanding of how this can be done, it is important to

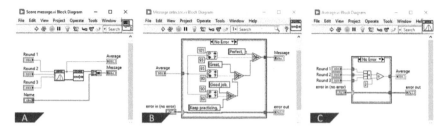

Figure 11.10   (A) Score message VI, (B) Message selector VI with error clusters and (C) Average VI with error clusters

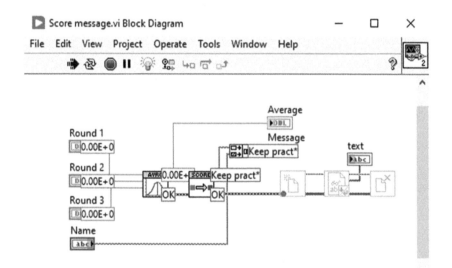

Figure 11.11   Controlling execution order using error cluster

remember the concept of data flow mentioned in Chapter 1, where it is explained that in order for one node to be capable of sending information through its output, all of its inputs must have received the necessary information, and the node needs to finish its execution. For example, let us say that for the VI shown in Figure 11.10(A) it is wanted to read a file but only after the "Message selector" subVI is executed. To do this, the functions "Open/Create/Replace File", "Read from Text File", and "Close File" need to be placed and connected as shown before in Figure 11.4. Then the error out of the "Message selector" subVI must be connected to the error in of the "Open/Create/Replace File" function as shown in Figure 11.11. As you can see, when running the program on highlight execution mode, the "Open/Create/Replace File" is waiting to receive the information on the error in terminal in order to be executed. In this case, the error cluster is used to ensure that a function does not execute until another function or subVI is executed.

11.2   Custom errors

The previous section explains how errors are produced when certain conditions are met, for example, when the user cancels the operation or when an invalid path is received. These errors predefined by LabVIEW^{TM} can also be shown when certain conditions on the VI are met and not only when a function produces the error. These errors can be defined using an error ring on Functions Palette> Programming>Dialog & User Interface. The error ring is as shown in Figure 11.12 (A), in this case it is an error cluster that does not have an error, it can be changed to the desired error by clicking the triangle on the right of the ring error, this will open the Select Error window as shown in Figure 11.12(B) where the No Error appears on the "No Error" Error Code Range, to select a different error, click on the Error Code Range, select a category and the list will be updated for the errors on that category. When the new error is selected, click the OK button, and the ring error will change to the new selected error.

The error ring can be used to show errors when certain conditions are met on VIs or subVIs, for example, the VI from Figure 11.13 is used to find a name on an

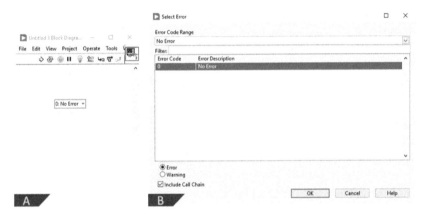

Figure 11.12   (A) Error ring on block diagram and (B) select Error window

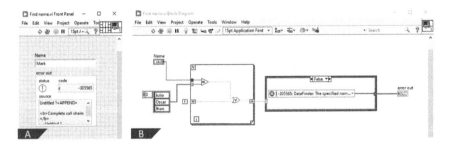

Figure 11.13   Find name VI. (A) Front panel and (B) block diagram

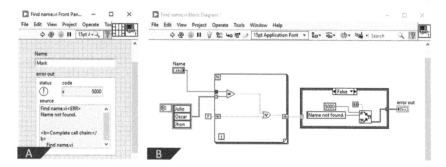

Figure 11.14   Creating an error defined by user on Find name VI. (A) Front panel and (B) block diagram

array, if the name is on the array the VI returns no error, if the name is not on the array the VI returns the predefined by LabVIEW^{TM} error code -305565 DataFinder: The specified name is invalid. This error code is found on the Select Error window on the DataFinder Error Code Range.

The VI shown in Figure 11.13 is used to call a predefined error code when a condition is met, but custom errors defined by the user can also be created. LabVIEW^{TM} has a list of available ranges reserved to create errors defined by the user; these ranges are: −8999 to −8000, 5000 to 9999, and 500,000 to 599,999. These errors are created using the Error Cluster From Error Code VI, which is found on Functions Palette>Programming>Dialog & User Interface. This VI is used as a subVI to generate custom errors with five basic inputs: the "error code" which can be any number within the ranges reserved for custom error codes, the "error message ("")" which is the error description that will appear on the error out cluster, the "error in" that works as in other functions, the "is warning" which is set to False by default, but when it receives a True value it changes the error into a warning, and finally, the "show call chain?" if also set to False by default but if it receives a True value includes a chain of callers from the VI that produced the error and shows it on the source of the error cluster. In Figure 11.14 the Error Cluster From Error Code VI is used instead of the error ring to generate a custom error with the code 5000, the message "Name not found". and the show call chain is set to True. As you can see on the front panel, the name "Mark" is searched on the list and since it is not within it, the VI generates the error as shown on the error out, where the status shows that an error occurred, the code value is 5000 and the source shows the message "Name not found". and it also indicates that the error occurred on the Find name.vi.

11.3   Error messages

In Section 11.1, it is explained that when an error occurs on a function that does not have wired their error in and error out, the program will pause and display an error window with the error information; afterward, it is explained that when the functions have their error in and error out connected, they will pass the error to the next function and if there is nothing else connected to this function, the error window will appear with the option to stop the execution or continue. This option can be used when the developer is working on the VI, but when the end user is using the program, this option is not available (remember, the automatic error handler is not available in final applications). Most of the time, the final user needs to know what causes the error and not all the engineering details behind it, so an error window with a message about the error can be enough information for the end user in the case of an error. To create different kinds of error windows, the Simple Error Handler can be used. This VI is found on **Functions Palette>Programming>Dialog & User Interface**. The Simple Error Handler VI is used to show error messages, it returns a description of the error and displays a dialog box (optionally). It has four inputs, "error code (no error:0)" calls the error code on its input, but if an error is received on error in the VI ignores the error code; "error source" is optional and it is used to describe the error source; "type of dialog" determines what type of dialog box to display depending on its value (values for the type of dialog shown in Table 11.1); "error in" describes the error that occurred before this function. The Simple Error Handler also has five outputs, "error?" returns True when an error occurs; "code out" returns the error code value from "error in" or "error code"; "source out" is a string that returns the source of the error; "error out" outputs the error information but, contrary to other functions that have the error out connected to other function when this terminal is connected, this function still shows the error window; "message" shows the information of the error code, source of the error, and a description of the error.

On the VI from Figure 11.15, the simple error handler is used to show the occurred error to the user. As you can see, the only input terminal connected to the simple error handler is the error cluster and the error window shows the default type

Table 11.1 Type of dialog values

Value	Type of dialog	Description
0	No dialog	Cancels the display of dialog box, it is useful when programmatic control over handling errors is needed.
1	OK message	The error window will be displayed with a single Continue button. If there is no input on the type of dialog, this value is used as default.
2	Continue or stop message	The error window will be displayed with two buttons: continue and stop.
3	OK message + warnings	The displayed window will show any warnings and one Continue button.
4	Continue/ stop + warnings	The displayed window will show any warnings and two buttons: Continue and stop.

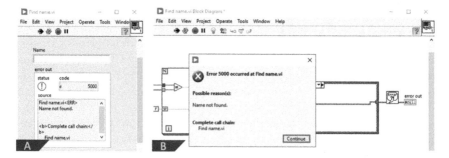

Figure 11.15   Find name VI with simple error handler. (A) Front panel and (B) block diagram and error window

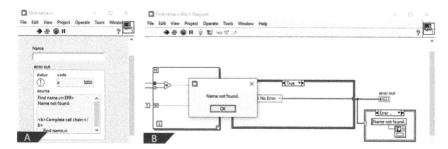

Figure 11.16   Find name VI with One Button Dialog Box. (A) Front panel and (B) block diagram and dialog box

of dialog window, displaying the message with a single continue button and the same error information as in the error out cluster indicator.

Another option to show a message to the user in case of an error is to use the dialog boxes. For example, in Figure 11.16, instead of using the simple error handler, a one button dialog box and a case structure is used to show the message "Name not found". On a dialog box with an "OK" button. This is a useful way to show an error in a different kind of window to the user. Also, if an action from the user is needed the "Two Button Dialog" and the "Three Button Dialog" can be used.

11.4   Error handling examples

This section provides an example of a VI that calculates the quotient and remainder when the calculate button is pressed (see Figure 11.17). The VI has two numeric controls, one for the dividend and one for the divisor; two numeric indicators, one for the remainder and one for the quotient. To calculate the values of the quotient and remainder, the function "Quotient & Remainder" is used.

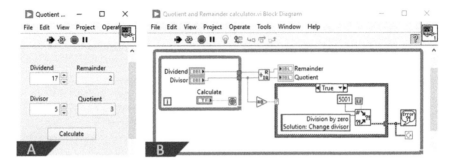

Figure 11.17   Quotient and remainder calculator VI. (A) Front panel and (B) block diagram

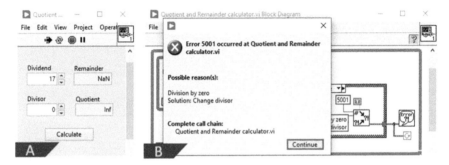

Figure 11.18   Quotient and remainder calculator error window. (A) Front panel and (B) block diagram and error window

When the divisor has a value zero, the "Quotient & Remainder" function returns "NaN" value for the remainder and "inf" value for the quotient, but for this case it is wanted that the VI displays an error window with the message "Division by zero Solution: Change divisor" and a continue button (see Figure 11.18(B)). After the user presses the continue button, the VI waits for the user to press the calculate button again and checks if the divisor is equal to zero to generate the error again, if the value is not equal to zero, the program stops. In this case, the error is handled so that the VI does not let the user end the program if a value different from zero is used for the divisor.

The VI showed before can be converted to a subVI with its respective error in and error out clusters as shown in Figure 11.19, where most of the code is inside a case structure with the "error in (no error)" connected to the selector. The inputs of the subVI are the "Dividend", "Divisor" and "error in (no error)". The outputs are the "Remainder", "Quotient", and "error out". When the subVI receives an error through the "error in (no error)" the subVI will not execute its normal function; instead, it will send the error received through the "error out" and the value of

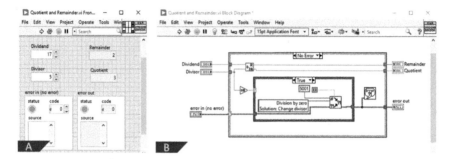

Figure 11.19   Quotient and remainder subVI. (A) Front panel and (B) block diagram

"NaN" for the remainder and quotient. If the subVI did not receive an error, it will continue with its normal execution and if the user enters a zero value on the divisor, the error window will be displayed and the error information will be sent through the "error out".

Chapter 12

Responding to the user interactions

As a program responds swiftly to the user's actions, it feels comfortable and works naturally with it. In this sense, traditional techniques such as polling can lose user actions. For this reason, in this chapter, the use of event structures is explained, which is an asynchronous communication structure that allows responding to all user actions, the chapter starts by describing what it is and how to use the event structure, it will show the use of data event nodes and event filter nodes, after that, an event state machine will be implemented, and finally, an example of Event-Driven State Machine will be implemented.

12.1 Event structure

The event structure responds to events related to user actions or programmed events. The event structure works asynchronously, in such a way that if two or more events occur "simultaneously", the event structure will queue them and execute one event for each iteration of the loop where the structure is placed (if there are three "simultaneous" events, the loop will need three iterations to manage all the events) [22]. Visually, the event structure is like the case structure, it has (1) Event Selector Label and (2) Timeout Terminal, additionally, depending on the event, it can have a (3) Data Node and/or a (4) Filter Node, see Figure 12.1.

Select the Programming >> Structures >> Event structure in the functions palette, To add a new event structure. The event structure is used in event-driven programming, this kind of programming has several advantages: (1) Eliminates the pooling of the program (pooling is referred to periodically monitor all the changes in the controls of the front panel), (2) the program is executed only when an event occurs (this gives the processor enough time to complete other tasks), (3) it is possible to change the behavior of certain events. The event structure must be placed inside a while loop, and you must consider that the structure will execute one event for each iteration of the loop.

- Tip #20: Avoid using more than one event structure inside a loop, avoid programming the same event in two different event structures.

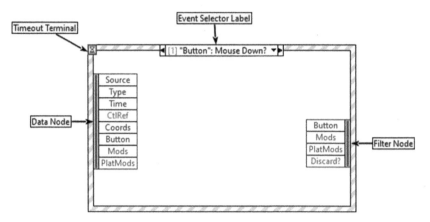

Figure 12.1   *Elements of an event structure, note that the Data Node and Filter Node will be available depending on the type of event*

12.2   Event-driven programming

With the aim to exemplify how to use the event structure, a basic calculator will be implemented, during this demonstration you will learn how to create events and how to use the data node and the filter node. First, in a new VI, a front panel is created as in Figure 12.2 (it is important to follow the next example to understand the use of events).

The next step is to create an event structure and place it inside a while loop, the block diagram should look like the one in Figure 12.3. At this point, the program will mark a broken arrow and cannot be executed.

Therefore, the first event to be programmed is the value change of the stop button, with which the program must be stopped. With this aim, you need to add a new event; in the edge of the event structure **Right click>>Add Event Case**, the **Edit Events** window will appear as in Figure 12.4.

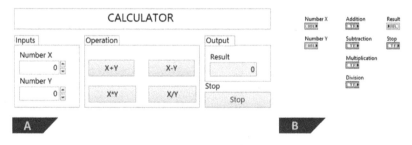

Figure 12.2   *(A) Calculator front panel HMI and (B) controls and indicators in the block diagram*

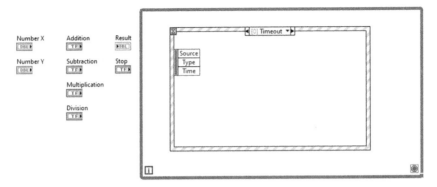

Figure 12.3   Creating and placing the event structure within a while loop. To create an event structure, select Programming>>Structures>>Event Structure

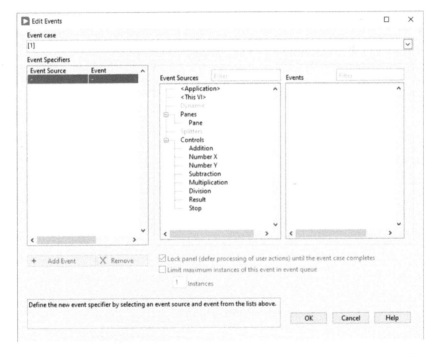

Figure 12.4   Edit Events window and the four main parts. (1) Event Case, (2) Event Specifiers, (3) Event Sources, and (4) Events

Before adding the event value change for the stop button, please identify four parts of the Edit Events window, (1) Event case: select a case and identify all the possible events that can trigger the case, (2) Event Specifiers: it allows adding new events that execute the code of the specified case, (3) Event Sources: contains all the sources that can activate an event, these sources are the controls, indicators, the front panel, the VI or the application, (4) Events: show all the possible events for each of the selected event sources, it should be noted that the type of event can be different between event sources. To add the value change event for the stop button, go to the Stop control within Event Sources, then select Value Change in Events (see Figure 12.5).

Finally, click OK in the Edit Events window, this will create a new case in the event structure, this case will be triggered when you click the Stop Button; however, when you are using the value change event of a latched Boolean button, it is always recommended to place the Boolean control inside the event case to avoid malfunction of the program. Once the Stop control is inside the event case, wire it to the while conditional terminal as in Figure 12.6.

Next, you have to create a case event for each Boolean button of the program (Addition, Subtraction, Multiplication, and Division), for this, you must add new case events by clicking on the edge of the event structure Right-click >> Add Event Case and selecting the value change event for each button (note that it is necessary to repeat this procedure four times). In the end, you will have four new event cases, place each Boolean control inside its corresponding event case and add a false constant to the boolean tunnel as in Figure 12.7.

Place the controls Number X and Number Y within the Addition event case, also, create an addition function and connect the inputs to Number X and Number

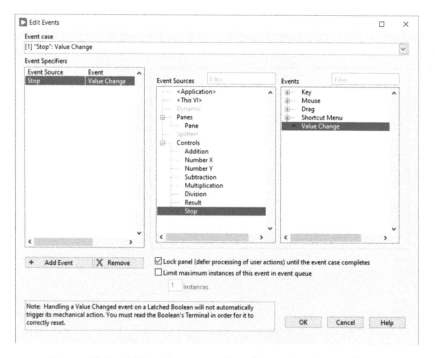

Figure 12.5   Adding the event value change for the stop button

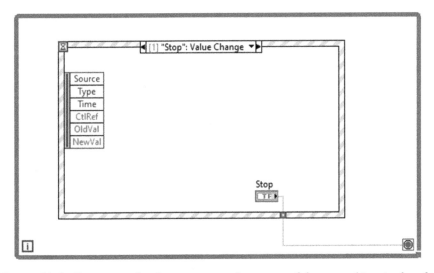

Figure 12.6   Event case for the stop event, the output of the control is wired to the conditional terminal of the while loop

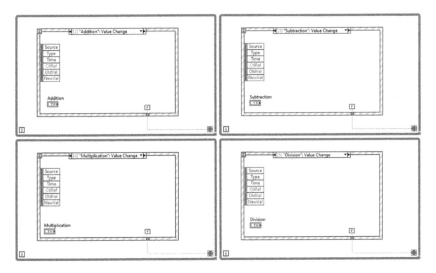

Figure 12.7   Event cases two, three, four, and five to detect the value change of each button

Y. Create three local variables of Number X and Number Y (right click on the variable >> create >> local variable), right click over each variable and select change to read. Place these variables in pairs within Subtraction, Multiplication, and Division event cases, perform the corresponding operation for each event case and wire the output to the Result indicator outside the event structure, as seen in Figure 12.8.

Now you can run the program, enter values in the controls Number X and Number Y, observe how the program responds quickly to any of the operations, also note that it is not necessary to temporize the program. Having created local variables to read Number X and Number Y will not cause race conditions. On the other hand, the Result indicator was left out of the event structure to be written in a single place of the program. If you are using Windows operating system, you can open the task manager and check the low consumption of hardware resources. In Figure 12.9, you can appreciate the result of a subtraction operation.

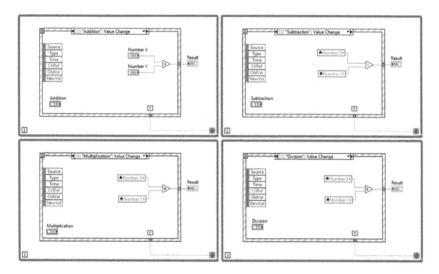

Figure 12.8   Event cases for the math operations using local variables

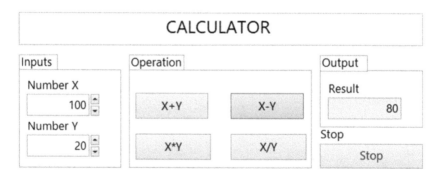

Figure 12.9   Subtraction operation using events, when you are running the program, observe the responding time without using temporization and the low consumption of hardware resources

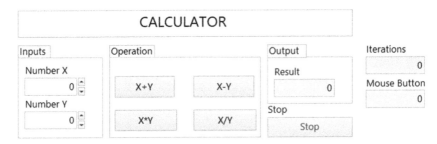

Figure 12.10   Adding the indicator Iterations (I32) and Button (U16) in the front panel

For the next part of the program, you will use the Even Data Nodes and Event Filter Nodes. Therefore, it is necessary to know their definitions:

Event Data Node: These are events that have already occurred, and that LabVIEW™ has processed.

Event Filter Node: These events have already occurred, and LabVIEW™ has not yet processed.

The Event Data Node provides data about the event that has already occurred, while the Event Filter Node, provides a way to modify the behavior of the event, which has not yet been processed. Event Data Nodes can be identified by the green arrow ⇨ in the Events of Edit Events window, while Event Filter Nodes can be identified by the red arrow ⇨. Next, modify the front panel to show the number of iterations of the while loop using even driven programming, in addition, the event data node will be used to identify which mouse button is being pressed (left or right button). Modify the front panel by creating the Iterations indicator with data type I32, and create the Mouse Button with data type U16, see Figure 12.10.

Wire the Iterations indicator to the iterations terminal of the while loop and add a new event case that is activated when a click is detected over the front panel. For this, go to the edge of the event structure, Right-click >> Add Event Case, select pane as event source and the mouse down as event, wire the Mouse Button indicator to the Button terminal in the data node. Figure 12.11 shows how to create the event case, and Figure 12.12 shows the resulting Block Diagram.

Run the program, you will see that Iterations will increase in one when you click over Number X or Number Y control to change the values, in fact, Iterations will increase if you click on any part of the front panel. Test the program by alternating left click or right click, the Mouse Button indicator will change between one and two, the terminal Button gives this information in the data node (Figure 12.12). The data node will change depending on the kind of event, for this event data node you can get

• Tip #21: It is important to note that iterations only changes when an event occurs, this helps to optimize the CPU requirements of the program.

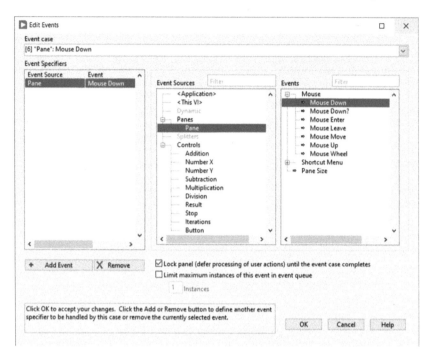

Figure 12.11   Creating the Mouse Down event for the pane

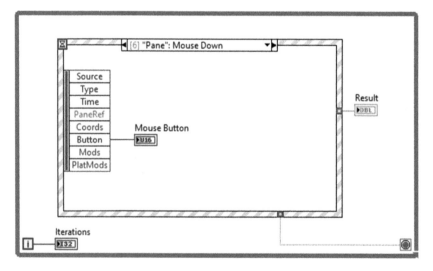

Figure 12.12   Created and wired Mouse Down event

information such as the coordinate position when you make a click over the front panel (Coords), if the click was a double click (Mods), if some special key as "Ctrl", "Alt", or "Shift" is pressed when you click over the front panel (PlatMods). The information obtained from the event data node can increase the functionality of your application and enhance the quality of the information obtained from the interface. It is important to note that if you click over Addition, Subtraction, Multiplication, or Division Buttons, the Iterations indicator will increase in two, this is because the two events are occurring "simultaneously", in this case, the event structure will execute one of the events and put in a queue the other one, the second event will be executed in the next iteration of the while loop, for this reason, the event structure is considered asynchronous, as the program can be processing one event and if one or multiple events occur "simultaneously", these will be placed in a queue.

Finally, for this program, the filter node will be used to change the normal behavior of an event. For this, an event case is created to detect the panel close event (clicking in the cross of the top right corner in the front panel) and filter the event. When the user clicks the panel close, a Two Button Dialog will be displayed and ask if you really want to close the program, this will give an opportunity to discard the event. With this aim, go to the event structure Right-click >> Add Event Case, in the Event Source, select <This VI> and in the Event select Panel Close? (Important: Select the Panel Close? event with the question mark and the red arrow ➡), see Figure 12.13.

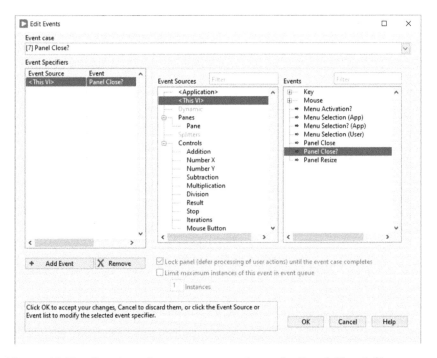

Figure 12.13   Creation of an event case to detect the Panel Close? filter event

Inside the new event case, create a Two Button Dialog, for it, in the functions palette, select Programming>>Dialog & User Interface>>Two Btn Dialog, wire the output of the function to the Discard? terminal of the event filter node. Create a string constant with the message: "Do you really want to close the program?" and wire it to the Message input of the Two Btn Dialog function, then create a string constant with the word "Yes" and another string constant with the word "No", wire the constant "Yes" to the F button name ("Cancel") input, and wire the constant "No" to the T button name ("OK") input, finally, wire a false constant to the Boolean tunnel of the event structure, the block diagram of this event case is shown in Figure 12.14. At this point, it is very important to save the

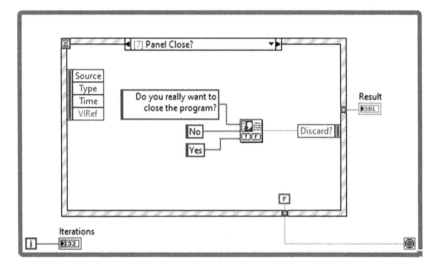

Figure 12.14   Using an event filter node to discard the panel close event

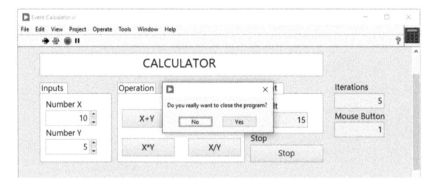

Figure 12.15   Two Button Dialog box display when the panel close event is activated by pressing cross in the top right corner of the front panel

program, because when testing the event "Panel Close?", there is the possibility of accidentally close the program and lose the last changes.

Next, test the program, go to the front panel and click on run, see how the program continues to perform the operations of addition, subtraction, multiplication, and division. Click on the cross (button panel close) that is in the upper right part of the front panel, observe that the event panel close occurs from the moment you press the button, however, LabVIEW^{TM} still does not process it and instead it shows the Two Btn Dialog (see Figure 12.15) that was programmed inside the event, when clicking on "No" a true is sent to the filter node and the event is discarded, when clicking on "Yes" a false is sent to the filter node and the event is processed.

12.3   Event-driven state machine

Event-driven programming has the advantage of responding quickly to all user interactions or external events; however, the code within each event case must be short for the proper function of the program. In this sense, there is the possibility of combining state machines with event-driven programming, to have an architecture that responds quickly to user actions while allowing complex code implementations.

The event-driven state machine is similar to the state machine; however, instead of performing continuous polling to monitor changes in the user interface, this type of programming has a "Wait for Event" state which monitors changes in

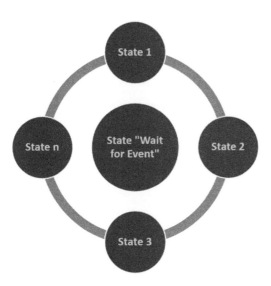

Figure 12.16   In an event-driven state machine, the "Wait for Event" state is the core of the design pattern, an event triggers the jump from "Wait for Event" to other states; however, the program always return to the "Wait for Event" state to monitor user actions or programmed events

the user interface (using an event structure) and depending on the user action it directs the program to its corresponding state, from this state the programs can be directed to different states, but finally returning again to "Wait for Event" state to monitor new events as shown on the diagram from Figure 12.16.

The design pattern event-driven state machine is widely used in test equipment for fast response interfaces, where each of the states represents a part of the test; however, given its versatility, it is often used for monitoring stations, data analysis, and data presentation.

The event-driven state machine design pattern uses a Wait for Event state, this state is regularly accessed to process all those events that were generated in the interface or those events generated by the user. Even so, if the program requires a process that runs frequently, it is possible to take advantage of the event Timeout of the event structure, this event runs if no event is detected within a certain period of time. In Figure 12.17, you can see the structure of an event-driven state machine, where the characteristic state is Wait for Event and the event structure.

With the aim to show how to implement an event-driven state machine, a signal generator will be programmed from scratch. The interface will have the control Amplitude (numeric control, double), Period (numeric control, double), Waveform Type (knob control, I32), Start/Stop (boolean control), Stop Program (boolean control), and as an indicator a Waveform Chart. You can design the interface as in Figure 12.18.

Before beginning with the block diagram, it is recommended to configure the control "Waveform Type" (knob control) to have the appearance of Figure 12.18 and desired behavior. To do this, open the properties of the Waveform Type control, Right-click >> Properties and select the "Data entry" tab, remove the use of default limits, and modify the minimum to zero, the maximum to two and the increment of one. Then go to the "Scale" tab and modify the scale range as

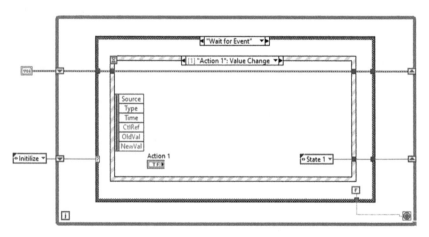

Figure 12.17   Event-driven state machine design pattern, the structure is like a state machine; however, this design pattern has a Wait for Event case to process the interface and user events

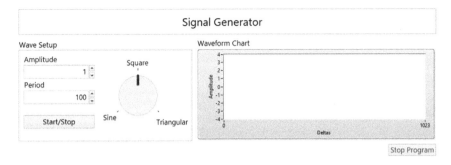

Figure 12.18   Front panel of the Signal Generator program

Figure 12.19   Modification of the knob control properties to obtain the appearance of Figure 12.18 and the desired behavior

minimum zero and maximum two. Finally, go to the "Text Labels" tab and add the labels Sine, Square, and Triangular, then select "Use text labels for scale markers" (see Figure 12.19), finally click on OK.

On the other hand, it is recommended to modify the scales of the Waveform Chart, with this aim, over the Waveform Chart **Right-Click>>Properties** and select "Scales", in the Y-axis remove the Autoscale option and modify the scale to −4 as the minimum and 4 as maximum, in the X-axis remove the Autoscale option and modify the name of the axes to Deltas, then modify the scale to 0 as the minimum and 1,023 as maximum as seen in Figure 12.20, click on OK. Finally, modify the mechanical action of the Start/Stop button to **Switch when Pressed**.

To start with the block diagram, you must create a state machine, for this, add a while loop with a case structure inside it. To propagate the data information of the program from one state to another use a cluster constant with **Current Data** (double), **Index** (I32), **Amplitude** (Double), and **Period** (Double), the information of this cluster will be sent from one iteration to another through a shift register. To create the shift register, right click on the input tunnel in the while loop and select **Replace with Shift Register** wire the cluster as in Figure 12.21. In addition, create an enum constant with the following elements in the list: **Initialize, Wait for**

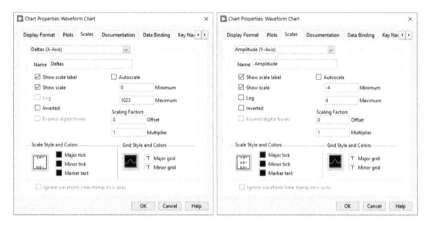

Figure 12.20   Modification of the Waveform Chart properties to adjust the scales of X and Y axes

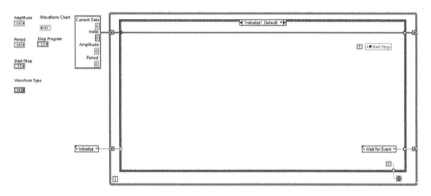

Figure 12.21   Initialize state of the event-driven state machine

Event, **Sine**, **Square**, **Triangular**, **Graph**, and **Stop**. Once the list is created, **Right-click >> Make type Def**. to create the type definition. Then wire the type definition to the while loop and then to the case selector of the case structure. Once wired, right click on the edge of the case structure, and select "Add Case for Every Value", now the case structure must have a case for each element in the enum type definition list. The state **Initialize** will return the Boolean control "Start / Stop" to false and will have a direct transition to the "Wait for Event" state, for this on the input tunnel of the while loop connected to the enum type definition, **Right-click >> Replace with shift Register** and within the **Initialize** case create a copy of the enum type definition and select the "Wait for Event" element, connect this copy to the shift register as shown in Figure 12.21. Finally, in this case, a false Boolean constant must be created and wired to the stop terminal of the while loop.

The next state to create is the Wait for Event state, this state monitors all the actions performed in the user interface, in addition, if the program does not detect any action from the user interface, and the value from the Start/Stop button is equal to one the program is directed to the state Sine, Square, or Triangular (selected by the control knob "Waveform Type") to display the waveform. With this aim, go to the state Wait for Event and create an Event Structure inside of it. Within the Timeout event case add the code to send the program to the Sine, Square, or Triangular state as selected, if the Start/Stop value is in one, otherwise the next state is the same Wait for Event state. The cluster information must propagate through the Wait for Event case and within the event structure, when exiting the events structure, the Amplitude and Period values from the user interface must be read, see the code implementation in Figure 12.22. Note that for the selection of the next state, the function Index Array is used to select one of the three enum constants (Sine, Square, and Triangular), taking advantage of the numerical output of the Knob Control.

Moreover, this event case from Figure 12.22 needs also to be activated when a value change is detected in the Start/Stop button, for this, click on the edge of the Event Structure and select "Edit Events Handle by This case", within the Edit Events window select Add Event and add the Value Change event for the Start/Stop control as shown in Figure 12.23, click OK. This event case now should be able to be triggered by the value change event of the Start/Stop control as in Figure 12.24.

> • Tip #22: To avoid repeating the same code for two or more different events, you can add more event sources to the event?case.

In addition, the event structure should monitor the value change of the Stop Program button and send the program to the Stop state when the change is detected. With this aim, add a new event case by Right-Click >> Add Event Case at the limit of the event structure, and select the value change event for the Stop Program button as in Figure 12.25.

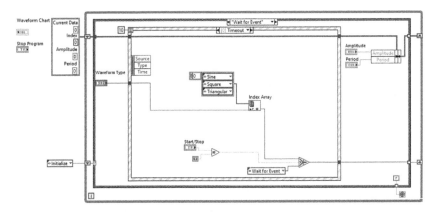

Figure 12.22   Time out event case of the wait for event case

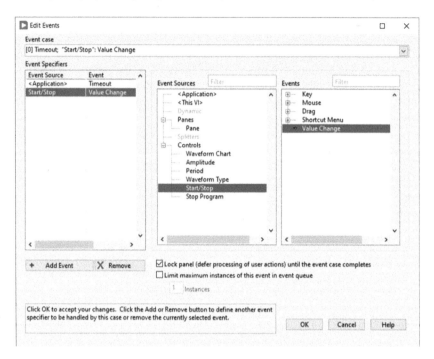

Figure 12.23   Selecting multiple event sources for a single event case in the Edit Events window

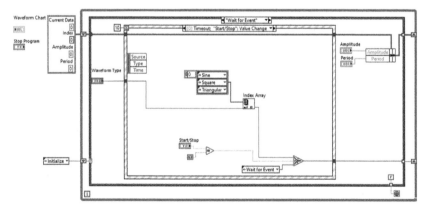

Figure 12.24   Event case with multiple triggers (Timeout and Start/Stop button Value Change)

The cluster information must propagate through Stop Program event case within the event structure, then place the Stop Program button inside the event case and create a direct transition to the Stop state using a copy of the Enum type definition constant as in Figure 12.26.

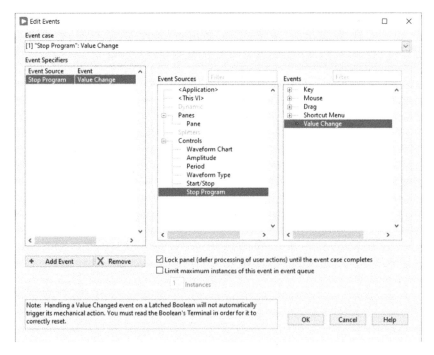

Figure 12.25   New event case for the value change in the Stop Program

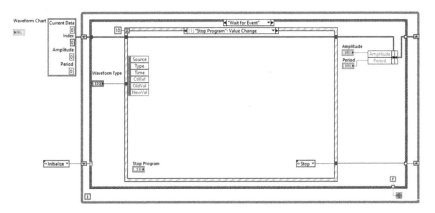

Figure 12.26   Event case for the Stop Program: Value Change

The next states (Sine, Square, and Triangular) are programmed using trigo-nometric functions. The scope of this section is about implementing an event-driven state machine, and this example is designed to be functional. However, it will not go into detail about the trigonometric functions for each waveform, just the general descriptions of the LabVIEW^{TM} functions are shown in Table 12.1. The

Table 12.1   Trigonometric and numeric functions used in the cases Sine, Square, and Triangular

Function	Name	Description	Functions palette
	Sine	Obtain the sine of the input, sine is in radians	Mathematics>>Elementary>> Trigonometric
	Negate	Negate the input value	Programming>>Numeric
	Inverse Sine	Obtain the arcsine of the input	Mathematics>>Elementary>> Trigonometric
	Increment	Increment in one the input	Programming>>Numeric

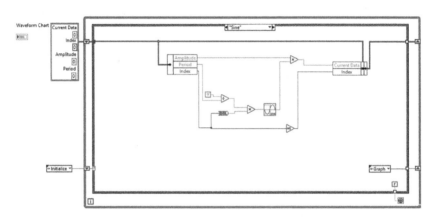

Figure 12.27   Sine State: generating a new value of a sine waveform using trigonometric functions

following explanation will focus on the transition between states and how to send information from one state to another.

To program the Sine state (Figure 12.27), the input information of Amplitude, Period, and Index is used, please note that the cluster helps to keep the order in the Block Diagram, in addition, the Index only increases when a new value of the signal is obtained (independent of the kind of signal), it is important to point out that when finishing generating the new value of the signal, it is performed a direct transition to Graph state, and this is important because it allows simplifying the code in such a way that the states "Square" and "Triangular" can use the same code in the Graph state.

For the Square and Triangular states, the transition is similar (direct transition to the Graph state) and the information that is propagated through the cluster is modified depending on each state. Figures 12.28 and 12.29 show the trigonometric functions for each state.

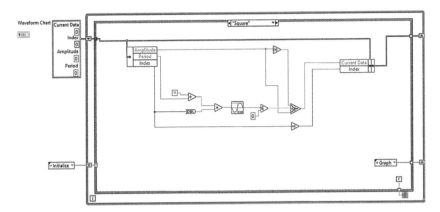

Figure 12.28   Square State: generating a new value of a square waveform using trigonometric functions

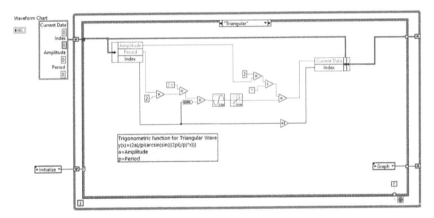

Figure 12.29   Triangular State: generating a new value of a triangular waveform using trigonometric functions

The next state is **Graph**, which obtains the amplitude value that was generated in any of the previous states (Sine, Square, or Triangular states), using the unbundle by name function to access the **Current Data** value from inside the cluster, this data is graphed using the Waveform Chart indicator. After graphing, the **Graph** state performs a direct transition to the **Wait for Event** state and sends a false value (using a constant) to the stop terminal of the while loop, see Figure 12.30.

Finally, the **Stop** state contains a true constant that is connected to the stop terminal of the while loop, additionally, a false constant is wired to a local variable of the Start/Stop button to restart it. The cluster wire is connected through the case structure to propagate the cluster information, finally, this case performs a direct

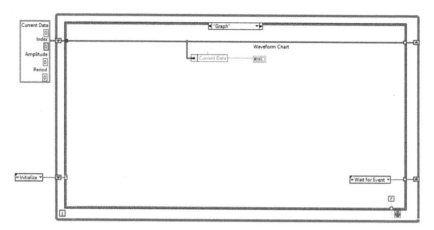

Figure 12.30   Plotting the amplitude value in the Graph state

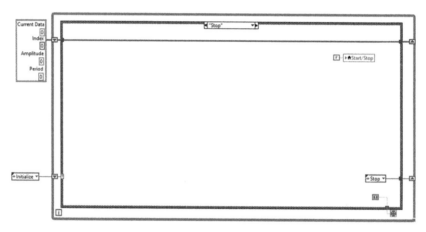

Figure 12.31   Stop State programming

transition to the same state (this is a good practice for states that are the last to be executed in the state machine) see Figure 12.31.

Now you can run the code and perform some tests with the program, observe in the task manager that when starting the program it consumes a minimum of resources, you can move the knob to any of the three waveforms to generate it and click on control Start/Stop, and observe how a new waveform is generated in real-time, in the same way, you can change the waveform and it automatically continues generating the selected waveform from the last value of the previous waveform (see Figure 12.32), the amplitude can be changed in real-time and the program can also be stopped by pressing the control Start/Stop.

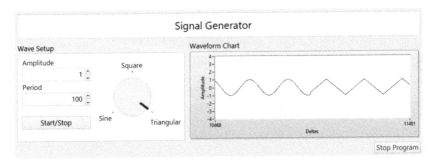

Figure 12.32   Running the signal generator program – Front Panel

12.4   Recommendations for event-driven state machines

1. Always use a constant enum type definition for state transitions.
2. Keep the code within the events structure compact and simple.
3. Do not use more than one event structure per loop.
4. Place the Boolean buttons inside the event structure to detect value changes.
5. If two independent events execute the same code, add an additional event in the same event case.

Chapter 13

The ATM review project

This chapter aims to review the topics covered so far in the book. The project consists of a VI that simulates an ATM that will require a card number and a PIN to log in and it will allow to check balance, change PIN, make withdrawals, and exit.

13.1 Creating a project with a VI and an auto-populating folder

In this section, a project will be created, as well as various VIs inside the same project and an auto-populating folder.

An auto-populating folder "is synchronized with a folder on disk and it is constantly updated to reflect the content of the folder on disk. This folder will update the content of the project folders when they change outside of LabVIEW^{TM}. The only disadvantage of the auto-populating folder "is that the project hierarchy will be the same as the system file.

13.1.1 Creating the project

1 – Open NI LabVIEW^{TM} 2020 and create a new project.

- Click on "Create Project".
- Select "Blank Project": and click "Finish".
- Save the project with the name "ATM" by going to File>Save As...

Note: Create this project inside a new folder for efficient resource use and VIs manipulation.

13.1.2 Creating a VI

1 – On the project explorer right click on "My Computer".

- Click on New>VI.
- Save the VI in the same way as the project with the name "Main" (Go to File>Save As...).

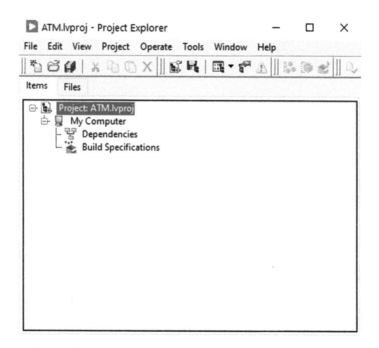

Figure 13.1   Project explorer window of the ATM project

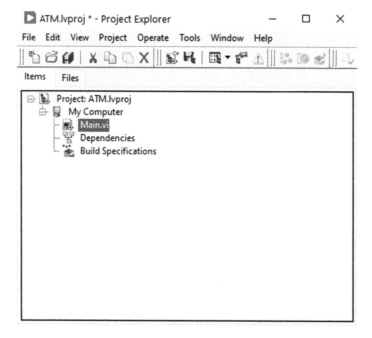

Figure 13.2   VI inside the project explorer

Note: Create this project inside a new folder for efficient resource use and VIs manipulation.

13.1.3   Creating folder (auto-populating)

1 – On the project explorer right click on "My Computer".

- Click on **Add>Folder (auto-populating)**.
- Create a new folder called "Resources"
- Save the folder on the project location

Note: It is important to have this Resources (auto-populating) folder inside the folder where the main project is being saved.

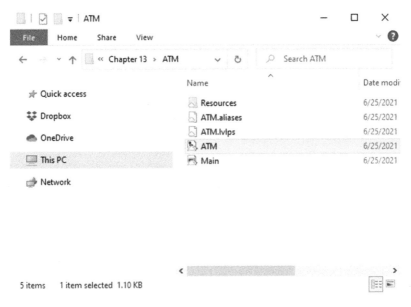

Figure 13.3   Creating resources folder

2 – For the last part, go to **File>Save All** on the project explorer to save the changes done in the project.

13.2   Creating user interface

In this section, the user interface will be created (the layout of the controls and buttons and the decorations for its presentation) using the VI made in the previous section. In order to perform this task, the following tools are explained (see Table 13.1).

Table 13.1   Tools for user interface creation

Tool name	Front panel	Description
Align Objects	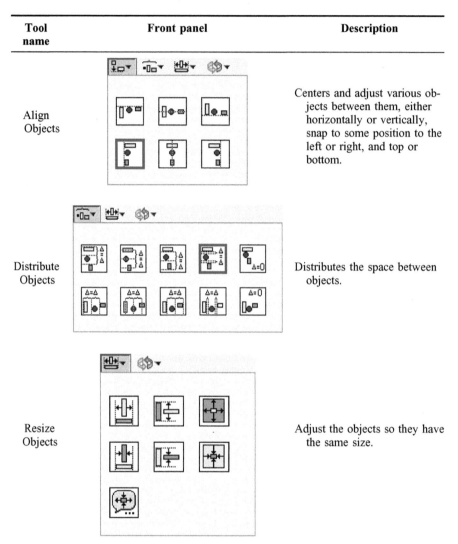	Centers and adjust various objects between them, either horizontally or vertically, snap to some position to the left or right, and top or bottom.
Distribute Objects		Distributes the space between objects.
Resize Objects		Adjust the objects so they have the same size.

Table 13.1   (*Continued*)

Tool name	Front panel	Description
Reorder	Group / Ungroup / Lock / Unlock / Move Forward Ctrl+K / Move Backward Ctrl+J / Move To Front Ctrl+Shift+K / Move To Back Ctrl+Shift+J	Creates groups of various objects and ungroups them, locks and unlocks them, this in order to facilitate the manipulation, movement or change some property of the objects, and finally move the objects forward, backward, to the back or front.
Text Settings	15pt Application Font / Font Dialog... Ctrl+0 / Application Font Ctrl+1 / System Font Ctrl+2 / Dialog Font Ctrl+3 / ✓ Current Font Ctrl+4 / Size ▶ / Style ▶ / Justify ▶ / Color ▶	Changes the font, size, style, position, and text color of an object or an independent text box.
Controls Palette	Controls / Search / NXG Style ▶ / Numeric / Boolean / String & Path / Data Containers / List, Table & Tree / Graph / Ring & Enum / Layout / I/O / Decorations	Contains a variety of controls and indicators for creating the user interface.

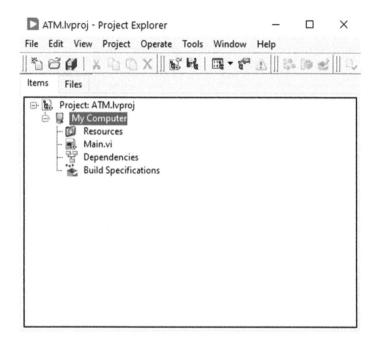

Figure 13.4   Resources inside the project explorer

13.2.1   Creating user interface controls

1 – Open the VI (Main) created in Section 13.1 and create the elements from Figure 13.5.

- Right click on the VI front panel to open the controls palette and select Numeric>Numeric control.
- Open the controls palette and select Boolean>Text Button.
- Open the controls palette and select Decorations>Flat Box.

Note: To copy an object, you can use the command Ctrl + left click on the object, hold the left click and drag to the desired position, in this way the object is copied with the same properties.

13.2.2   Adjusting interface

1 – Change the properties of the objects, such as text, size, alignment, and font.

- Select the text of the first and second numeric control with double click, change the labels to "Card Number" and "PIN", modify the size to 24 with Text Settings and intern text to 18, and center intern text.
- Change the intern text of the button to "Log In".
- Right click on numeric controls, go to Properties, and uncheck the "Show increment / decrement buttons" option.

- Remove the label "Button" inside properties, deselecting the option "Visible" in "Label", modify the intern text size to 18 and expand the button.

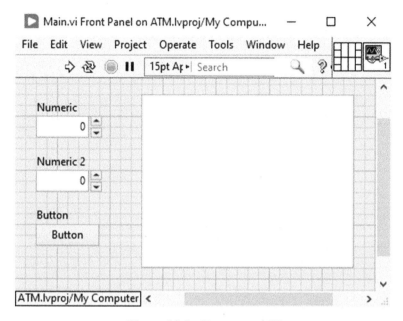

Figure 13.5   Front panel VI

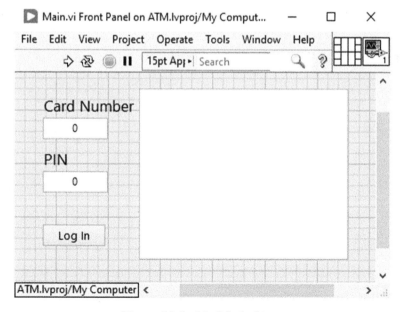

Figure 13.6   Modified objects

2 – Adjust the controls in relation to each other in size and alignment.

- Resize the width of the numeric controls by selecting both controls and use the tool **Resize Object>Maximum Width** to adjust the size of both objects to the maximum width.
- Select the three objects and align them using the tool **Align Object>Horizontal Centers**.

Note: If the object label is used, it must be adjusted to the center, otherwise at the moment of lining up, the objects will not align correctly.

- Selecting the three elements, use the tool **Distribute Object>Vertical Gap** to adjust the space between them and group them using the tool **Reorder>Group**.

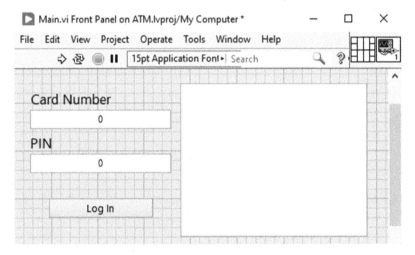

Figure 13.7   Adjusted elements

3 – Decorate and create a title for the interface.

- Select the Flat Box and send it to the back with the tool **Reorder>Move to Back**, expand the block and adjust it for the group of objects.
- Lock the flat box, so it does not accept changes. Use the tool **Reorder>Lock** to lock it.
- Add another flat box for the title as in Figure 13.8; double click on the front panel to create a text and write the text "**ATM**", place it up and adjust with the flat boxes placed before (see Figure 13.8).

Note: You can make the user interface user-friendly using other controls, such as the NXG Style controls palette.

4 – Using the tools mentioned in this section creates the user interface in Figure 13.9.

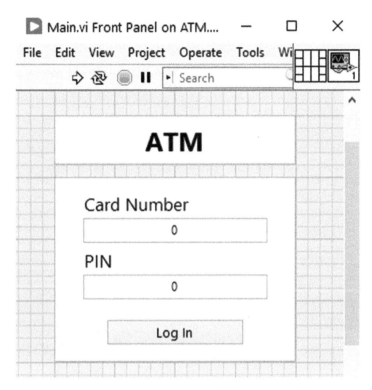

Figure 13.8   Log In section of the user interface

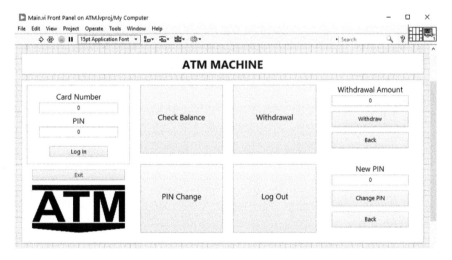

Figure 13.9   Finished user interface

13.3   Creating event state machine

In this section, an event state machine will be created.

A state is a part of a program that satisfies a condition, performs an action, or waits for an event. A state machine is a design pattern where a state diagram or a flowchart is implemented. It consists of a set of states and a transition function that assigns the next state. Commonly, it is used to create programs where depending on an action performed by the user, the program performs a transition to different states. Another common use is for test process, where each state represents a segment of the process.

For the specific case of the developed program (ATM), the state machine will be used for the different available operations, as the card login, balance check, withdrawal, PIN change, etc.

With this aim, the functions of the block diagram shown in Table 13.2 will be used.

13.3.1   Creating the state machine

1 – Open the ATM project made in previous sections.

- Open the VI "Main".
- Open the block diagram window by going to Window > Show Block Diagram.

Note: To change easily between the front panel and the block diagram, you can use the command CTRL + E.

- Add the components shown in Table 13.2 from the functions palette on the block diagram as shown in Figure 13.10.

2 – Create the list of items for the state machine on the enum constant.

- Right click on the enum constant and select Edit Items.
- As in Figure 13.11, add the following elements in Items:
  o   Start
  o   Wait for event
  o   Log In
  o   Check Balance
  o   Withdrawal
  o   PIN Change
  o   Money Withdrawal
  o   Back
  o   Save File
  o   New PIN
  o   Exit Program
  o   Log Out

3 – Change enum constant to type definition.

- Right click on the enum constant and select Make Type Def.
- Right click on the enum constant and select Open Type Def.

Table 13.2   Functions used for the event state machine

Function name	Block diagram	Description
While loop	**While Loop**	Located on **Functions > Programming > Structures**. Repeats the code continuously inside of its sub-diagram until a specific condition occurs.
Event structure	**Event Structure**	Located on **Functions > Programming > Structures**. Waits for an event to occur, then executes the appropriate case to handle the event.
Case structure	**Case Structure**	Located on **Functions > Programming > Structures**. Contains one or more sub-diagrams or specific cases. These will execute depending on the input of the case selector.
Enum constant	**Enum Constant**	Located on **Functions > Programming > Numeric**. Contains a list of Items. Each item within an enum includes an integer number of 16 bits and a string.

- A new VI that contains only the front panel will open.
- Save the file inside the **Resources** folder with the name "**States**", see Figure 13.12.

4 – Setting up the state machine.

- Place the **case structure** inside the **while loop**.
- Right click on the edge of the **while loop** and select **Add Shift Register**.
- Connect the **enum constant** to the **shift register** and case structure as shown in Figure 13.13(A).

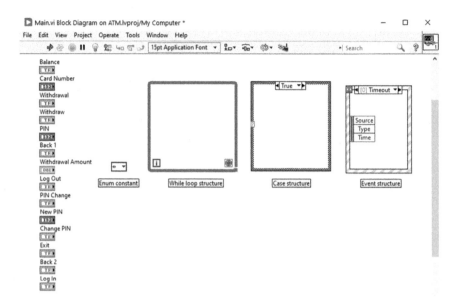

Figure 13.10   New components on the block diagram

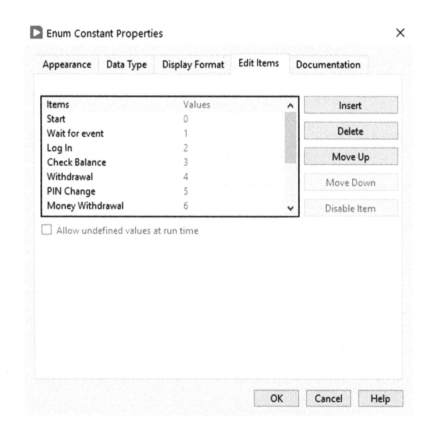

Figure 13.11   Items within the Enum Constant

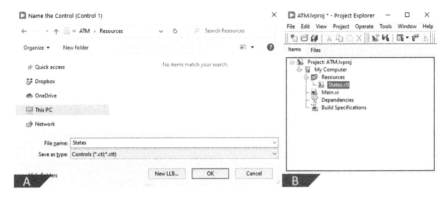

Figure 13.12   (A) Saving states.ctl on Resources folder and (B) States.ctl inside the resources folder on the ATM project

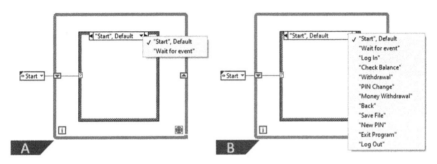

Figure 13.13   (A) Setting up state machine and (B) adding case for every value

Note: Observe that not all the items of the enum constant were added as cases on the case structure; only two cases were added since initially the case structure has only two cases.

- Right click on the **case structure**, select **Add Case for Every Value**. This will add a case for every element of the enum control, as shown in Figure 13.13(B).
- Insert the **event structure** inside the **case structure** in the case **Wait for Event** as shown in Figure 13.14.
- Add an event for the case "**Exit**" in the **event structure**. Right click on the edge of the event structure and select "**Add Event Case...**".
- On **Event Sources**, select the button **Exit**, with the "**Value Change**" event as shown in Figure 13.15, then click on OK.
- Place the terminal of the **Exit control** inside the **Exit event** of the **event structure**.
- Clone the **enum constant** and place it inside the **event structure**, selecting the item **Exit Program** and connecting it to the **shift register** to the right of the **while loop** structure as shown in Figure 13.16.

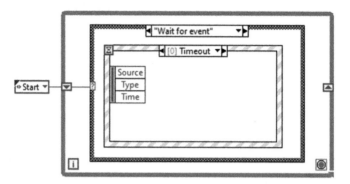

Figure 13.14   Event structure inside the case structure

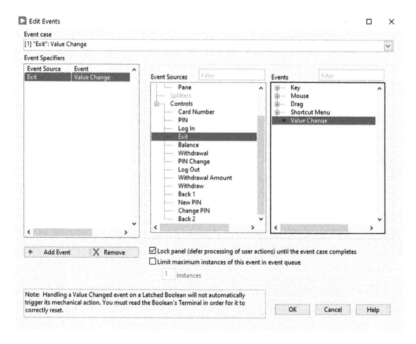

Figure 13.15   Creating an event

- Select the case **Exit Program** on the **case structure** and insert a **true** constant by going to **Functions palette** > **Boolean** > **True Constant,** connect it to the **stop** terminal of the **while loop,** which is at the bottom right of the while loop structure as shown in Figure 13.17.

Note: Observe in Figure 13.17 the arrow button used to execute the program is broken. The broken arrow is because the tunnels on the case structure do not have any

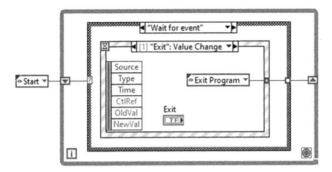

Figure 13.16   Exit terminal and enum constant inside event structure

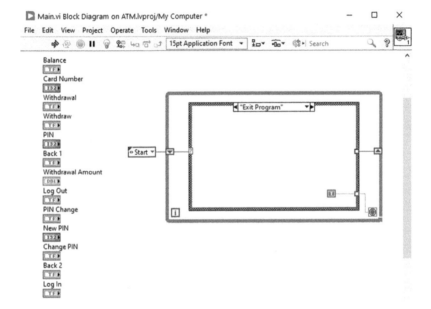

Figure 13.17   Exit Program case

data for the other cases. LabVIEW^{TM} indicates the undefined data of the other cases with a white color in the tunnels. To solve this problem, right click on the tunnel and select the option "Use Default If Unwired". The subsequent cases will be programmed later. Note that the program can now be executed, as shown in Figure 13.18.

- Clone the enum constant, select the "Wait for event" item and place it inside the Start case on the case structure and connect it to the shift register.

  Note: Always try to work on the block diagram horizontally for a better observation of the data flow in debug mode.

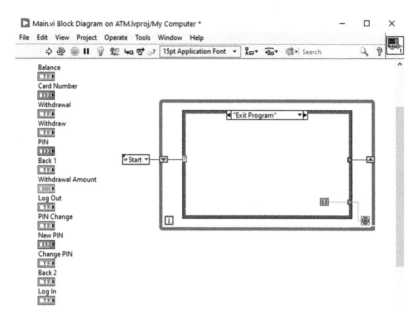

Figure 13.18   Tunnels changed to use the default if unwired

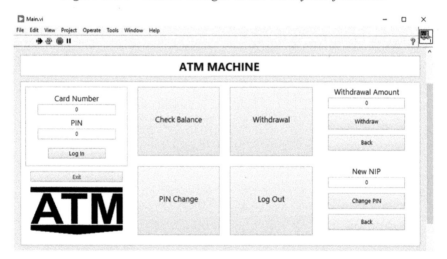

Figure 13.19   Program in execution to verify the case Exit program

5 – Run the program and verify errors.

- Save the program.
- Go to the front panel, click the **run** button to execute the program.
- Press the **Exit** button, and the program should exit immediately.

Note: Observe how the black top-left arrow indicates that the program is running correctly (see Figure 13.19).

- Run the program again using the Highlight Execution tool located on the top part and click the button Exit again.
- Observe the data flow going out of the event structure and going into the shift register, as shown in Figure 13.20.

Note: Observe in Figure 13.20 how the value "Exit Program" leaves the event structure and arrives at the shift register to the right side. Then observe in

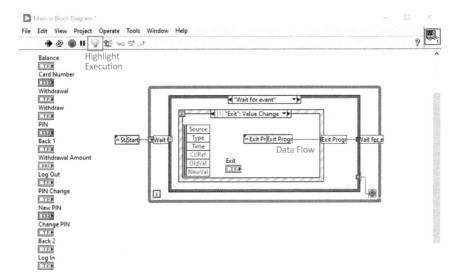

Figure 13.20   Data flow of the Exit button

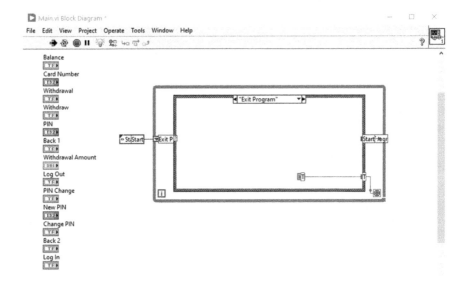

Figure 13.21   Changing case structure to Exit Program case

Figure 13.21 how it comes out from the shift register on the left side to change the case structure to Exit Program.

Note: Observe how the true constant leaves the Exit Program case to arrive in the Stop of the while loop structure to stop the program completely.

13.4   Creating property nodes and arrays

This section focuses on the creation of property nodes and arrays. The used functions on this sections are shown on Table 13.3.

Property nodes allow access to properties of an object, either to change its color, size, position, etc.

Table 13.3   Functions used on this section

Function name	Block diagram	Description
Array constant	Array Constant	Located on Functions > Programming > Array. Create an array inside the block diagram.
Numeric constant	Numeric Constant	Located on Functions > Programming > Numeric. Create a numeric constant value inside the block diagram.
Search Unsorted 1D array	Search Unsorted 1D Array.vim	Located on Functions > Programming > Array. Search a specific element inside a one-dimensional array.
Index Array	Index Array	Located on Functions > Programming > Array. Returns the element or sub-array of an n-dimensional array starting from the value indicated on the specified position.

Table 13.3 (*Continued*)

Function name	Block diagram	Description
Compound Arithmetic	Compound Arithmetic	Located on **Functions** > **Programming** > **Boolean**. Performs arithmetic operations on one or more inputs; depending on the Compound Arithmetic **Mode**, the input data type can be numeric, matrix, cluster, or boolean.
Equal?	Equal?	Located on **Functions** > **Programming** > **Comparison**. Returns a True if the first value is equal to the second value.
Not Equal?	Not Equal?	Located on **Functions** > **Programming** > **Comparison**. Returns a True if the first value is different from the second value.
One Button Dialog	One Btn Dialog	Located on **Functions** > **Programming** > **Dialog & User Interface**. Creates a dialog box that contains a message and a single button.
String Constant	String Constant	Located on **Functions** > **Programming** > **String**. Creates a string constant on the block diagram.

Arrays are data structures that consist of elements and dimensions. The elements are the indexed data that compose the array, and these can be numeric data, Boolean, paths, strings, waveform, and clusters. An array can have one or more dimensions, but it cannot have more than one data type.

13.4.1 Creating property nodes

1 – Open the ATM project.

- Open the VI "Main".
- Open the block diagram window.
- Right click on the numeric control "Card Number" select the option Create>Property Node>Disabled, do the same for "PIN", "Log In", "Log Out", "PIN Change", "Withdrawal", and "Balance". Place the created property nodes inside the case structure on the Start case.
- Create a property node to modify the property "Visible", in the same way as in the previous step. Right click on the object and go to Create>Property Node>Visible for the controls "Withdraw", "Back 1", "Withdrawal Amount", "Change PIN", "Back 2", and "New PIN". Place the created property nodes inside the case structure on the Start case.
- Arrange the property nodes inside the start case as shown in Figure 13.22.

Note: Observe how some property nodes are in reading mode. In order to be able to modify the properties, the property nodes need to be changed to write. To do this, right click on each node and select "Change All To Write", see Figure 13.23.

- Make the change to all the property nodes and compare the property nodes from Figure 13.22 and Figure 13.24 and see how they change from output to input.
- Right click on the left side of the property node of "Card Number" where there is the word "Disable" and select the option Create>Constant, do the same for "Withdrawal" and "Withdraw".
- Change the option of the constant created for the "Withdrawal" property node to "Disabled and Grayed Out", see Figure 13.25.

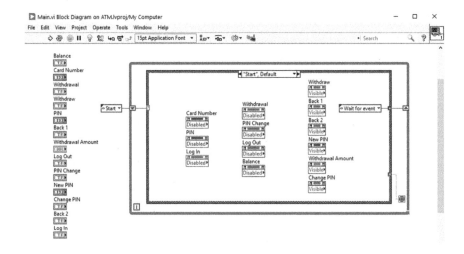

Figure 13.22   Property nodes on start case

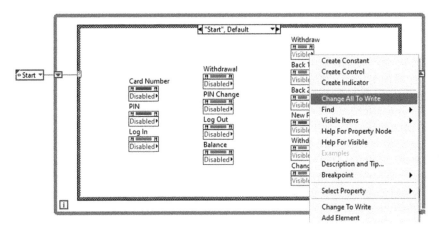

Figure 13.23 *Changing a property node from reading to writing the property*

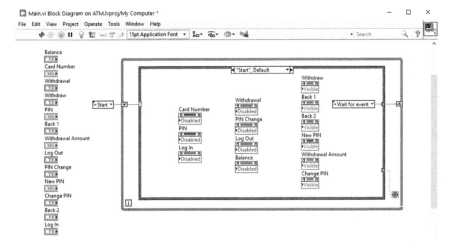

Figure 13.24 *Property nodes on write mode*

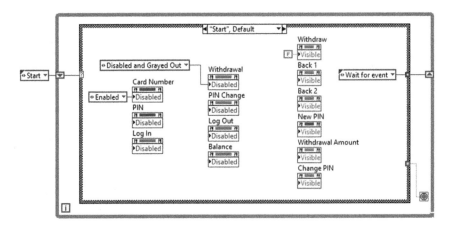

Figure 13.25 *Constants on property nodes*

- Connect the property nodes as in Table 13.4, see Figure 13.26 for reference.
- Insert a false constant and connect it to the Boolean tunnel on the bottom part of the case as in Figure 13.26.

  2 – Create new events.

- Go to the case "Wait for event", create a new event on the event structure for the buttons "Log In" and "Log Out" with the event value change and place the buttons in their respective event.
- Clone twice the "Enum Constant" with the element "Log In" and "Log Out".
- Place the "Enum Constant" with the element "Log In" inside the event "Log In" and the Enum Constant with the element "Log Out" inside the event "Log Out", see Figure 13.27.

Table 13.4   Property node connections

Property node	Input
Card number	Enabled
PIN	Enabled
Log In	Enabled
Withdrawal	Disabled and Grayed Out
PIN Change	Disabled and Grayed Out
Log Out	Disabled and Grayed Out
Balance	Disabled and Grayed Out
Withdraw	False Constant
Back 1	False Constant
Back 2	False Constant
New PIN	False Constant
Withdrawal Amount	False Constant
Change PIN	False Constant

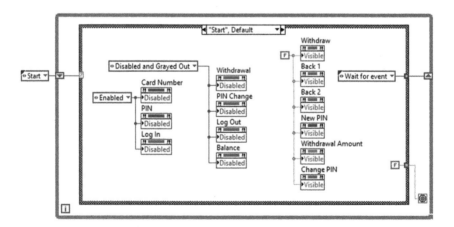

Figure 13.26   Initialization of properties and the stop constant in the Start case

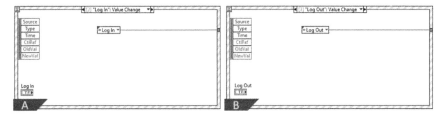

Figure 13.27   (A) Log In event and (B) Log Out event

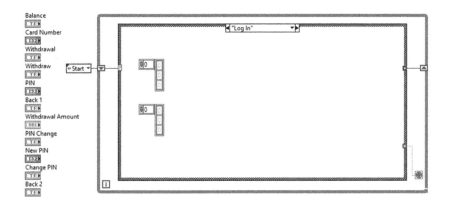

Figure 13.28   Arrays on the Log In case

3 – Define the case "Log In".

- Insert an "Array Constant" inside the case "Log In" of the case structure, right click on the block diagram and select Functions>Programming>Array>Array Constant.
- Insert a "Numeric Constant" inside the "Array constant" to create a numeric array.
- Expand the array downside to create an array with three elements and clone this array as shown in Figure 13.28.
- Create a label for each array, right click on the array and go to properties, this will open the array properties window. On the appearance tab and check the visible checkbox under the "Label" option and write "Card number" on the blank space. Do the same for the other array constant, but write "PIN" instead. The labels should appear as shown in Figure 13.29.
- Create three values on "Card Number" and "PIN" with a length of eight and four characters respectively, see Figure 13.30.
  - Card Number
    - 12345678
    - 11112222
    - 87654321

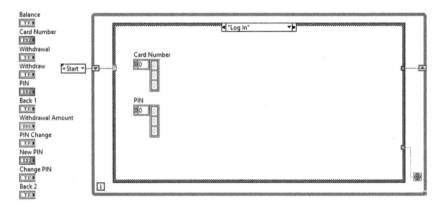

Figure 13.29   Labeled arrays

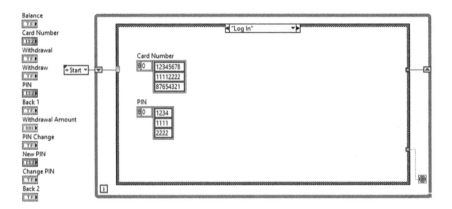

Figure 13.30   Arrays with values

○   PIN
  ○   1234
  ○   1111
  ○   0000

- Place the numeric controls "Card Number" and "PIN" inside the case.
- Insert "Search Unsorted 1D Array" inside the Log In case, connecting the "Card Number" array to the connector "Unsorted 1D Array" and the numeric control "Card Number" to the connector "element" of the "Search Unsorted 1D Array", see Figure 13.31.
- Insert an "Index Array" inside the case and connect the "PIN" array to the connector "array" and the output of the "Search Unsorted 1D Array" with the connector "index" of the "index array" function, see Figure 13.32.

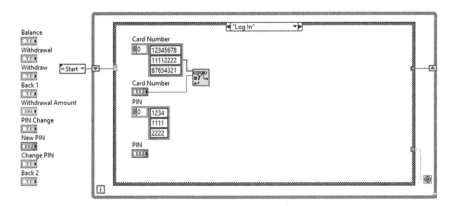

Figure 13.31   Card Number array connected

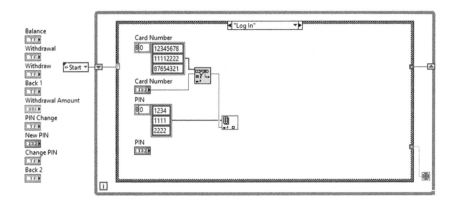

Figure 13.32   PIN array connected

- Add an "Equal?" comparator and two "Not equal?" comparators inside the case.
- Connect to the input of the "Equal?" comparator the output of the "Index Array" and the numeric control "PIN".
- Insert a "Numeric Constant" with value "0", and connect it to the input of the comparator "Not Equal?" to be compared with numeric control "Card Number".
- Insert a "Numeric Constant" with value "0", and connect it to the input of the "Not Equal?" comparator to be compared with the numeric control "PIN", see Figure 13.33.
- Add "Compound Arithmetic", expand down to get three inputs, then change the comparison mode by left clicking on the symbol and selecting Change Mode>AND.

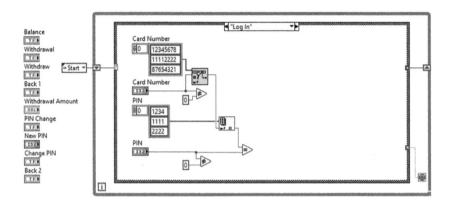

Figure 13.33   Connecting the comparisons of Log In case

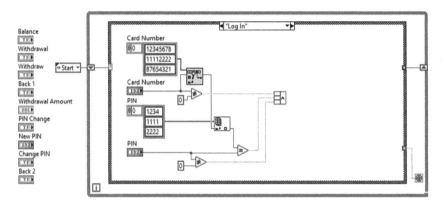

Figure 13.34   Connected comparators to the compound arithmetic function

- Connect the outputs of the comparators "Equal?" and "Not Equal?" to the inputs of the "Compound Arithmetic", see Figure 13.34.
- Add "Case Structure" inside the same case and connect it to the output of the "Compound Arithmetic" to the created case structure, as shown in Figure 13.35.
- Inside the "True" case of the case structure, add property nodes for the controls "Log In", "PIN", and "Card Number" with the constant "Disabled and Grayed Out", and for the controls "Balance", "Withdrawal", "PIN Change", and "Log Out" with the constant "Enabled", see Figure 13.36.
- Clone the "Enum Constant (Start)" and place it inside the case "Log In", change the enum element to "Wait for Event", and connect it to the shift register tunnel.
- Add "One Button Dialog" and "String Constant" inside the false case, connect the "String Constant" to the input of the "One Button Dialog".
- Place the text "Incorrect PIN or Card Number" inside the string constant, see Figure 13.37.

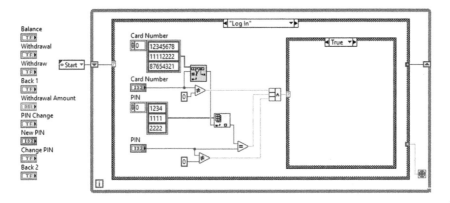

Figure 13.35   Case structure within case Log In

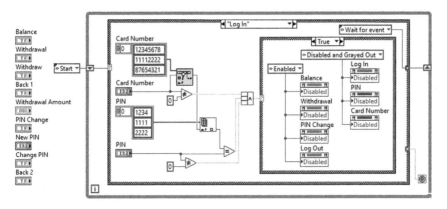

Figure 13.36   True case of the case structure within the Log In case

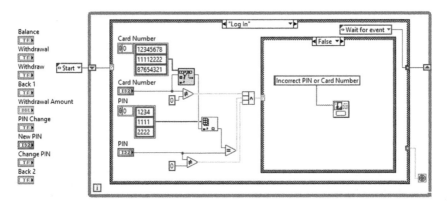

Figure 13.37   False case of the case structure within the Log In case

3 – Define the case "Log Out".

- Select the "Log Out" case on the case structure and place the "enum Constant (Start)" inside.
- Connect the "Enum Constant (Start)" to the tunnel of the "Shift Register" at the right side of the case structure, see Figure 13.38.

Note: The case "Log Out" will change the state of the system going to the "Start" case, making the ATM asks for the "Card Number" and "PIN".

- Execute the program with the following values and click on the "Log In" button, see Figures 13.39 and 13.40.
  o "Card Number": 12345678
  o "PIN": 1234

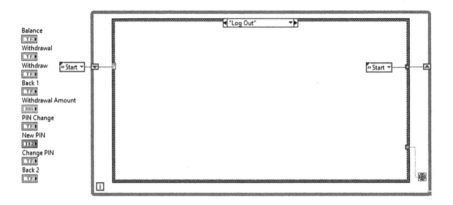

Figure 13.38   Log Out case

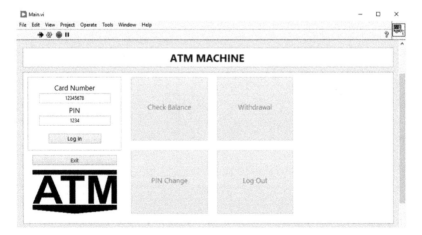

Figure 13.39   Value input

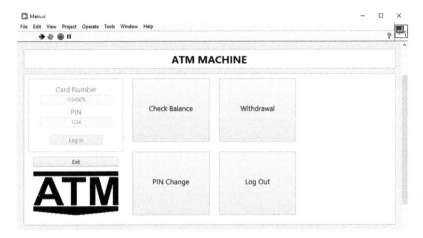

Figure 13.40 Logged In after clicking Log In

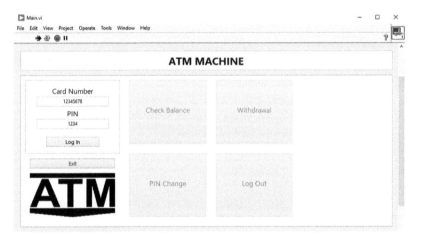

Figure 13.41 After clicking the Log Out button, the program asks for a valid Card Number and PIN again

Note: Observe the change between Figures 13.39 and 13.40, the controls "Card Number", "PIN", and "Log In" are disabled and the controls "Check Balance", "Withdrawal", "PIN Change", and "Log Out" are enabled, this is due to the property nodes.

• Click the "Log Out" button.

Note: Observe that the ATM comes back to the initial state with the controls "Card Number", "PIN", and "Log In" enabled and the controls "Check Balance", "Withdrawal", "PIN Change", and "Log Out" disabled, see Figure 13.41.

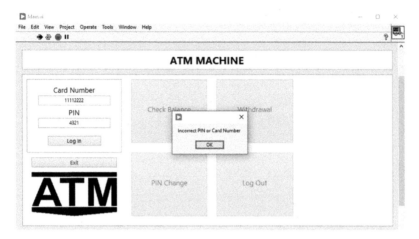

Figure 13.42   Incorrect data

- Add new values for "Card Number" and "PIN", then click "Log In" and compare it with Figure 13.42.
  - "Card Number": 11112222
  - "PIN": 4321

Note: Observe how a new window opens with the message "Incorrect PIN or Card Number". This is because the "PIN" value does not match with the "Card Number" (the nip was not found, or they are not in the same index), in other words, it is not the right "PIN" for the "Card Number".

13.5   Reading and writing files

In this section, different low-level functions will be used to write and read files in a structured way.

File read is used to obtain data from a file, which can be lectures of an instrument or an Excel file; in the specific case of the program under development, this functions will be used to read the card number and PIN. To do this, the functions from Table 13.5 will be used.

13.5.1   Creating user files

1 – Open ATM folder.

- Open the "Resources" folder.
- Right click and create a text file with the name "Users" by selecting New>Text Document. See Figure 13.43.
- Open "Users" text file.
- Add the following values inside the text file with Tab separation and Enter. See Figure 13.44.

Table 13.5 Functions used for reading and writing files

Function name	Block diagram	Description
Open/Create/Replace File	Open/Create/ Replace File	Located on Functions> Programming>File I/O. Opens, creates, or replaces a file.
Close File	Close File	Located on Functions> Programming>File I/O. Closes an open file.
Read Text File	abc Read Text File	Located on Functions> Programming>File I/O. Reads a specified number of characters or lines of a file.
Build Path	Build Path	Located on Functions> Programming>File I/O. Creates a new file direction by appending a name or a relative path to an existing path.
Application Directory	Application Directory	Located on Functions> Programming>File I/O> File Constants. Returns the file path of the application directory.
Cluster Constant	Cluster Constant	Located on Functions> Programming> Cluster, Class & Variant. Creates a cluster constant inside the block diagram.

(Continues)

Table 13.5   (Continued)

Function name	Block diagram	Description
Unbundle By Name	Unbundle By Name	Located on **Functions> Programming> Cluster, Class & Variant.** Returns the cluster elements by their given name.
Bundle By Name	Bundle By Name	Located on **Functions> Programming> Cluster, Class & Variant.** Replaces one or more cluster elements.
Match Pattern	Match Pattern	Located on **Functions> Programming> String.** Search within a string for a particular expression.
String Length	String Length	Located on **Functions> Programming> String.** Returns the number of characters inside the string.
Tab Constant	Tab Constant	Located on **Functions> Programming> String.** Creates a horizontal tab value.
Decimal String To Number	Decimal String To Number	Located on **Functions> Programming> String>Number/ String Conversion.** Converts the numeric characters of the string to a decimal integer.

Table 13.5   (Continued)

Function name	Block diagram	Description
Fract/Exp String To Number	Fract/Exp String To Number	Located on **Functions> Programming> String>Number/ String Conversion.** Interprets the characters from 0 through 9, +, −, e, E, and the decimal point of a string to a double numeric constant.
Greater?	Greater?	Located on **Functions> Programming> Comparison.** Sends a True if the first value is greater than the second and a False in the opposite case.
Select	Select	Located on **Functions> Programming> Comparison.** In the case of a True value on its input, it sends the upper input value to the output, and in case of a False value, it send the bottom value to the output.
Build Array	Build Array	Located on **Functions> Programming> Array.** Concatenates multiple arrays or appends elements to an n-dimensional array.
Invoke Node	Invoke Node	Located on **Functions> Programming> Application Control.** Applies a method or an actions to a reference.

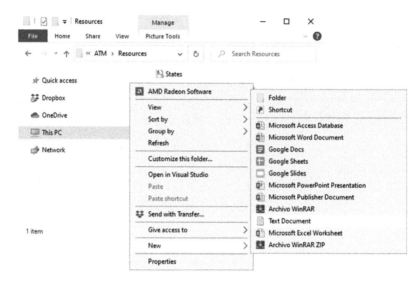

Figure 13.43   Creating a text file

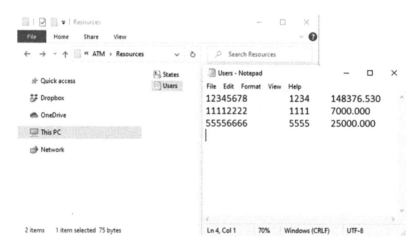

Figure 13.44   Values on the text file

- 12345678   1234   148376.530
- 11112222   1111   7000.000
- 55556666   5555   25000.000

2 – Open the ATM project.

- Open the **Main** VI.
- Open the block diagram window.

- Create outside the while loop a "Cluster Constant" and place four "Array Constant" inside it. See Figure 13.45.
- Modify three of the "Array Constant" to arrays of integer numeric constants with the labels "Card", "PIN", and "User Index", modify the last array constant to an array of double numeric constant with the label "Balance".
- Create a "Shift Register" inside the while loop and connect the cluster to the left side of the "Shift Register". See Figure 13.46.

Note: Observe how the cluster changed its color in Figure 13.46; the arrays now have defined data types as numeric constants, while in Figure 13.45, the cluster was in color black because the array constants did not have a defined data type.

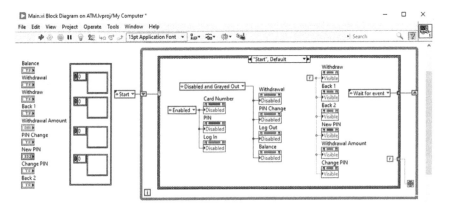

Figure 13.45   Outside the while loop, a black box with four array constants is the cluster constant

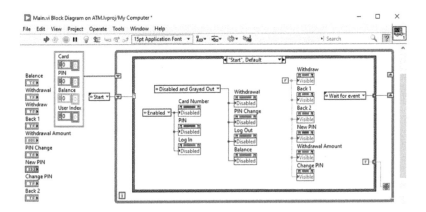

Figure 13.46   Cluster – shift register connection

- Within the Start case Insert a "Bundle By Name" and connect the "Shift Register" connected to the "Cluster Constant" to the "Input Cluster", and the output of the "Bundle By Name" to the "Shift Register" on the right side.
- Pull down the options of the "Bundle By Name" to see the elements of the cluster.
- Use the option "Use Default If Unwired" on the output tunnel of the case connected to the "Shift Register" of the cluster. See Figure 13.47.
- Insert a "While Loop" inside the "Start" case and place a "Case Structure" inside the "While Loop", see Figure 13.48.

Note: To have a good perspective of the data flow in debugging mode it is preferable to order the components to have a clean workspace inside the block

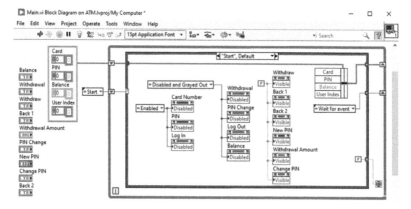

Figure 13.47   Cluster connection within the Start case

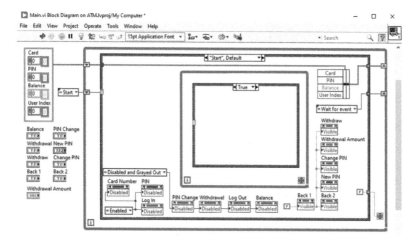

Figure 13.48   While Loop and Case Structure inserted into Start case

diagram; for example, observe the change of position of the property nodes from Figures 13.47 to 13.48.

- Insert "Application Directory", "Build Path", and "String Constant".
- Connect the output of "Application Directory" to the input "base path" of the "Build Path" and the "String Constant" to the input "name or relative path" of the "Build Path".
- Write on the "String Constant" the value of "Resources\Users.txt". See Figure 13.49.
- Insert "Open/Create/Replace File", "Read Text File", and "Close File".
- Create a constant on the input terminal "operation" of "Open/Create/Replace File", Right clicking on it and selecting Create>Constant with the option of "open"
- Connect "Open/Create/Replace File", "Read Text File", and "Close File", the input and output cluster errors, as well as the top inputs and outputs "refnum out", "file", and "refnum".
- Connect the output of the "Build Path" to the input "file path" of the "Open/Create/Replace File". See Figure 13.50.
- Place a "Shift Register" at the while loop inside the Start case, then connect the "text" output of the "Read Text File" in it. See Figure 13.51.
- Insert "String Length", "Greater?", and "Numeric Constant" inside the while loop.
- Connect the "Shift Register" to "String Length" and compare it with a "Numeric Constant" of value "0" using the comparator "Greater?".
- Connect the output of the "Greater?" comparator to the "Case Structure", see Figure 13.52.
- Insert three "Match Pattern", two "Decimal String to Number" and a "Fract/Exp String to Number" inside the true case.

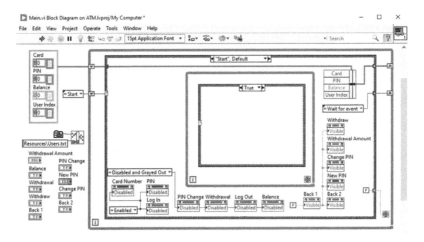

Figure 13.49   Creating the path to the file Users.txt

220   *Graphical programming using LabVIEW^{TM}: fundamentals and advanced techniques*

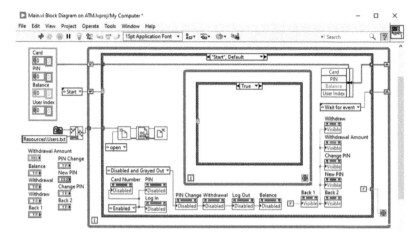

Figure 13.50   File functions connection to open, read a file, and close it

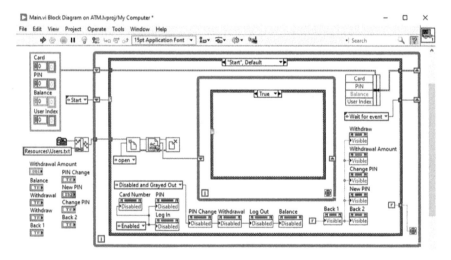

Figure 13.51   Connecting the text information of the file to the shift register of the while loop within the start case

- Connect them as shown in Figure 13.53.
- Insert two "String Constant", one with an "Enter" value and the other with a "Tab Constant".
- Connect the "String Constant" with the "Enter" value in the first "Match Pattern" in the terminal "regular expression", do the same with the "Tab Constant" for the other two "Match Pattern". See Figure 13.54.

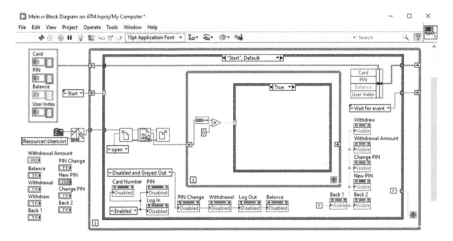

Figure 13.52   Creation of input case for the case structure inside the while loop

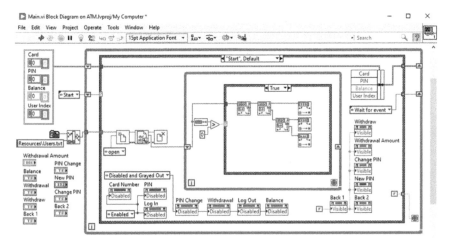

Figure 13.53   Connection of the true case, this case will be used to obtain each card number, PIN, and Balance

Note: The first "Match Pattern" determines the rows by searching for an "Enter", and the other two "Match Pattern" determines the columns by searching the "Tab" spaces. These search functions are used to obtain the data inside the "Users" text file; this data is necessary to log in the ATM.

- Insert "String Length", "Greater?", "Numeric Constant", "Select", "True Constant", and "False Constant" inside the true case.
- Connect the output "after substring" of the first "Match Pattern" to the "Shift Register" at the right side of the while loop and to the "String Length".

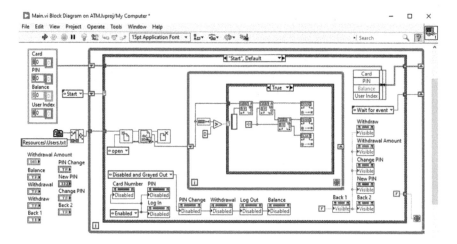

Figure 13.54   Match Pattern Connections

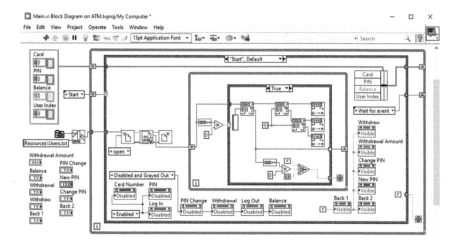

Figure 13.55   A comparison is used to monitor the length of the string. This string diminishes its length as the information from the string is obtained. If the current string is equal to 0, the while loop within the Start case stops

- Compare the output of the "String Length" with "Numeric Constant" of value "0" using the "Grater?" comparator.
- Connect the output of the "Greater?" comparator to "Select"
- Connect the "False Constant" to the "True" input of the "Select" and the "True Constant" on the "False" input of the "Select".
- Connect the output of the "Select" to the "Stop" of the while loop.
- Change the created tunnel (from "Select" to "Stop") to "Use Default If Unwired". See Figure 13.55.

- Connect the outputs "number" of the "Decimal String To Number" to the inputs of the "Bundle By Name", the first one on "Card", the second on "PIN", and the output of the "Fract/Exp String To Number" to the input "Balance" of the "Bundle By Name". See Figure 13.56.

Note: Observe how the connections are broken. This is because "Card", "PIN", and "Balance" are arrays. To fix this, the outputs of the while loop must be indexed, to do this, right click on the tunnel of the while loop and select Tunnel Mode>Indexing, this will convert the output into an array. See Figure 13.57.

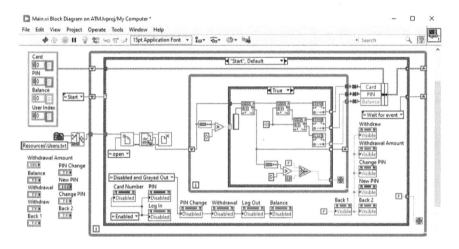

Figure 13.56   Bundle by name connections

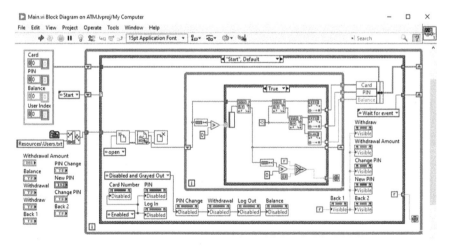

Figure 13.57   Indexed tunnels are used to send the obtained information from the file to the cluster constant

- Go to the "False" case and add two "Numeric Constant" with value "0", "DBL Numeric Constant" with value "0" and a "True Constant".
- Connect them as shown in Figure 13.58.
- Insert "Invoke Node". Right click on the top part of the node and go to Select Class>VI Server>VI>VI.
- Select the method of the "Invoke Node" on the bottom part and change it to Default Values>Reinitialize All To Default. See Figure 13.59.
- Go to the "Wait for event" case.
- Connect the left cluster tunnel with the right cluster tunnel as shown in Figure 13.60.

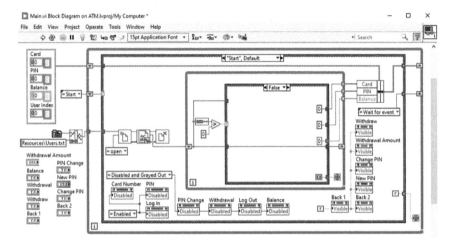

Figure 13.58   Defining the outputs of the False case

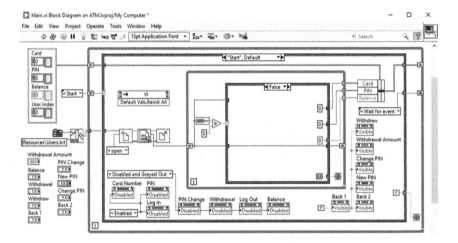

Figure 13.59   The Invoke Node in the Start Case initializes all the controls and indicators to their default values

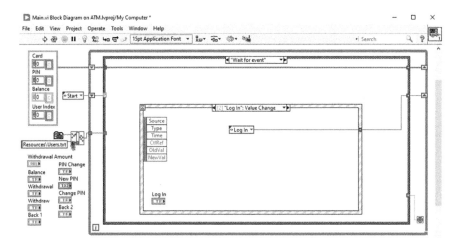

Figure 13.60   Cluster connection on wait for event case

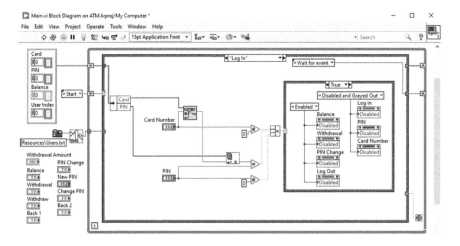

Figure 13.61   Change of arrays for Unbundle By Name

Note: If the cluster is not connected on the wait for event case, the cluster data will be lost and the program will fail when trying to log in since it will have the default values.

3 – Go to the "Log In" case.

• Insert "Bundle By Name".
• Connect the "Shift Register" cluster on the left side on the "Unbundle By Name" and drag it down to obtain "Card" and "PIN".
• Substitute the arrays "Card" and "PIN" (these arrays were defined as constants in Figure 13.37, Section 13.4.1) for the values of "Unbundle By Name" of "Card" and "PIN". See Figure 13.61.

- Insert "Build Array" and "Bundle By Name" inside the "True case".
- Connect the output terminal "index element" of the "Search 1D Array" to the "Build Array".
- Connect the cluster to the "Bundle By Name" and select "User Index" with left click. See Figure 13.62.

Note: When the PIN and card numbers are correct, the index position value of the card number will be saved on the user index to follow-up of the user on the ATM.

- Create a constant array on the "False case" with the label "User Index".
- Insert a "Bundle By Name" and a "One Button Dialog"
- Connect the cluster to the "Bundle By Name" and select "User Index" with the left click.
- Connect the array "User Index" to the "Bundle By Name". See Figure 13.63.

Note: When the PIN or the card number is invalid, an empty array will be sent to the user index. This action clears the User Index array of the cluster, so the account can be accessed in case of an error.

4 – Check correct operation.

- Enable the "Highlight Execution" on the block diagram.
- Run the VI and observe the data flow. See Figure 13.64.

Note: Observe how the data flows from the users file inside the while loop, doing the data separation using the "Enter" constants and the "Tab" spaces, and at the end it sends the three first values of the corresponding card number and PIN. Also observe Figures 13.65 and 13.66.

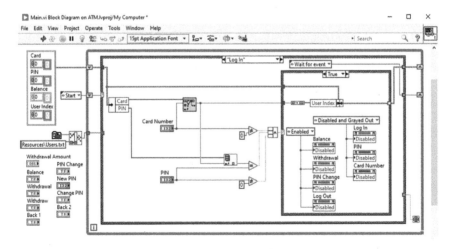

Figure 13.62   Case True inside Log In case

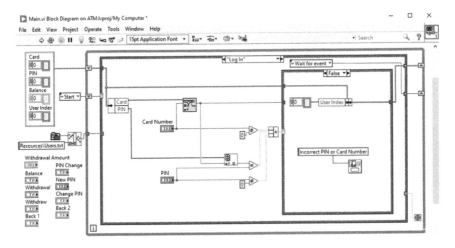

Figure 13.63   False case of the Log In case

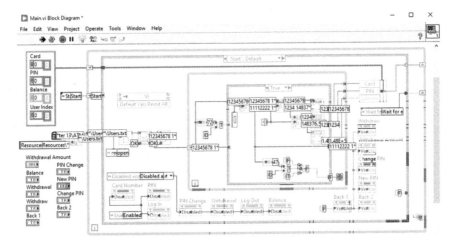

*Figure 13.64   Follow-up of the users file first row of data going into the array
inside the cluster*

- Observe how when all the values of the file are captured they are sent to the cluster and the case will change to "Wait for Event". See Figure 13.67.
- Enter the following values for "Card Number" and "PIN" in the front panel and click on "Log In". See Figure 13.68.
- 12345678   1234

Note: Observe that the "Search 1D Array" function searches the card number on the "Card" array which is inside the cluster. In case of finding the card the index

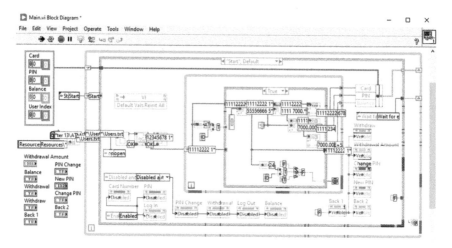

Figure 13.65   Follow-up of the users file second row of data going into the array inside the cluster

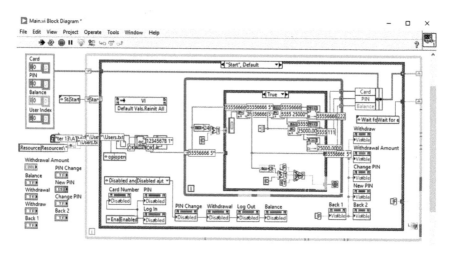

Figure 13.66   Follow-up of the users file third row of data going into the array inside the cluster

is obtained. This index is pointed out on the "**PIN**" array, if the pointed PIN is equal to the one typed by the user a True value will be sent to the case structure, where this index will be written on "**User Index**" of the cluster to be able to work with the data of this user in future states. Also observe that some controls on the front panel are enabled and other disabled as shown on Figure 13.69.

- Click the "**Log Out**" button, write the value "**0**" for "**Card Number**" and "**PIN**", click the "**Log In**" button, and observe the data flow. See Figure 13.70.

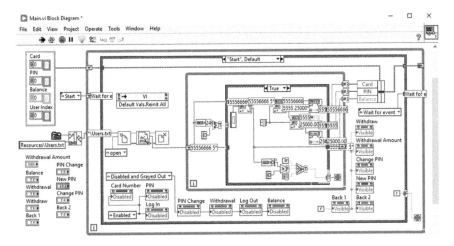

Figure 13.67   All the information of the file is sent to the cluster, and the state machine performs a transition to wait for event

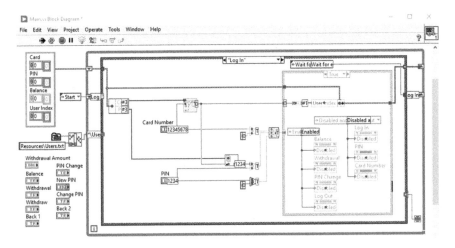

Figure 13.68   Block diagram of a successful log in

Note: Observe how the False case of the Log In state is reached, then the dialog box with the "Incorrect PIN or Card Number" message will appear and the elements of "User Index" will be erased, see Figures 13.70 and 13.71.

Accessing and modifying the cluster account information

In this section, the access and modification of data from a cluster inside a VI will be practiced.

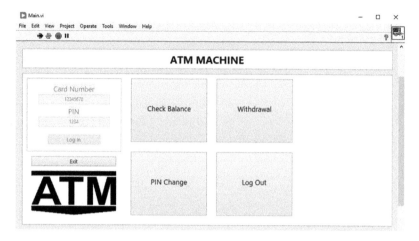

Figure 13.69   View of the Front panel in a successful log in

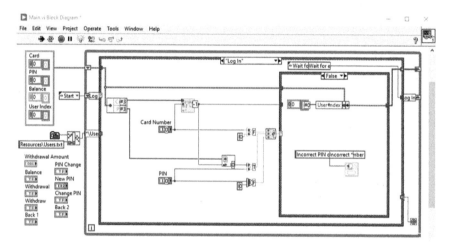

Figure 13.70   Data flow of a failed log in attempt

In this section, new cases will be programmed to perform the account balance check and to modify the PIN. With this aim, the front panel controls to change the PIN will be visible, and the new PIN will be validated in the number of characters. To do this, the functions from Table 13.6 will be used.

13.5.2   Creating the event Check Balance

1 – Open the ATM project

- Open the VI "Main"
- Go to the "Wait for event" case and add an event to the event structure for the "Balance" button with value change.

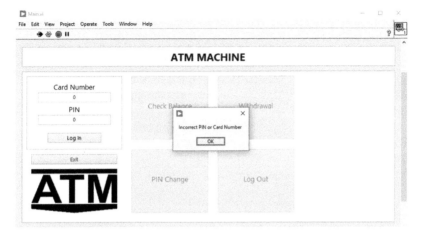

Figure 13.71   Front panel of the failed log in attempt

Table 13.6   Functions with arrays and strings used in this section

Function name	Block diagram	Description
Index Array	Index Array	Found on **Functions > Programming > Array**. Returns the element of an n-dimensional array starting from the indicated index.
Concatenate Strings	Concatenate Strings	Found on **Functions > Programming > String**. Concatenates inputs of strings and arrays of 1D strings in one string output.
Format Into String	Format Into String	Found on **Functions > Programming > String**. Converts to a string format, path, timestamp, boolean, enumerated type, or numeric data into text.
Replace Subset	Replace Subset	Found on **Functions > Programming > Array**. Replaces an element or subarray inside an array from a point indicated on the index.

- Clone the "Enum Constant (Start)" which is outside the while loop, change the value of the clone to "Check Balance", place it inside the "Balance" event and connect it to the "Shift Register" to the right side of the case. See Figure 13.72.
- Go to the case "Check Balance" on the case structure.
- Insert "Unbundle By Name", "Format Into String", "Concatenate String", "One Button Dialog", two "Index Array", and three "String Constant". See Figure 13.73.
- Connect the cluster from the left "Shift Register" to the "Unbundle By Name" and pick the values "Balance" and "User Index".

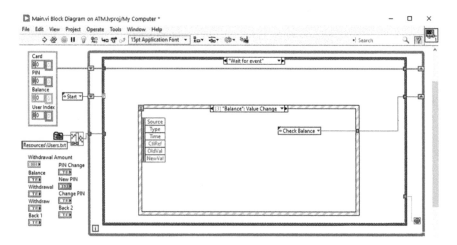

Figure 13.72   Creating the "Balance" event

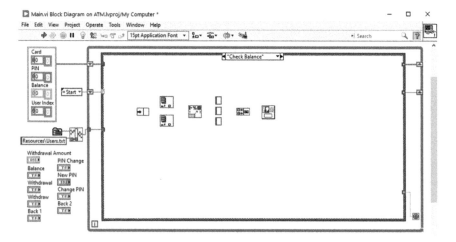

Figure 13.73   Functions added inside the "Check Balance" case

- Connect each of the outputs of the "Unbundle By Name" ("Balance" and "User Index") to an "Index Array". See Figure 13.74.
- Create a numeric constant with value "0" on the "index" input of the "Index Array" connected to "User Index".
- Connect the "element" output to the "index" input of the "Index Array (Balance)".
- Connect the "element" output to the "input 1" of the "Format Into String"
- Connect a "String Constant" with the value of "%.3f" to the "format string" input of the "Format Into String". See Figure 13.75.

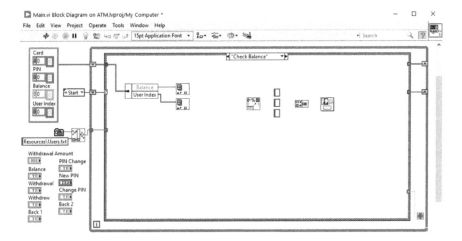

Figure 13.74   Connections of Balance and User Index to two Index Array

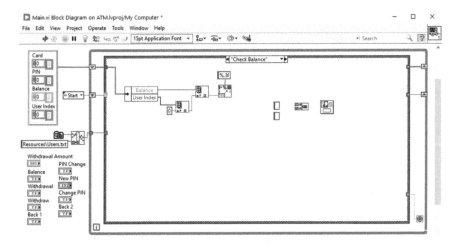

Figure 13.75   Index Array and Format Into String connections

- Change the values of the other two string constants to "Your balance is: $" and " dollars", including a space before dollars.
- Drag down the "Concatenate Strings" to have three inputs and connect the "String Constants" and the "Format Into String" in the following order:
  o   "Your balance is: $"
  o   Output "resulting string" of "Format Into String"
  o   " dollars"

- Connect the output "concatenated strings" of the "Concatenate Strings" to the input "message" of the "One Button Dialog". See Figure 13.76.
- Connect the cluster at the input of the case structure on the left side to the output tunnel of the case structure going into the "Shift Register"
- Clone the "Enum Constant (Start)" which is outside the while loop, change the value of the clone to "Wait for event" and place it inside the case "Check Balance" and connect it to the tunnel of the "Shift Register" to the right side of the case. See Figure 13.77.

13.5.3   Programming PIN change

1 – Create events for the buttons "PIN change" and "Back 2".

- Go to the case "Wait for event" and create an event for "PIN change" that sends the program to the "PIN Change" case. See Figure 13.78.
- Create an event for the button "Back 2" that goes to "Back" case. See Figure 13.79.
- Modify the case "PIN Change" of the case structure, adding property nodes for "New PIN", "Change PIN" and "Back 2", with the "Visible" property and a "True" constant connected.

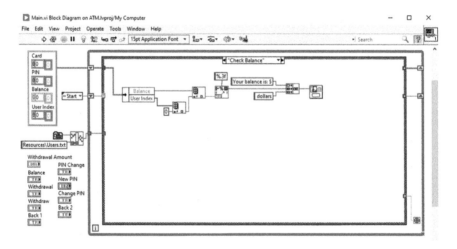

Figure 13.76   Connecting functions with Arrays and Strings to display the balance message

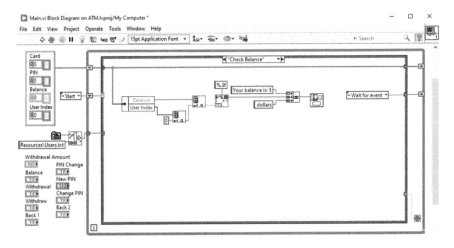

Figure 13.77   Cluster and enum constant connection

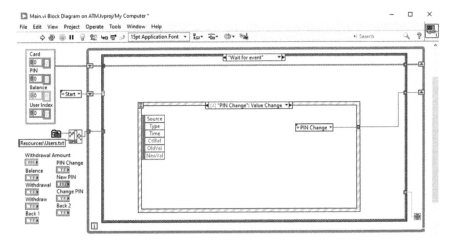

Figure 13.78   Creating PIN Change event

- Clone "Enum Constant (Start)" with the value "Wait for event". Perform the connections as see in Figure 13.80.
- Go to the case "Wait for event" and create an event for "Change PIN" that sends the program to the "New PIN" case. See Figure 13.81.
- Go to the case "New PIN" of the case structure and insert the following functions: "Unbundle By Name", "Index Array", "Format Into String", "String Length", "Not Equal", and "Case Structure".
- Insert the numeric control "New PIN" inside the case. See Figure 13.82.

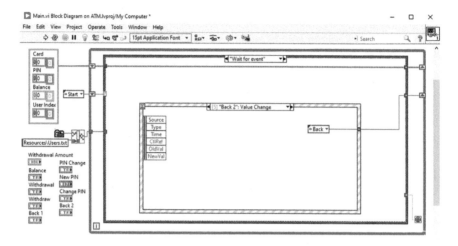

Figure 13.79   Creating Back 2 event and returns to the Back case

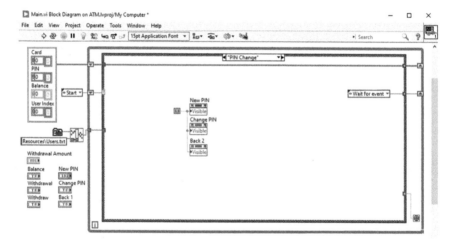

Figure 13.80   Modification of the PIN Change case

- Connect the left side cluster to "Unbundle By Name" unbundle the values of "PIN" and "User Index".
- Connect the output "User Index" from the cluster to the input "array" of the "Index Array" and the "PIN" output to the case structure, also add a numeric constant with value "0" and connect it to the "index" input of the "Index Array".
- Connect the numeric control "New PIN" to the "Input 1" input of the "Format Into String" and to the case structure. See Figure 13.83.

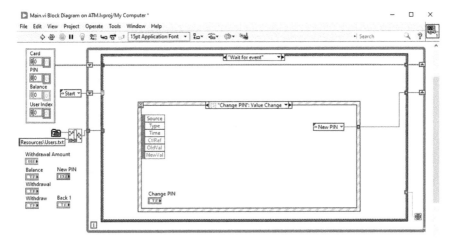

Figure 13.81   Creating "Change PIN" event

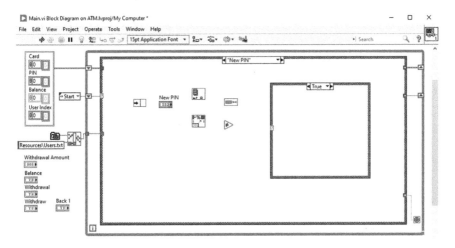

Figure 13.82   Elements added on "New PIN" case

- Create a numeric constant with the value "4".
- Connect the output "Resulting String" from "Format Into String" to the input of "String Length", compare the output of the "String Length" with the "Not Equal?" function and the numeric constant "4" (this is to validate that the PIN is four characters long).
- Connect the output of the "Not Equal?" comparator to the selector terminal of the case structure.
- Connect the output "Element" from the "Index Array" to the case structure. See Figure 13.84.

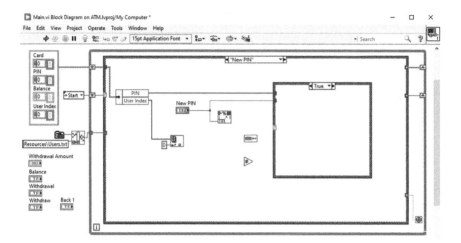

Figure 13.83   Connecting the Array information of PIN and User Index of the cluster in the case "New PIN"

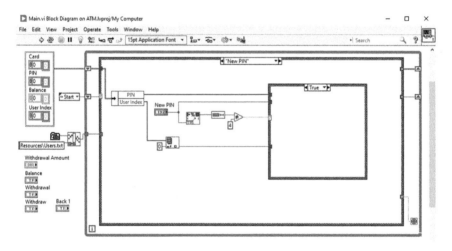

Figure 13.84   PIN length validation

- Inside the "False" case insert the functions: "Replace Subset", "Bundle By Name", "Format Into String", "Concatenate Strings", "One Button Dialog", and a "String Constant" with value "Your new PIN is".
- Connect the cluster to the "Bundle By Name" with the value bundle of "PIN".
- Connect the "PIN" output of the "Unbundle By Name" to the "array" input of the "Replace Subset" and the "output array" to the "PIN" input of the "Bundle By Name" and the output to the cluster tunnel to the right. See Figure 13.85.

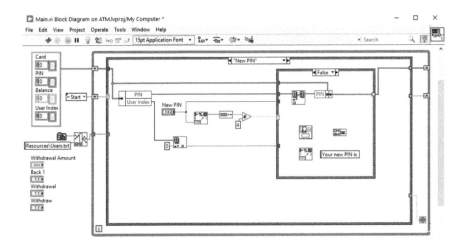

Figure 13.85   First Part of the PIN cluster connection

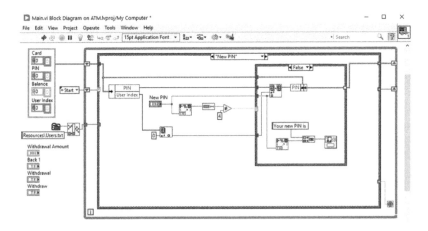

Figure 13.86   New PIN capture and new PIN message

- Connect the output of the numeric control "New PIN" to the input "new element/ subarray" of the "Replace Subset" and the "input 1" of the "Format Into String".
- Connect the "element" output of the "Index Array" to the "index" input of the "Replace Subset".
- Connect the "String Constant" of "Your new PIN is " with the "resulting string" output of the "Format Into String" using the "Concatenate Strings" function and the output to the "message" input of the "One Button Dialog". See Figure 13.86.
- Change to the "True" case and add a "One Button Dialog" with text input "The PIN must be four digits long".
- Connect the cluster as shown in Figure 13.87.

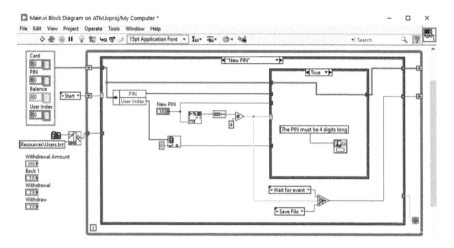

Figure 13.87   True case and transition selection between two possible states

- Outside the case add a "Select" function with an "Enum Constant (Wait for event)" connected to the "T" input and an "Enum Constant (Save File)" connected to the "F" input.
- Connect on the "S" input of the "Select" function the output of the "Not Equal?" comparator.
- Connect the output of "Select" to the input of "Shift Register" used for the states at the right, as shown in Figure 13.87.

2 – Modify the "Back" case.

- Add property nodes for "New PIN", "Change PIN", and "Back 2" with the "Visible" property connected to a "False" constant.
- Add property nodes for "Balance", "Withdrawal", and "PIN Change" with the "Disabled" property connected to an "Enabled" constant.
- Add an "Enum Constant (Wait for event)" and connect the cluster as shown in Figure 13.88.

3 – System operation check.

- Use "Highlight Execution" to follow the program through the block diagram.
- Log in with the card number "11112222" and PIN "1111". See Figure 13.89.
- Click on "PIN Change" and observe the data flow as shown in Figures 13.90 and 13.91.

Note: Observe that when "PIN Change" is pressed, the program transitions to "PIN Change" state.

Note: On the "PIN Change" state can be observed how the controls "New PIN", "Change PIN", and "Back 2" become visible.

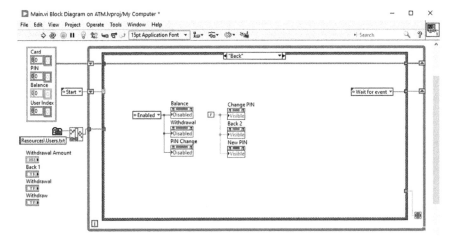

Figure 13.88   Back case modification

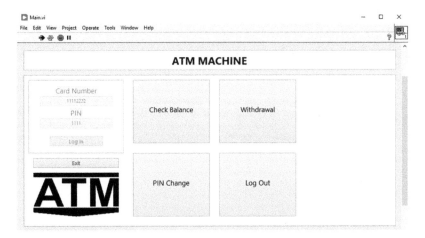

Figure 13.89   Front Panel after introducing a valid Card Number, PIN, and pressing Log In

- Insert the new PIN "1234" on the front panel and click on "Change PIN". See Figure 13.92.
- Observe the data flow when changing the PIN as shown in Figures 13.93 and 13.94.

Note: The length of the new PIN is compared with the constant "4" to validate it, if it is not correct, the program will go back to the "Wait for event" case and wait for a valid PIN with four characters.

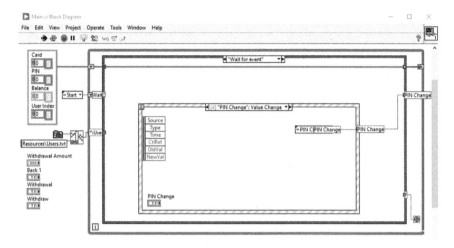

Figure 13.90   Data flow to PIN Change

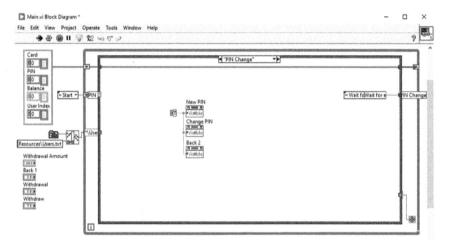

Figure 13.91   In PIN Change state, the controls to perform the PIN change become visible

13.6   File save and rewrite

In this section, new states will be created to modify the balance and save the latest data on the same file. These modifications will be validated to not exceed the amount of the accounts. To do this, the functions from Table 13.7 will be used.

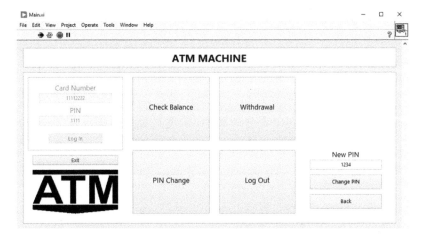

Figure 13.92   PIN Change

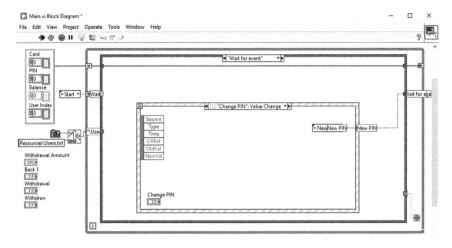

Figure 13.93   Data flow for the event Change PIN that sends to the New PIN state

13.6.1   Creating events

1 – Open the ATM project.

- Open the "Main" VI.
- Create the event "Withdrawal" inside the event structure.
- Clone the "Enum Constant (Start)" which is outside the while loop and drop inside the new event case, change the value of the clone to "Withdrawal",

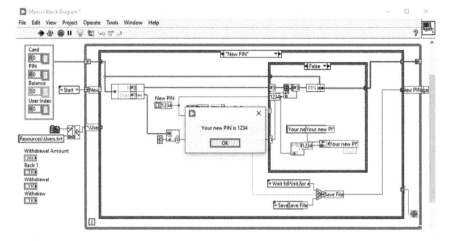

Figure 13.94   After a successful change in the PIN, the message is displayed by the One Button Dialog

Table 13.7   Functions used to save files

Function name	Block diagram	Description
Subtract	Subtract	Located on **Functions > Programming > Numeric.** It makes the subtract arithmetic operation.
Transpose 2D Array	Transpose 2D Array	Located on **Functions > Programming > Array.** Change the axis direction of a 2D array.
Write Delimited Spreadsheet.vi	Write Delimited Spreadsheet.vi	Located on **Functions > Programming > File I/O.** Saves a 1D or 2D array inside an existing file open inside a VI.
For Loop	For Loop	Located on **Functions > Programming > Structures.** Creates a loop with N number of iterations, where N is the number of times that the loop will be repeated.

connecting it with the "Shift Register" at the right of the case as shown in Figure 13.95.

- Repeat the same process of the previous point for the events "Back 1" and "Withdraw", but with the "Enum Constant (Back)" inside of "Back 1" and the "Enum Constant (Money withdrawal)" inside the event "Withdraw". See Figures 13.96 and 13.97.

- Go to the case "Withdrawal" and add the property nodes for "Withdraw", "Withdrawal Amount", and "Back 1" with the "Visible" property and a "True" constant.

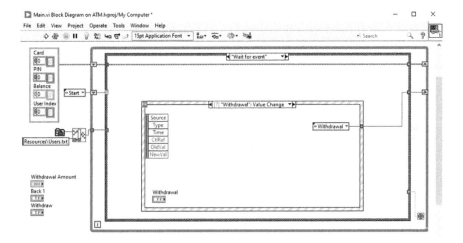

Figure 13.95 Creating withdrawal event

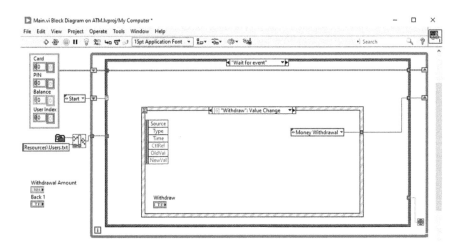

Figure 13.96 Creating the withdraw event

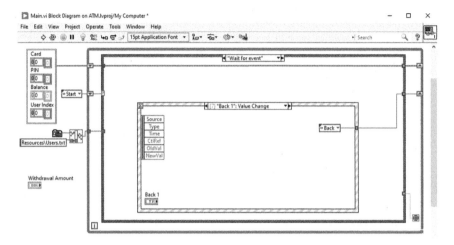

Figure 13.97   Creating the Back 1 event

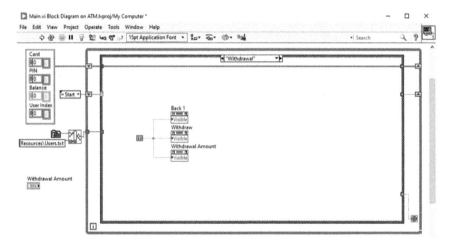

Figure 13.98   Property nodes on Withdrawal case

- Connect the cluster to the "Shift Register" as shown in Figure 13.98.
- Add property nodes for "Balance", "Withdrawal", and "PIN Change" with the property "Disabled" and connect them with a constant "Disabled and Grayed Out".
- Clone the "Enum Constant (Start)" and change the value of the clone to "Wait for event" and place it inside the case "Withdrawal" and connect it to the tunnel of the shift register to the right. See Figure 13.99.

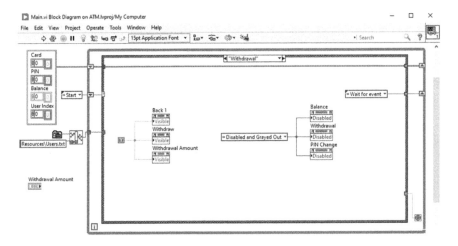

Figure 13.99   *Disabled and Grayed Out property nodes*

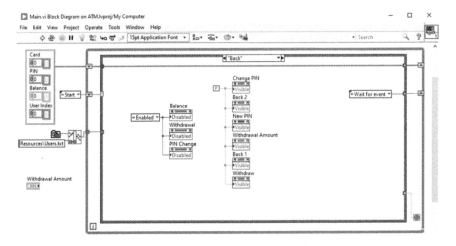

Figure 13.100   *New property nodes on the Back case*

- Go to the "Back" case, create the property nodes for "Withdrawal Amount", "Withdraw" and "Back 1", and connect them to the "False" constant, which is already inside the case. See Figure 13.100.
- Go to the case "Money Withdrawal" on the case structure.
- Add "Unbundle By Name", connect on its input terminal the cluster that comes from the tunnel connected to the shift register on the left side and expand it to show the four values of the cluster.
- Add "Greater?", "Case Structure", two "Index Array", and place the numeric control "Withdrawal Amount" inside the case. See Figure 13.101.

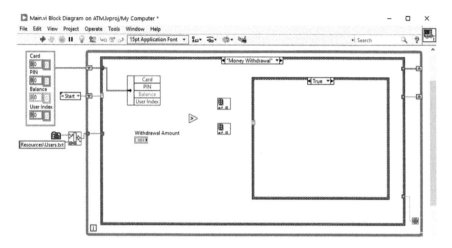

Figure 13.101   Adding functions of the Money Withdrawal case

- Connect the cluster values "Balance" and "User Index" to the input "array" of each of the "Index Array", connect the input "index" of the "Index Array (User Index)" a "0" constant and on the input "index" of the "Index Array (Balance)" the output "element" of the "Index Array (User Index)".
- Connect the numeric control "Withdrawal Amount" to the "x" input of the "Greater?", and on the "y" input of the "Greater?" connect the output "element" of the "Index Array (Balance)", connect the output of "Greater?" to the case structure.
- Create a popup message inside the "True" case using "One Button Dialog" with the message "Insufficient balance for transaction".
- Connect the cluster by the "True" case, as shown in Figure 13.102.
- Add inside the "False" case the functions "Subtract", "Bundle By Name", "Replace Array Subset", "Format Into String", "Concatenate Strings", "One Button Dialog", and two "String Constant" with the texts "Your new balance is: $" and "dollars". See Figure 13.103.
- Connect the cluster to "Bundle By Name" and select the "Balance" value.
- Connect the "x" and "y" inputs of the "Subtract" to the numeric control "Withdrawal amount" and the output "element" of the "Index Array (Balance)", respectively. Connect the output of the "Subtract" to the input "new element/subarray" of the "Replace Array Subset" and to the input "input 1" of the "Format Into String".
- For the "Replace Array Subset", connect the value "Balance" of the "Unbundle By Name" to the "array" input and the "element" output of the "Index Array (User Index)" to the "index" input, and the output "output array" of the "Replace Array Subset" to the input if the "Bundle By Name" of the value "Balance".

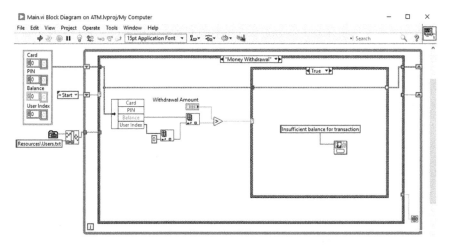

Figure 13.102   Connection of the Money Withdrawal when the withdrawal amount is greater than the account balance

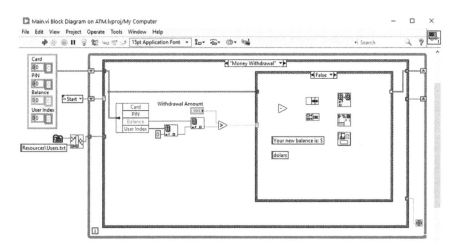

Figure 13.103   Functions and constants in the False case within Money Withdrawal state

- Add a string constant with "%.3f" on the "format string" input of the "Format Into String".
- Connect to the inputs "Concatenate Strings" in the following order:
  - The constant "Your new balance is: $".
  - The output "resulting string" of the "Format Into String".
  - String constant " dollars".

- Connect the output of the "Concatenate Strings" to the input "message" of the "One Button Dialog". See Figure 13.104.
- Add a "Select" comparator with a value of "Enum Constant (Wait for event)" on the "T" input and a value of "Enum Constant (Save File)" on the "F" input.
- Connect the output of the "Greater?" comparator to the input "s" of the "Select" function, and its output to the "Shift register" to the right. See Figure 13.105.

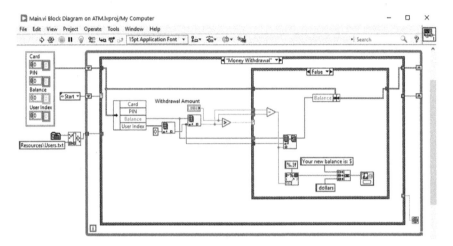

Figure 13.104   Connection of the Money Withdrawal when the withdrawal amount is less than the account balance

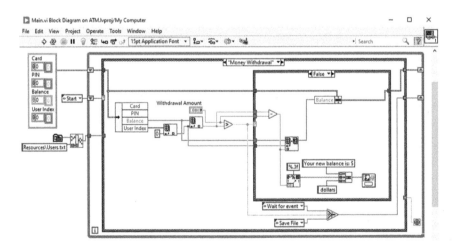

Figure 13.105   Adding a case selector for the state transition to Wait for Event or Save File

13.6.2   Creating Save File case

1 – Go to Save File case

- Add the following components: "For Loop", "Build Array", "Transpose 2D Array", "Write Delimited Spreadsheet.vi", and "Unbundle By Name". Connect the "Unbundle By Name" to the cluster and unbundle the "Card", "PIN", and "Balance" values. See Figure 13.106.
- Add three "Format Into String" inside the "For Loop"
- Connect the following cluster values from the "Unbundle By Name" on the inputs "Input 1" of the "Format Into String":
  - o   Card
  - o   PIN
  - o   Balance

- Add a string constant on the input "format string" with the value "%.3f" on the "Format Into String (Balance)". See Figure 13.107.
- Drag down the "Build Array" to obtain three inputs
- Connect the outputs "resulting string" of the "Format Into String" functions into the three inputs of "Build Array".
- Connect the output "appended array" of the "Build Array" to the input "2D array" of the "Transpose 2D Array" and the output "transposed array" to the input "2D data" of the "Write Delimited Spreadsheet.vi".
- Connect the output "appended path" of the "Build Path" (located on the left side of the block diagram) to the "file path" of the "Write Delimited Spreadsheet.vi".
- Add an "Enum Constant (Back)" and connect it to the shift register at the right. See Figure 13.108.

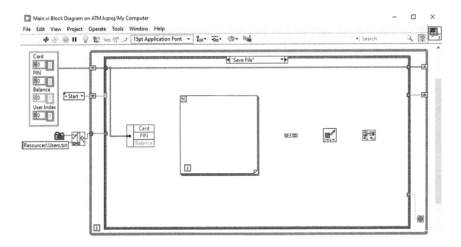

Figure 13.106   It is suggested to add the nodes in the shown order to facilitate the wiring

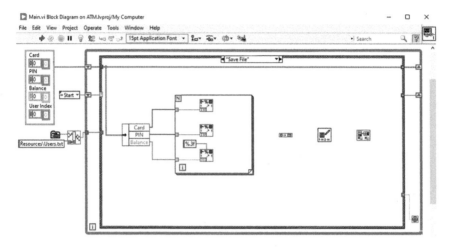

Figure 13.107   The formats into string converts the card number, PIN, and balance of each user into strings

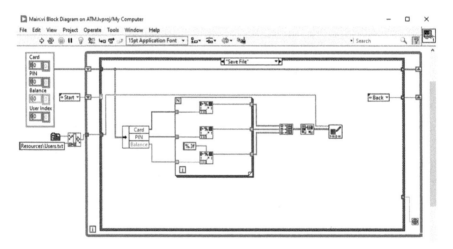

Figure 13.108   The Card, PIN, and Balance information is "Format" to strings and saved

2 – System operation check

• Use "Highlight Execution" to follow the data flow on the block diagram.
• Log In with the card number "12345678" and PIN "1234". See Figure 13.109.
• Click on "Check Balance" and observe the data flow as shown in Figures 13.110 and 13.111.

Note: Observe how the program performs a transition to the "Check Balance" case when clicking the "Check Balance" button.

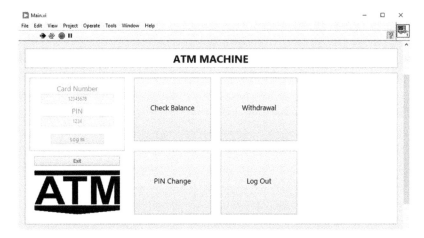

Figure 13.109   Logging In

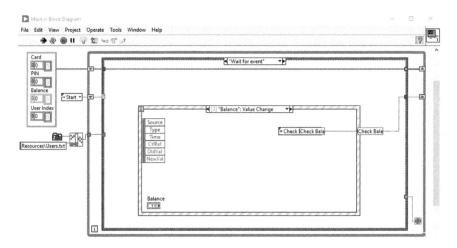

Figure 13.110   Data flow to check the balance

Note: Continuing with the data flow, when entering the "Check Balance" case, it can be observed how the message with the current balance is shown to the logged in user; after that, the program comes back to the "Wait for event" case.

- Click on "Withdrawal" and observe the data flow. See Figure 13.112.
- Observe the withdrawal data flow as shown in Figures 13.113 and 13.114.

Note: The controls used for the withdrawal are shown, and the secondary controls for account operations are disabled as shown in Figure 13.115.

- Enter the amount of $500 dollars and click on the withdraw button. See Figure 13.116.
- Observe the withdraw data flow as shown in Figures 13.117 and 13.118.

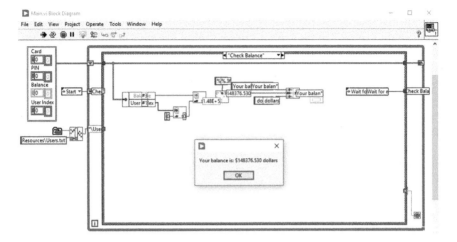

Figure 13.111   Current balance message

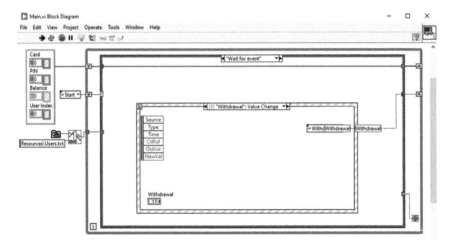

Figure 13.112   Withdrawal button

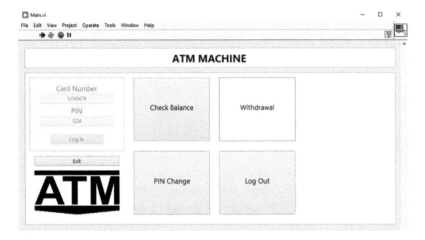

Figure 13.113   Withdrawal event data flow

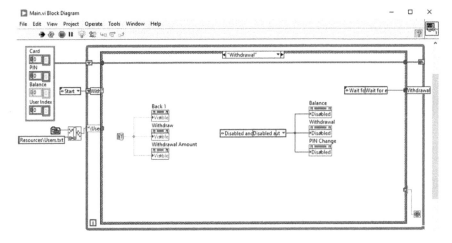

Figure 13.114　Withdrawal case data flow

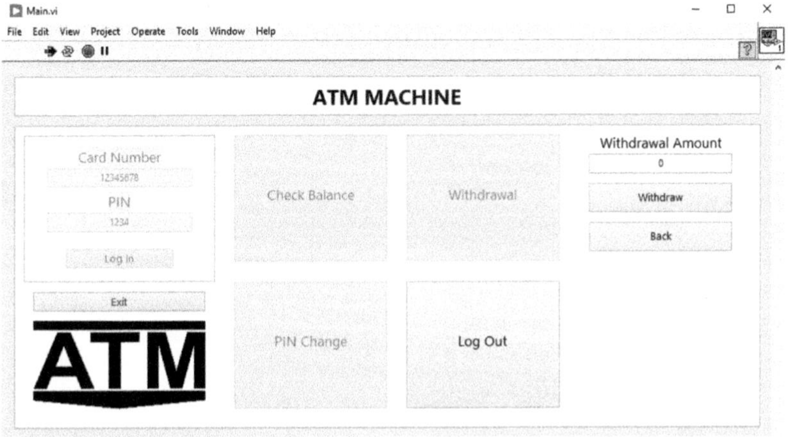

Figure 13.115　Front Panel controls after pressing the button Withdrawal

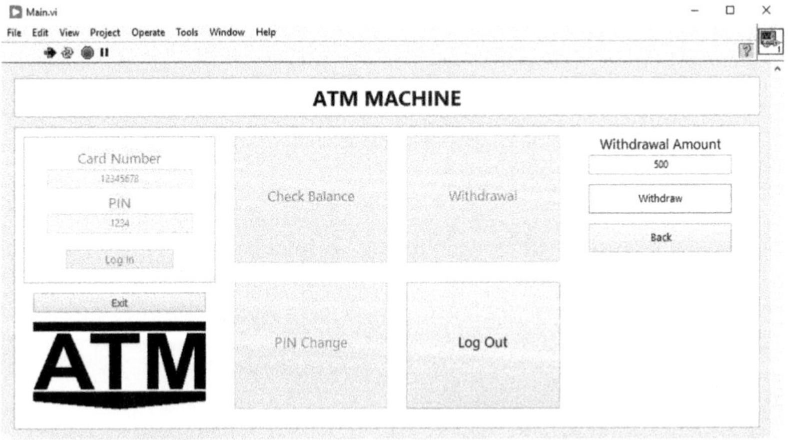

Figure 13.116　Entering a withdrawal amount

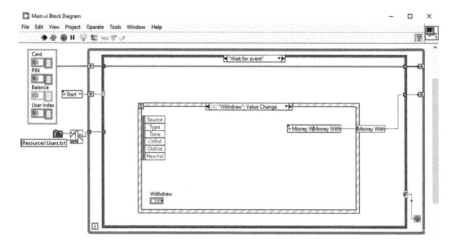

Figure 13.117   Withdraw event data flow

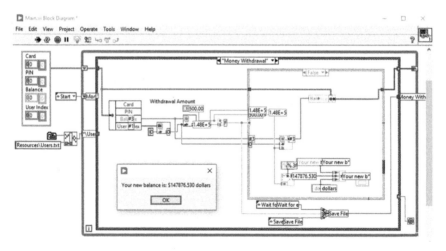

Figure 13.118   Money withdrawal data flow and the message display of the one-button dialog after performing the withdraw

Note: Compares the withdrawal amount with the amount the user has on the Users.txt file, if the amount is less than it has, the specified amount will be withdrawn, and the available balance will change, sending a message with the new amount changing the value inside the Users.txt file as shown in Figure 13.119.

Note: Once the file is saved, the program will go to the Back case to disable the controls as shown in Figure 13.120.

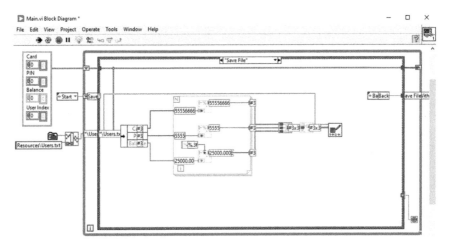

Figure 13.119 Data flow of the Save File case to update the information in Users. txt

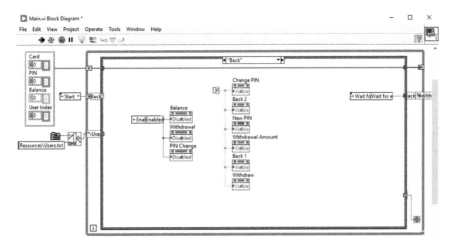

Figure 13.120 Data flow of the Back case

Note: Withdrawal controls are hidden, and the secondary controls are enabled for account operations as shown in Figure 13.121.

- Click again on the "Withdrawal" button, enter the amount of $500,000 dollars and click the button "Withdraw" as shown in Figures 13.122 and 13.123.

Note: When the withdrawal amount exceeds the available balance, the program will go to the wait for event case to wait for a correct value, or the user can go back to the main menu.

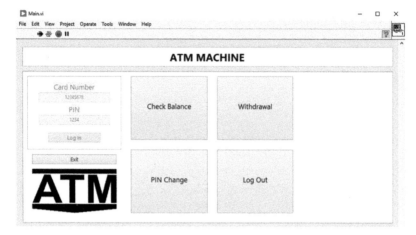

Figure 13.121   Front Panel appearance after all the controls for Withdrawal are Hidden; on the other hand, Check Balance, Withdrawal, and PIN Change are enabled

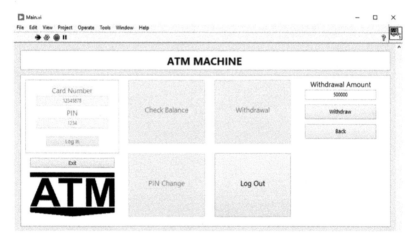

Figure 13.122   Entering a withdrawal amount greater than the account balance

13.7   Last adjustments and VI documentation

In this section, the user file will be modified to show fewer decimal points, and the VI will be changed to work with two decimal points on the Format Into String functions. Also, notes will be included in all cases to have sufficient documentation for developer peers and facilitate future code maintenance.

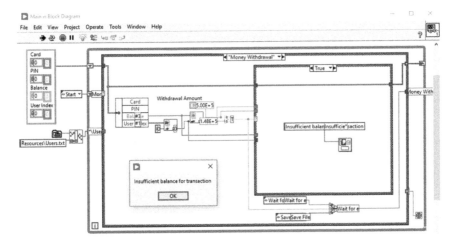

Figure 13.123   A message of Insufficient balance for the transaction is displayed

13.7.1   Modify text file and case parameters

1 – Open ATM project

- Open the "Users" file.
- Modify the last values of the balance column in a way that there are only two values after the decimal point. See Figure 13.124.

  2 – Modify the cases "Save File", "Check Balance", and "Money Withdrawal (False)"

- Modify the "format string" of each "Format Into String" inside each case.
- See Figures 13.126, 13.127, and 13.128.

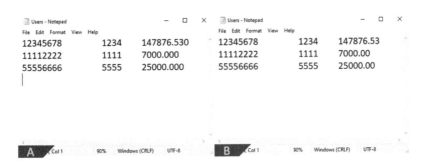

Figure 13.124   (A) Users file without modification and (B) users file with the modification

Figure 13.125   *Modifying the string format from three decimal points to two (%.3f to %.2f)*

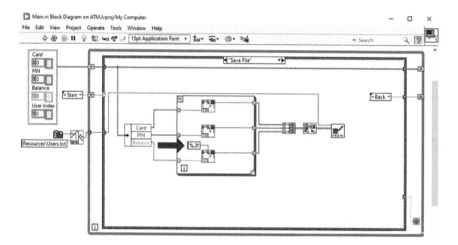

Figure 13.126   *Save File case modification*

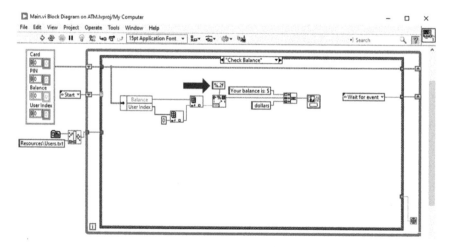

Figure 13.127   *Check Balance case modification*

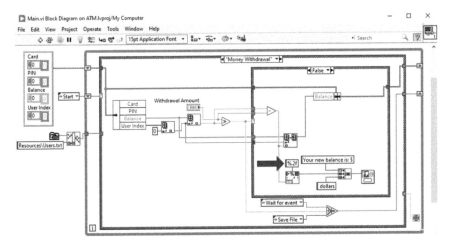

Figure 13.128   Money Withdrawal case modification

13.7.2   VI documentation

1 – Add notes for VI documentation.

- Double click on the block diagram to create a text box and add the notes shown in Figure 13.129.
- Add the following note on the case "Wait for event". See Figure 13.130.
- Add the following note on the "Log In" case and the subcase (True-False). See Figures 13.131 and 13.132.

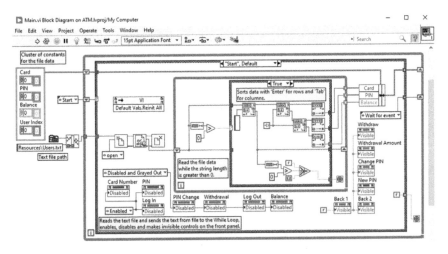

Figure 13.129   Start case documented

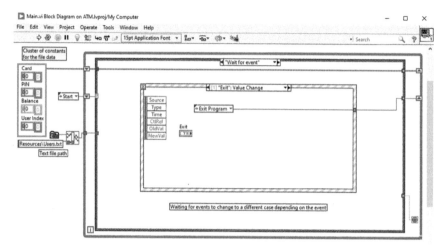

Figure 13.130   Wait for event case with documented

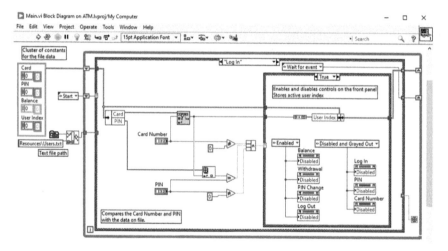

Figure 13.131   Log In case (True) documented

- Add the following note on the "Check Balance" case. See Figure 13.133.
- Add the following note on the "Withdrawal" case. See Figure 13.134.
- Add the following note on the "PIN Change" case. See Figure 13.135.
- Add the following notes on the "Money Withdrawal" case and on the sub-cases (True-False). See Figures 13.136 and 13.137.
- Add the following note on the "Back" case. See Figure 13.138.
- Add the following note on the "Save File" case. See Figure 13.139.

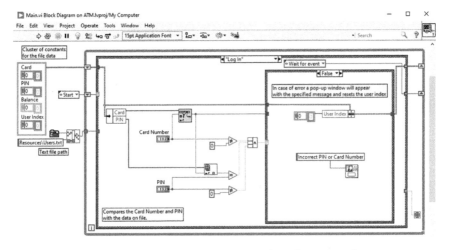

Figure 13.132   Log In case (False) documented

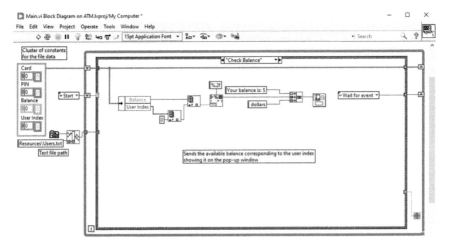

Figure 13.133   Check Balance case documented

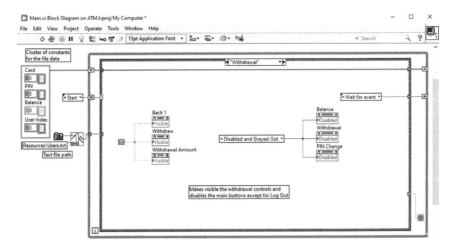

Figure 13.134   Withdrawal case documented

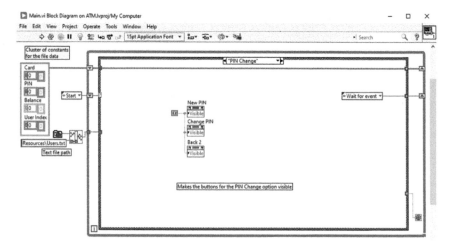

Figure 13.135   PIN Change case documented

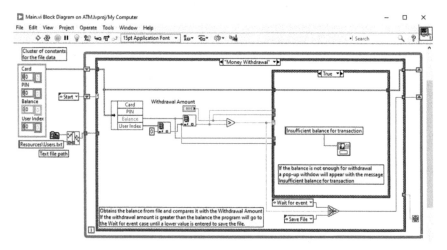

Figure 13.136   Money Withdrawal case (True) documented

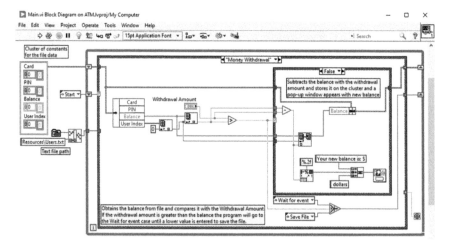

Figure 13.137   Money Withdrawal case (False) documented

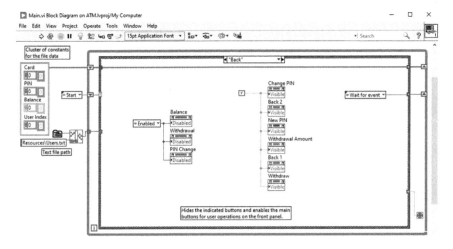

Figure 13.138   Back case documented

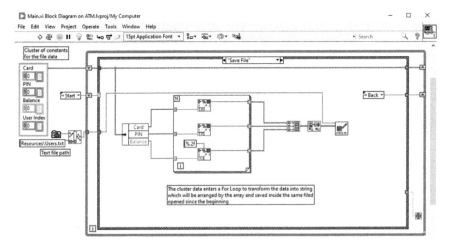

Figure 13.139   Save File case documented

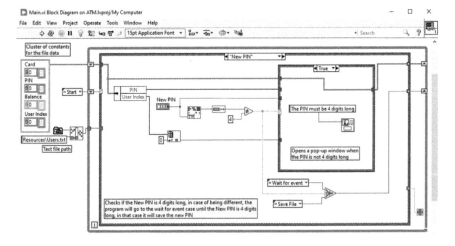

Figure 13.140   New PIN case (True) documented

- Add the following notes on the "New PIN" case and on the subcases (True-False). See Figures 13.140 and 13.141.
- Add the following note on the "Exit Program" case. See Figure 13.142.
- Add the following note on the "Log Out" case. See Figure 13.143.

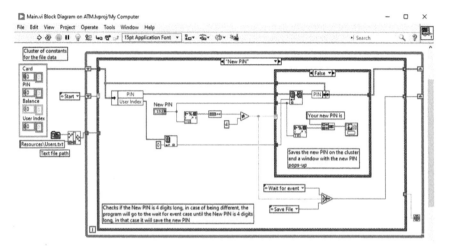

Figure 13.141   New PIN case (False) documented

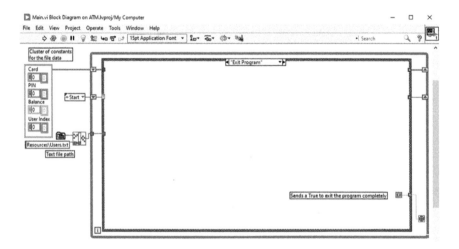

Figure 13.142   Exit Program case documented

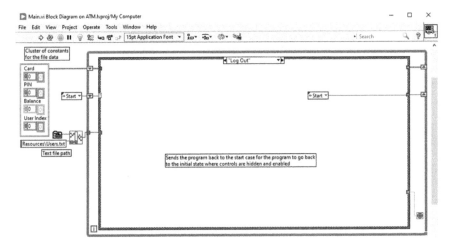

Figure 13.143   Log Out case documented

Chapter 14

Communication between loops at different rates

The inherent parallelism of LabVIEW^{TM} allows concurrent execution of tasks, however, without an efficient mechanism to let the efficient communication between loops, the produced information that is communicated between parallel loops can be duplicated or lost. In this sense, this chapter explains the use of asynchronous communication methods between loops such as producer–consumer design pattern and event-driven producer–consumer design pattern, which allow solving some classic problems in this type of programming [23].

14.1 Asynchronous communication

Asynchronous communication allows you to send and receive information without wires and process the information at different instants of time. In fact, up to this chapter, some asynchronous communication techniques have already been implemented, for example, event structures are a good example of asynchronous communication, these structures can detect two or more events "simultaneously"; however, this structure will only process one event for each iteration of the loop where the structure is within. This type of asynchronous communication is good for processing interface events; however, not very useful when you want to process information that is generated faster than it can be processed. For this, there are functions with queues, which allow the data to be processed as it is generated.

14.1.1 Queues

Queues are one of the ways in which LabVIEW^{TM} handles asynchronous communication and is one of the most efficient when it comes to processing information as it is generated. Queues in LabVIEW^{TM} are similar to other text-based programming languages. The queues work by default in a FIFO (first-in, first-out); however, they can be configured to operate in different ways. To understand what a queue is, imagine a bank line, where the first customer who arrives is the one who is attended, so the clients who arrive later are lined up to wait their turn to be attended by the cashier. In this example, the clients are the ones who "produce" the requests; each one will have a different request, some to open an account, some for withdrawals, and some for deposits. On the other hand, the cashier is the one who "consumes" or processes each of the requests, see Figure 14.1. Note that if a new

Figure 14.1   Graphical representation of FIFO (first-in, first-out) using a bank line as an example

client arrives and the cashier is busy, the client only has to line up and wait for their turn to be attended, in this way, no request is lost.

LabVIEW^{TM} uses different functions to implement queues, these functions can be accessed from the function's palette at Programming>>Synchronization>>Queue Operations. Table 14.1 contains a description of each queue function.

14.1.2   Producer–consumer design pattern

The producer–consumer design pattern uses queues and is created to execute processes where the generation of the information is at a different rate than the loop where the information is processed, or when the trigger to generate this information is given by an external source (for example, when a DAQ has its sample rate). It is not necessary to start the producer–consumer design pattern from scratch, you can begin working with this pattern by going to File>>New, then select VI>>From Template>>Frameworks>>Design Pattern>>Producer/Consumer Design Pattern (Data), see Figure 14.2.

By default, LabVIEW^{TM} generates the following design pattern (Figure 14.3). Note that the design pattern consists of two while loops, the first or upper while loop is known as the producer loop, and the lower while loop is known as the consumer loop. Also, note that at the left of the design pattern is the Obtain Queue function, this function creates the queue with the specified data type, by default, the design pattern is created with a string data type (using the string constant at the Obtain Queue input); however, you can create a queue of any data type as integers, Booleans, doubles and even clusters, which are highly useful, etc. Within the producer loop, there is a case structure, which attends a condition to add elements to the queue. In this template, the case selection terminal of the case structure is set to false by default, this will be modified later to control when to add an element to the queue. Also, note that the reference created from the Obtain Queue function must be wired to all the functions that work with the same queue, however, this reference does not send information, it is only a pointer in memory to the queue. Therefore, the information that is queued using the Enqueue Element function is information that can automatically be accessed from any part of the program using the Dequeue Element

Table 14.1   Functions with queues

Function	Description
Obtain Queue	Creates a reference to a queue. The required input of this function is the datatype of the queue.
Enqueue Element	Adds an element at the end of the queue. The required inputs are the queue reference and the element.
Lossy Enqueue Element	Returns the element at the front of the queue without removing it from the queue. The required input is the reference.
Get Queue Status	Returns information as the number of elements in the queue, the name of the queue, and pending elements to insert or remove. The required input is the reference.
Release Queue	Release a reference to a queue, freeing up memory space. The required input is the reference.
Lossy Enqueue Element	Adds an element to a queue and remove an element from the front in case of no space in the queue. The required inputs are the queue reference and the element.
Enqueue Element At Opposite End	Adds an element at the front of the queue. The required inputs are the queue reference and the element.
Dequeue Element	Returns the element at the front of the queue, removing it from the queue. The required input is the reference.
Flush Queue	Returns all the elements from the queue as an array and removes all the elements from the queue. The required input is the reference.

function (as long as they have the same reference as input). The consumer loop is the second loop, which uses the Dequeue Element function to access the elements in the queue. In the producer–consumer design pattern, it is common to observe that the elements accessed in the queue contain information about the case that must be executed within the consumer loop. Finally, if the producer loop ends, it deletes the reference to the queue, which will cause an error in the consumer loop, then the consumer loop will automatically be closed (for this template).

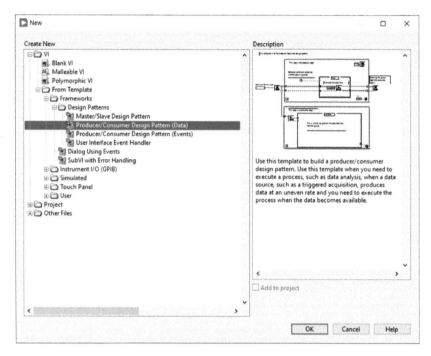

Figure 14.2   Creating a producer/consumer design pattern from a template

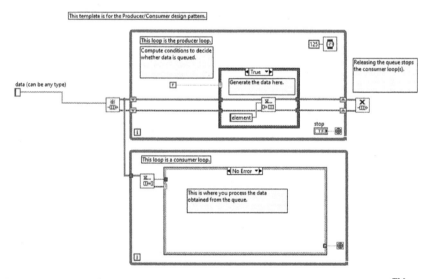

*Figure 14.3   Producer–consumer design pattern obtained from LabVIEW^{TM}
templates*

14.2   Example of asynchronous communication with producer–consumer design pattern

To practice implementing the producer–consumer design pattern, a program will be developed to send requests from the producer loop to wait sometime in the consumer loop. The consumer loop will be occupied attending these requests for as long as necessary, however, you will notice that the user interface continues accepting additional requests. The number of elements in the queue can be observed by the corresponding indicator. To do this, and from the consumer–producer design pattern, modify the user interface to have the following appearance (Figure 14.4).

In the case of the Boolean controls, it is suggested that the labels have the same name as the texts of the Boolean control, this name will identify the Boolean controls in the block diagram, it is recommended to hide the labels of the Boolean controls to not to repeat the same text in the front panel. Regarding the Enum indicator, it must contain three elements in the list, which are the same that will be used to create constants within the block diagram, the elements in the enum can be seen in Figure 14.5.

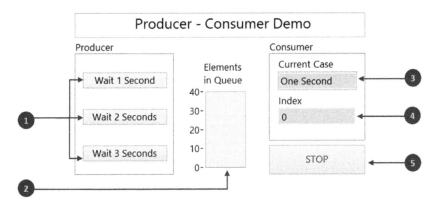

Figure 14.4   *Front panel of producer–consumer demo. (1) Boolean controls, (2) tank style numeric indicator (I32), (3) enum indicator, (4) numeric indicator (I32), and (5) Boolean control*

Items	Values	
One Second	0	
Two Seconds	1	
Three Seconds	2	

Figure 14.5   *List of items inside the enum indicator, note that this same list will be used for the enum constants inside the block diagram*

In Figure 14.6, you can appreciate in the block diagram the appearance of the producer–consumer design pattern after the modification to implement the proposed application, note that there are no wires between the producer loop and the consumer loop, boot are independent, the only wire in common is the reference from the Obtain Queue function; however, this cable does not have data, it only has a reference to a position in memory of the queue. Following, a complete explanation of the program will be provided.

To start with the program, a **cluster constant** is created with the **enum constant Consumer Case** and the **integer I32 constant Index** within it. The **enum constant Consumer case** has the same elements as shown in Figure 14.5. The cluster constant is connected to the **element data type** input of the **Obtain Queue** function (Figure 14.7). As this program only has one queue, the output reference of

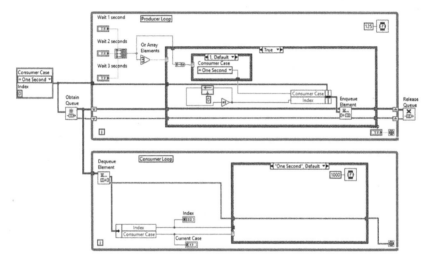

Figure 14.6   Block diagram of the developed producer–consumer demo

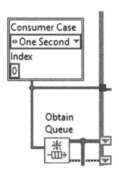

Figure 14.7   Declaring the element data type (a cluster with an enum constant and integer I32) of the queue

the Obtain Queue function will be connected to all the reference inputs of the functions to work with queues of this program.

Within the producer loop, the condition to produce new elements to the queue is when one of the three Boolean buttons (Wait 1 second, Wait 2 seconds, Wait 3 seconds) is pressed, with this aim, an array of Booleans has been created using the Build Array function (for more information you can check Section 5.1.1), the array is the input of the Or Array Elements function, this function returns a true if any of the elements of the array is true (this can happen only if any of the Wait buttons is pressed), see Figure 14.8. The output of Or Array Elements is connected to the case selector terminal in the case structure and the Boolean array is connected to an input tunnel to the case structure, this array will be used to determine which of the buttons is being pressed (see Figure 14.8).

Suppose any of the wait buttons is pressed. In that case, the true case is selected, and an enum constant with the same elements of Figure 14.5 is added to the queue, as well as the current index (the index corresponds to the number of times that any of the three wait buttons have been pressed), see Figure 14.9.

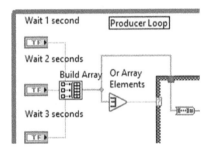

Figure 14.8   Using an array of Booleans to determine if any of the buttons are pressed to access the true case and Enqueue a new element

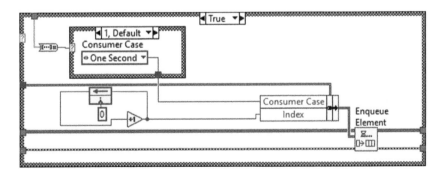

Figure 14.9   After any of the three wait buttons is pressed, the True case is selected to Enqueue new Elements

The enum constant will be used to identify the state to be executed in the consumer loop. Note that to determine the nested case to be executed in the producer loop, the Boolean array is used, which is converted to a 32-bit integer using the Boolean Array to Number function [▣-ᴵ▣], the resulting integer is connected to the case selector terminal of a nested case structure to obtain the enum constant to add to the queue (see Figure 14.9). In Table 14.2, you can see the resulting integer values after converting the Boolean array to a number and the possible selected case (the integer values are in function of which wait button is pressed).

Remember that queues can add a single element at a time (of a defined data type), therefore, since the creation of the queue it was defined as cluster data type, which allows multiple elements to be sent simultaneously within the cluster. Once the user selects the waiting time (by clicking one of the three possible wait buttons), the selected enum constant and the index are bundled to the cluster, see Figure 14.9. It is important to note that the index uses a feedback node initialized to zero and that it will increase by one every time the true case is selected. After using the Bundle by Name function, the cluster is added to the queue using the Enqueue Element function, see Figure 14.9.

Otherwise, when no wait button is pressed, the false case of the producer loop is selected and this "leisure" time is used to consult the number of elements in the queue and update the Elements in Queue indicator using the function Get Queue Status, to provide visual feedback in the front panel about the awaiting elements to be processed in the queue, see Figure 14.10.

Finally, the consumer loop processes all the elements that have been added to the queue from the producer loop, for this the Dequeue Element function is used to return the first element that has been queued and that has not yet been processed. Since the element is cluster type, the unbundle by name function is used to access the Index and the Consumer Case, where the Consumer Case is wired to the case

Table 14.2   *Integer values after converting the Boolean array to number, and the possible selected case*

Boolean array value			Integer value	Selected case
0	0	1	1	◄1, Default ▼► Consumer Case ◄▸One Second ▼
0	1	0	2	◄2 ▼► Consumer Case ◄▸Two Seconds ▼
1	0	0	4	◄4 ▼► Consumer Case ◄▸Three Seconds ▼

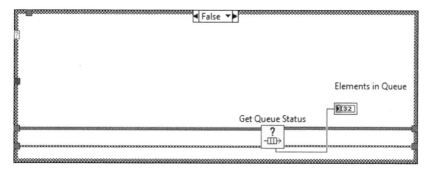

Figure 14.10   Using the Get Queue Status function to obtain the number of awaiting elements in the queue

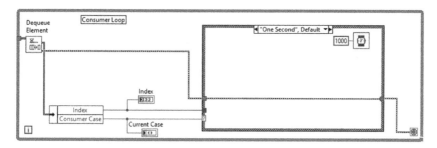

Figure 14.11   Consumer loop: using the Dequeue Element function to get an element from the queue, unbundle the cluster, and select the case

selector to determine what state should be executed, while the index shows the action that is currently attended, see Figure 14.11.

Note that the possible cases within the consumer loop are the same as those in Figure 14.5, each of these cases only waits for its corresponding time given by the Wait function. For this program, the states only wait a certain period of time; however, these states are usually used to execute code asynchronously to the user action or external event that is captured in the producer loop and generates new elements, and where the processing time of these elements (consumer loop) is longer than the time to produce new elements (producer loop) hence the need for queues.

In Figure 14.12, the front panel of the Producer–Consumer Demo program running is presented. Note that when you press any of the three Wait buttons consecutively (faster than the waiting time), none of the waiting times is lost, each one of the actions is stored in the queue and waits to be attended. The Consumer container shows the state that is currently being attended and the index of the action corresponding to the state.

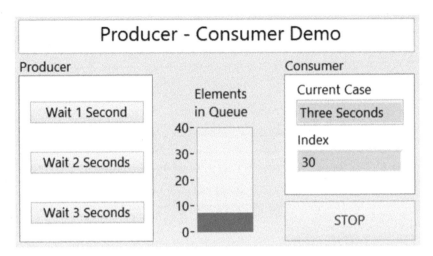

Figure 14.12   Front panel of the Producer–Consumer Demo with 30 actions already attended and around 8 actions in the queue

In addition, the indicator Elements in Queue of Figure 14.12 shows the number of elements in the queue waiting to be attended, this indicator is updated when no action is detected on any of the three wait buttons.

The previous program is a good example of how queues work, however it has a disadvantage, and that is that actions that occur in the production loop can still be lost, this is due to the entire loop is working by pooling (see the Wait function used to temporize the loop). This can be improved if the producer cycle works through events.

14.3   Event-driven producer–consumer design pattern

The event-driven producer–consumer design pattern is similar to the producer consumer of Section 14.1.2, the main difference is in the use of an event structure within the producer loop to add new elements to the queue. It is not necessary to start the event-driven producer–consumer design pattern from scratch, it is possible to start working with this pattern by going to File>>New, then select VI>>From Template>>Frameworks>>Design   Pattern>>Producer/Consumer   Design Pattern (Events), see Figure 14.13.

After creating the design pattern, see Figure 14.14, it is observed that adding elements to the queue is performed through the event value change of the Boolean Enqueue Element button; however, it is possible to add multiple events to trigger the addition of new elements to the queue, or additional event cases can be created to have different elements to add to the queue. This design pattern intends that the user interface remains fluid and that none of the performed actions are lost.

So, it is possible to perform an update to the program of Section 14.2 to operate by events, so Figure 14.15 shows the modification to the block diagram to

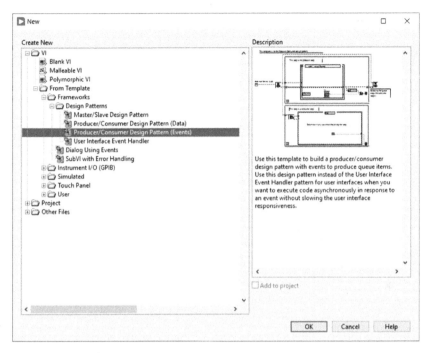

Figure 14.13   *Creation of an event-driven producer–consumer design pattern from a template*

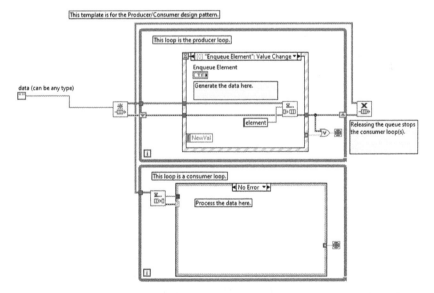

Figure 14.14   *Event-driven producer–consumer design pattern obtained from LabVIEW^{TM} templates*

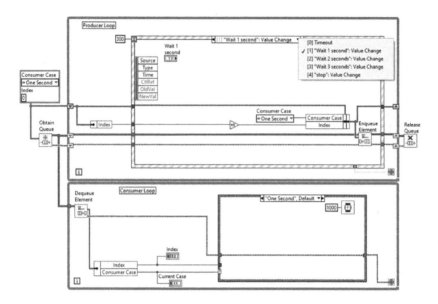

Figure 14.15   Block diagram of the modified producer–consumer demo

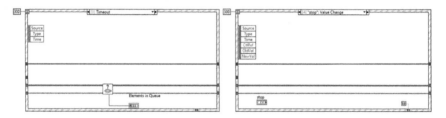

Figure 14.16   Code within Timeout event case and stop event case

implement the event-driven producer–consumer design pattern. From the Block Diagram, it can be appreciated that an event case has been created for each of the front panel buttons, in addition, there is a timeout case event that is executed every 300 milliseconds (if none event is detected). Each Wait event case sends a different enum constant and index in a cluster to the consumer loop using the Enqueue Element function.

On the other hand, the event case Timeout shows the number of elements in the queue, through the Get Queue Status function and the Elements in Queue indicator. The input data in the event case tunnels must be propagated to the next iterations. Finally, the event case Stop detects the value change in the stop Boolean button, sends a true to the stop terminal of the while loop (if it is pressed), subsequently the reference to the queue is destroyed, which causes an error in the consumer loop and stops the program. The Timeout event case and stop event case are shown in Figure 14.16.

14.4   Recommendations

- The producer–consumer design pattern is useful for applications that require data acquisition and processing at different rates.
- Use event-driven producer–consumer design pattern for a fluent user interface, avoid losing user actions (by pooling) or synchronize loops.
- Avoid processing information in the producer loop.
- Use a case structure within the consumer loop to manage all the possible states of your program.

Chapter 15

Preventing race conditions

Race conditions are common errors in parallel applications. These occur when the order in execution of events produces information loss due to a variable being written from different parts of the program. Therefore, this chapter explains race conditions and how to prevent them. Additionally, the use of functional global variables to avoid race conditions is presented, in addition, practical examples for their use are explained.

15.1 What are race conditions?

A race condition is a common problem in concurrent programming languages. It occurs when a variable is written in different parts of the code simultaneously, leaving the variable with another value from expected [24]. For example, Figure 15.1 shows two algorithms that can generate a race condition. Let us say that the value of X is 10 and the Algorithm 1 starts executing first and reads the value of X, then algorithm two reads the value of X. The next step for Algorithm 1 is to compute X = X + 5 leaving X with a value of 15, then Algorithm 2 will compute X = X + 2, but for Algorithm 2 the value of X is still 10 since it is the value that it read on its previous state, so the value of X for Algorithm 2 will be 12. The last step for Algorithm 1 is to write the value of X and for this algorithm is 15, then the algorithm will overwrite the previous value and set it to 12. This is where the problem of race condition happens, because the expected value of X after executing both algorithms is 17, but it ended up being 12 instead due to the parallel execution of both algorithms.

When programming in LabVIEW^{TM}, there are many ways where race conditions can occur, generating errors in the program. Most of the time they occur when using local or global variables as shown in Figure 15.2, where the example from Figure 15.1 is programmed in LabVIEW^{TM} running 1,000 times each algorithm using local variables. As you can see on the front panel, the value of X is 6,305 while the expected value for X was 7,000 for that number of executions. This happens because sometimes one algorithm reads the value of X before the other algorithm finishes writing the value of X, this is like ignoring the computation of X in the iteration where it happened and this is why the value of X is always less than 7,000.

Another common way where race conditions occur is while using global variables. These variables work similarly to local variables, but they can be used

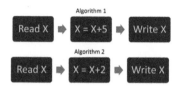

Figure 15.1   Race condition between two algorithms

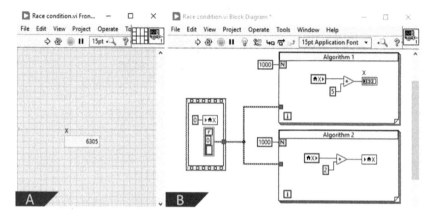

Figure 15.2   Race condition between two For Loops on LabVIEW^{TM}. (A) Front
panel and (B) block diagram

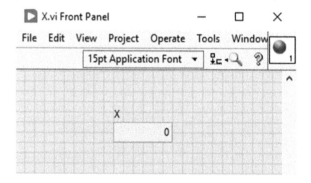

Figure 15.3   X Global variable window

across different VIs. To create a global variable, go to File>New... and on the
"New" window select the folder called "Other Files" then select "Global
Variable" and click the "OK" button. This will open a front panel like a window as
in Figure 15.3, this window does not have a block diagram, it is used to place a
control or indicator that will be used as the global variable. After the global variable
is created and saved, this file can be dragged into another VI and used in a similar

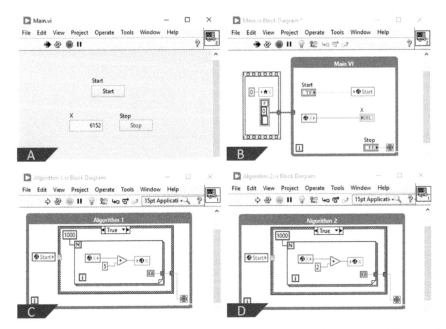

Figure 15.4   Race condition between two Vis. (A) Main VI front panel, (B) main VI block diagram, (C) Algorithm 1 block diagram, and (D) Algorithm 2 block diagram

way as the local variables, the difference is that the value of this global variable can be updated from different VIs. For example, in Figure 15.4 two global variables are used on different VIs. These VIs generate the same race condition as in Figure 15.1, but execute the algorithms from different VIs. The main VI is used to monitor the value of the X global variable and start Algorithms 1 and 2 simultaneously. Algorithms 1 and 2 execute 1,000 times when they receive a true value from the Start global variable and when the for loop finishes executing the VIs stop. As you can see from Figure 15.4A the value for X is different from 7,000 which was the expected value for this variable, but since race conditions also occur between these VIs, some values of X were ignored during the execution of the algorithms. Note that all the VIs need to be executed before pressing the Start button on the Main VI.

15.2   Preventing race conditions

Now that the concept of race condition is understood, it is important to have it in mind while programming. The best way to avoid race conditions is to write the variable from one part of the code only, for example the VI from Figure 15.2 can be modified as shown in Figure 15.5, where the two algorithms are now in one for loop and in order to do the operation or $X = X + 2$ it has to wait for the operation $X = X + 5$ to be finished. As you can see, this code will always give the same value

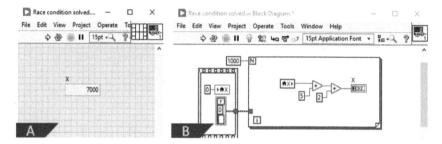

Figure 15.5   Race condition solved VI. (A) Front panel and (B) block diagram

for X when it is executed and the other code most times X had different values due
to the race conditions.

• Tip #23: One way to detect that the code has a race condition is to pay
attention when executing the code multiple times and some values change
running under the same conditions. Most times this behavior is due to race
conditions.

Sometimes the solution for race conditions cannot be solved, as in the example
from Figure 15.4, where one part of the code is forced to execute until the other part
finished its execution and writing the variable from just one part of the code. When
a variable needs to be modified from multiple parts of the code, race conditions can
be prevented using functional global variables, a design pattern explained in the
next section.

15.3   Functional global variables as prevention of race conditions

The functional global variable is a design pattern used to avoid race conditions
when a variable needs to be modified from multiple parts of the code or even from
different VIs. This design pattern is implemented as a subVI, it is used to retain data
between consecutive calls of this subVI. The functional global variable uses a while
loop or a for loop that only iterates once and it has an uninitialized shift-register.
This shift-register is used to retain data on the subVI (functional global variable) so
that the next time it is called from the main VI the functional global variable retains
the last value. Since subVIs have to wait to finish their execution in order to be
called again (non-reentrant VI) this ensures that the variable is being modified only
from one part of the code preventing race conditions.

The functional global variable design pattern is as shown in Figure 15.6. It
consists of the elements inside the error case structure. The action control is an enum
control, which in this case has two items "Write" and "Read". The case structure that

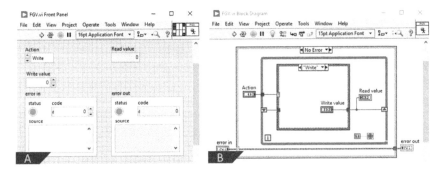

Figure 15.6   Functional global variable subVI. (A) Front panel and (B) block diagram

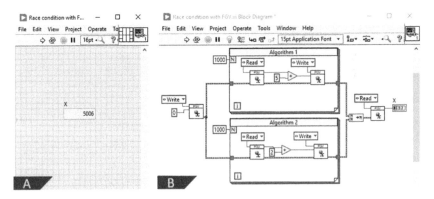

Figure 15.7   Wrong attempt to solve a race condition using functional global variable. (A) Front panel and (B) block diagram

is connected to the enum control has the "Write" case, which saves a new value into the shift register; and the "Read" case, which is used to send the value to the "Read value" indicator, this case has no elements inside it just connects the left tunnel from the shift-register with the right tunnel. The while loop has a shift-register uninitialized, it is important that the shift-register is not initialized because in this way when the functional global variable subVI is called again, the last value from the last execution will be stored in the shift-register.

The functional global variable can be modified to fulfill the needs of the application and it must be carefully used in order to avoid race conditions. For example, let us say that the VI from Figure 15.2 needs to be executed with both algorithms running on different for loops, this could be solved implementing a functional global variable, but using the functional global variable from Figure 15.6 will result in a race condition as shown in Figure 15.7, where the value of X is still not as expected due to race conditions while reading and writing the value on the functional global variable.

A valid approach to implement a functional global variable in this VI is to include the algorithms into the functional global variable a shown in Figure 15.8. In Figure 15.8(A), the structure of the functional global variable is shown, and the cases are shown in Figure 15.8(B). As you can see the cases included are one for the operations of Algorithm 1 and one for Algorithm 2, also a case to initialize the functional global variable is included.

These modifications make up for an easier implementation of the functional global variable on the main VI and a better way to prevent race conditions. The modified functional global variable is implemented on the VI as shown in Figure 15.9, as you can see on the functional global variable on the left is used to initialize the value and then the error clusters are used to force the execution of the algorithms to wait after the value is initialized, then Algorithms 1 and 2 execute 1,000 times and the error clusters are used again to force the last functional global

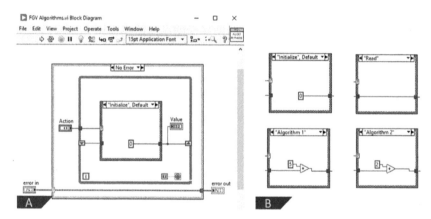

Figure 15.8   Modified functional global variable. (A) Block diagram and (B) functional global variable cases

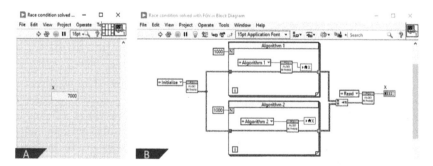

Figure 15.9   Race condition solved with functional global variable. (A) Front panel and (B) block diagram

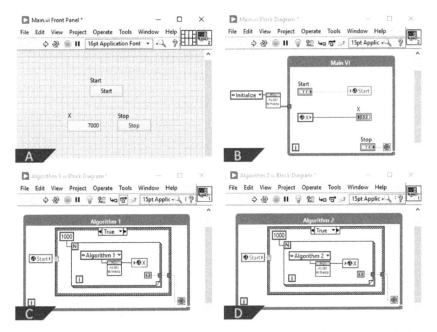

Figure 15.10   Race condition between two VIs solved with functional global variable. (A) Main VI front panel, (B) main VI block diagram, (C) Algorithm 1 block diagram, and (D) Algorithm 2 block diagram

variable to wait for these executions. The local variables in this case are used only to show the value of X.

The same functional global variable can be applied to programs that execute with multiple VIs as shown in Figure 15.10, where the functional global variable is initialized on the Main VI. On the other VIs, the functional global variable is called to execute Algorithm 1 or Algorithm 2 depending on the VI and since the functional global variable is a subVI it will not create a race condition. The global variables in this case are used only to read the value of X.

15.4   Race condition prevention examples

This section presents some examples of different VIs where race conditions can happen and how to prevent them. The first example is the VI from Figure 15.11, which the task is to create a copy of a text file before it is modified. The original file's content is "OriginalText" and should be saved into a new text file called "copy.txt". In this case there is a race condition, because in the way it is programmed, the file "original.txt" can be modified before the copy is created, resulting in a copy with the new data of the "original.txt", when the intention is to create the copy before modifying it. Another possible result is that the file "copy.txt" is created as a blank file.

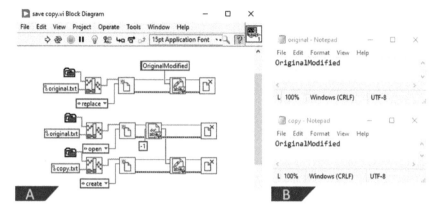

Figure 15.11   Save file VI with race condition. (A) Block diagram and (B) original.txt file and copy.txt file

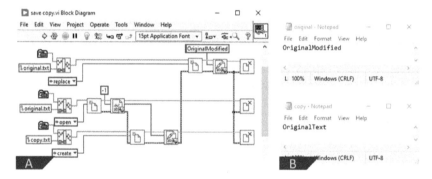

Figure 15.12   Save file VI without race condition. (A) Block diagram and (B) original.txt file and copy.txt file

This is a common race condition in parallel (concurrent) programming and it can be easily avoided by forcing the order of execution with data flow as shown in Figure 15.12. As you can see, the order of execution is controlled with the error clusters, it starts from the "Open/Create/Replace File" function at the left, then the data from the file "original.txt" is read and sent to the "Write to Text File" function, which will save the data in a newly created file called "copy.txt", then the file "original.txt" will be replaced with the new data. Using the error cluster ensures that the execution order is as intended because there is no way to know which step will execute first in the other form.

Chapter 16
Advanced use of software resources

The way in which the information is written in a file depends on the application, for example, it is not the same to write information referring to text that the user is providing as part of a form than writing the information that is being acquired from data acquisition system (DAQ), in this sense, you need to know efficient ways to work with this kind of information. Therefore, this chapter explains the different types of available files, how to create multichannel files for acquisition tasks, and functions for using relative paths. Other functions to implement sophisticated solutions with files will be explored.

16.1   Types of files

There are many different types of files to use in LabVIEW^{TM}. In Chapter 7, the ASCII Files were used for datalog, however, there are binary files that are files optimized for writing information from data acquisition systems. Next will be listed different kinds of files with their respective advantages.

16.1.1   ASCII files

This kind of file is used to interchange information between different programs. Several database programs accept ASCII files (Excel, Access, SQL, Oracle, etc.); therefore, a good use for these types of files is to exchange information or create human-readable files. ASCII files have the advantage of being able to be formatted in such a way that they can be interpreted in other programs by delimited file extensions such as CSV or TXT extensions [25].

16.1.2   Binary files

These files are used for high-speed data acquisition systems to save information (e.g. from analog input channel) into the file. There is not a straightforward way to read a binary file, if you open this file from a text editor, you will only see different kinds of symbols without any particular meaning for a human being. So, it is important to know how the binary file was written, the data types, and codification [26].

16.1.3   TDMS files

This is a structured binary file from National Instruments^{TM}, is optimized and provides functions to save information from multiple channels, and has properties about the saved data [27]. Use this kind of file to save information from high-speed data acquisition systems.

16.2 Working with relative paths

A path is a hierarchical directory with references to other computer files or other directories. The path is made by a Workspace and the Base Name of the file, for example, the following path C:\User\Project\ExamplePath.vi have "C:\Users\Project\" as Workspace and ExamplePath.vi as Base Name. In graphical user operative systems (as Windows) it is common to use the term "Folder" as a friendly term for directories.

LabVIEW^TM has several functions that allow users to define their own paths, e.g. to save a new file in a custom or relative location (relative to the application or a specific folder), leaving aside hard coding paths that cannot be changed runtime. In Section 7.1, Table 7.3, were explained functions to work with paths, as Build Path, Application Directory, and Path Constant; however, there are additional functions to work with relative paths, and other functions recommended for developing mode as in Table 16.1.

You can use these functions to automatically obtain a specific path Workspace and add a Base Name. Figure 16.1 shows the use of Get System Directory to create the path to a Measurement.csv file within the Public Documents folder of a PC.

Table 16.1   Functions to work with relative and specified paths

Function	Description	Location
Recommended functions for Runtime		
Application Directory.vi	Obtains the path of the application, if it is not an application, obtain the path of the project, if it is not a project, obtain the path of the main VI.	Functions>>Programming >>File I/O
Get System Directory.vi	Return standard system directories for different operating systems (e.g. Home, Desktop, or Documents)	Functions>>Programming >>File I/O
Recommended functions for Developing Mode		
Default Directory	Returns the path to the Default Directory (this path can be modified in tools>>options>>paths)	Functions>>Programming >>File I/O
Temporary Directory	Returns the path to the Temporary Directory (this path can be modified in tools>> options>>paths)	Functions>>Programming >>File I/O

Figure 16.1   Using Get System Directory to automatically obtain the Public Documents folder in a computer with Windows Operative System

Table 16.2   List of available system directories from the Get System Directory function

1. User Home	2. Public Application Data
3. User Desktop	4. Public Preferences
5. User Documents	6. System Core Libraries
7. User Application Data	8. System Installed Libraries
9. User Preferences	10. Application Files
11. User Temporary	12. Boot Volume Root
13. Public Documents	14. Public Cache

Table 16.2 contains the complete list of possible directories to be created using the Get System Directory Function. Additional information to this function is available in the LabVIEW^{TM} Help.

16.3   Binary files

16.3.1   *Writing two-channels binary files*

Binary files are a particular type of files, which are not (directly) human-readable, however, they are highly used with high-speed data acquisition systems to store measurement information. Binary files require fewer bits to represent numbers than ASCII files and allow random access to the file. However, a disadvantage of binary files is that it is needed to know in advance how it was encoded and the data types that are being used. Without this information, it is difficult to access the stored data coherently.

Table 16.3 shows functions commonly used with binary files, functions for reading, writing, and getting the file size, these functions can be accessed from Functions>>Programming>>File I/O.

The functions as Open/Create/Replace File, Build Path, or Close File are the same for binary files or ASCII files (see Table 7.3 of Section 7.1); however, the functions to read or write binary files are different. For binary files, it is important to consider how the information is structured/encoded, for example, Figure 16.2 shows the block diagram to save two waveforms, one for a sine signal and the other for a cosine signal, notice that there is no special notation in the file, and for each iteration of the for loop, the cosine value is written followed by the sine value.

Table 16.3   Functions to read, write, and get the file size of a binary file

Function	Description
Write to Binary File	Writes binary information to a file. The required input is "data"; however, it is recommended to wire the file reference when it is used within a loop. If no reference is wired, the function shows a file dialog box.
Read from Binary File	Reads binary information to a file. It is recommended to wire the data type input, and reference. If no reference is wired, the function shows a file dialog box.
Get File Size	Returns the number of bytes in a file.

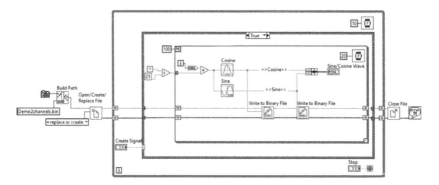

Figure 16.2   Block diagram of a program that saves two waveforms (sine/cosine) in a binary file

Table 16.4   Bytes size in disk for commonly used numeric data types in measurement tasks

Data type	Bytes in disk
I8	1
I16	2
I32	4
I64	8
Double	8
Extended double precisión	16

To read the file, it is necessary to know the size in bytes for each data type. For example, the file in Figure 16.2 stores 200 double numbers, of which 100 numbers represent the sine waveform and 100 numbers represent the cosine waveform, if each double number measures 8 bytes (64- bits), the number of bytes inside the file will be 1,600 bytes (200 × 8 = 1,600). Table 16.4 shows the size in bytes for different numeric data types typically used in measurement tasks.

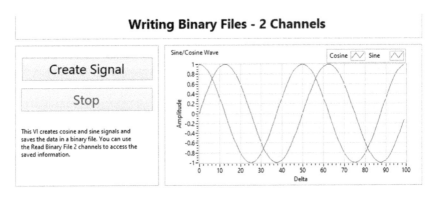

Writing Binary Files - 2 Channels

Figure 16.3   Front panel of the Write Binary File 2 channels.vi

In Figure 16.3, you can see the front panel/user interface corresponding to the code presented in the block diagram of Figure 16.2. When running the program and the Create Signal button is pressed, the VI display both the sine waveform and the cosine waveform on the Sine/Cosine Wave chart.

16.3.2   Reading two-channels binary files

Use the Writing Binary Files – two Channels to create the demo2channels.bin multichannel file, writing binary files is a typical task in acquisition systems, and this file can be read using the block diagram of Figure 16.4. A complete explanation of the block diagram is presented after a few recommendations.

Before starting the reading of any binary file, it is necessary to have the following information:

1. The data type of the data to read from the file.
2. The number of elements to read from the file.
3. The structure of the information (number of channels, how were saved the information of the channels).

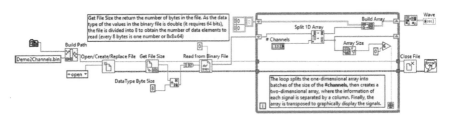

Figure 16.4   Block diagram to read a two-channel binary file, the program calculates the number of elements to read and separate the two channels by odd and pair value position within the file

As mentioned in Section 16.1, Types of files, binary files are commonly used in tasks that require high-speed DAQ, to save information from one or more channels. Therefore, for these cases, the information to be written within the binary file is numeric. In Table 16.4, you will find the different numeric data types typically used in measurement tasks, as well as the required number of bytes for each of them. This information is used to obtain the number of data elements to read within a file.

To read the file information, start by opening the file from an application folder, as shown in Figure 16.5.

The file reference is passed to the Get File Size function, which returns the size of the file in bytes. To determine the number of elements that will be read from the file, it is necessary to divide the number of bytes in the file by the bytes of the element data type to read, in this case, since the data type to read is double, the file size is divided by eight. If the data type had been a 32-bit integer, it must be divided by four. You can use Table 16.4 as a reference to get the size in bytes for each data type. The number of elements to read is wired to the count input of the Read from Binary File function and a constant of the kind of data type to read is wired to the data type input, as seen in Figure 16.6. The output of Read from Binary File is an array of double numbers with all the data stored in the binary file.

To split the signal information from different channels, knowing how the file was written is necessary. For this case, it is known that the binary file contains two waveforms (two channels), and the data is interspersed between the information of

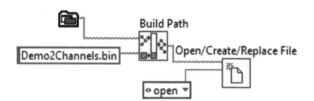

Figure 16.5   Opening the Demo2Channels.bin file created in Section 16.3.1 (note that the low-level functions to open binary files are the same as ASCII files)

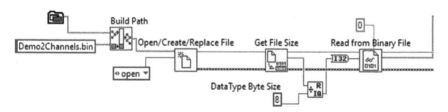

Figure 16.6   Obtaining an array with all the signals information from Demo2Channels.bin. At this point, the data from cosine and sine signals is mixed

the cosine wave and the information of the sine wave (see Figure 16.2, the block diagram of write binary files – two channels). Therefore, each sample of the waveform can be obtained in batches of the size of the number of channels (for this case batches of two) using the function Split 1D Array, and then build an array of two dimensions where each column represents the information of a different channel. Finally, the two-dimensional array is transposed to arrange each channel by row, and the data can be graphed in the wave indicator. The block diagram to graphically obtain the signal information from the data in the binary file is shown in Figure 16.7.

After running the block diagram of Figure 16.4, the signals from the binary file are shown in the Front Panel of Figure 16.8, it can be observed how the cosine and sine waveforms are obtained. The only input needed from the user is the # Channels. So the

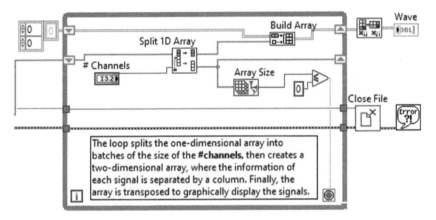

Figure 16.7   This loop creates a two-dimensional array where each column represents a different channel, then the array is transposed to arrange the channels by row and to send the signal information to the wave graph indicator

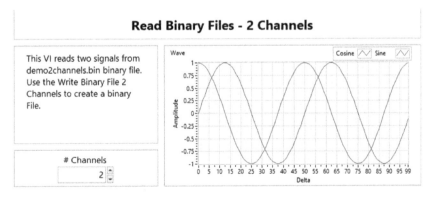

Figure 16.8   Front panel of the read binary files – two channels

current program can be adapted to read more channels from the same file; however, proper modifications must be performed to the program to write binary files.

16.4   Working with files and folders

In addition to working with functions to write or read files, LabVIEW^{TM} has advanced functions that can copy files, erase the file or move the file, and other functions or VIs that allow knowing file properties, creating folders, or obtaining file extensions. To access these functions you have to access **Programming >>Fil I/O>>Adv File Funcs** from the functions palette, where you will find the following functions to work with files:

It is possible to use the **Advance File functions** to create folders into a directory automatically. For example, if a program needs to create three folders, it is possible to use a for loop to repeat the **Create Folder** function three times and

Table 16.5   Functions to move, copy, delete, obtain properties or data of files and folders

Function/VI	Description
Move	Moves a File or Directory from one path to another
Copy	Copies the File or Folder without losing the original File/Folder
Delete	Deletes a File or Folder
File/Directory Info	Provides information of the File or Directory such as Size or last modification date
Create Folder	Creates a New Folder in the specified path
List Folder	Returns two string arrays, one with the list of folders and the other with the list of files (within the folder, not subfolders). This function can also be used to search files or folders wiring the input "Pattern"
Check if File or Folder Exists.vi	Checks if a file or folder exists. This VI is helpful to ask the user if he wants to replace a file or folder before performing the action
Get File Extension.vi	Gets the file extension

use the iteration terminal to distinguish between folders. However, this operation can cause an error if the folder already exists, so it is recommended to use the Check if File or Folder Exists.vi before creating a folder. The Create Folder functions can be used if the folder does not exist. Figure 16.9 can be appreciated the block diagram of the proposed code.

On the other hand, if the folder exists, the program must warn that the folder or folders already exist and stop the for loop immediately, with this aim, a One Button Dialog is used within the True case, see Figure 16.10.

Additionally, it is possible to obtain further information about all the files and folders within a Folder. For example, in Figure 16.11 shown a block diagram to get information from C:\Using Folder Functions (the same folder of Figure 16.9), the block diagram uses File Directory Info and List Folder functions. Suppose the input path to File/Directory Info corresponds to a directory. In that case, the function returns the Size as the number of elements within it, and returns True to the directory terminal. If the path corresponds to a file, File/Directory Info gives the number of bytes of the file. It is possible to obtain the last modification date of the file or folder using the File directory Info. In addition, the List Folder function brings two arrays, one with a list of filenames and another with a list of folder names. For Figure 16.11, only a list of Folder Names is needed. Another way to see the number of folders in a directory is using the array size function to the Array Folder Names, see Figure 16.11.

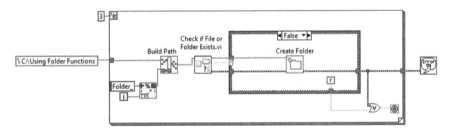

Figure 16.9   Block diagram to create three folders in C:\Using FolderFunctions, the new folders are made only when the Folder_#, does not exist

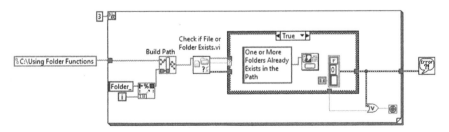

Figure 16.10   Block diagram that checks if a folder already exists. In a true case, the program warns the user and stop the for loop

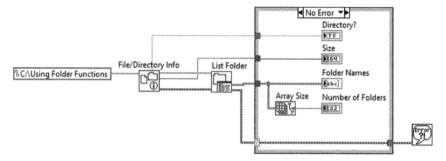

Figure 16.11   Using File/Directory info and list folder functions to obtain information from a directory

Figure 16.12   Front panel that shows information from the directory as Folder Names, Number of folders within the directory, and a Boolean indicator to see if the selected path is a directory or a path

The front panel with the indicators of Figure 16.11 can be seen in Figure 16.12; note how all the folder names are listed, and the output Size and Number of folders are the same as this directory only have folders within it.

In the same way, it is possible to move, copy, or delete a file. With this aim, the Example.txt file will be created inside C:\Using Folder Functions\Folder_0. Once created, the Copy function copies the file to the C:\Using Folder Functions\ Folder_1 directory. The block diagram of Figure 16.13 shows the implementation of the code that programmatically allows copying from one folder to another. The program first checks the existence of the Example.txt file and the C:\Using Folder Functions\Folder_1 destination directory.

Suppose one of the paths C:\Using Folder Functions\Folder_0\Example.txt or C:\Using Folder Functions\Folder_1 do not exist, in that case the program shows a One Button Dialog message indicating the "Warning" (it is not correctly a warning as it is not part of an error cluster, it is only a warning message), see Figure 16.14.

To finish this chapter, it is recommended to perform some modifications to the program of Figures 16.13 and 16.14 to move and delete files. These functions are

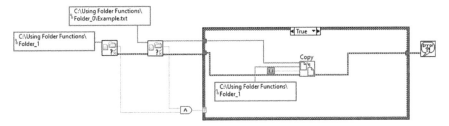

Figure 16.13   Using the copy function to copy Example.txt from Folder_0 to
Folder_1. If the file already exists, it is replaced (see the true
constant input to Copy Function)

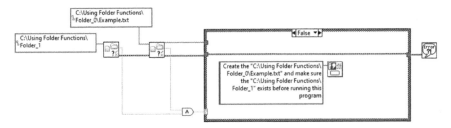

Figure 16.14   If one of the paths do not exist a one button message is shown to
the user

similar to the copy file function, and it is an excellent way to put what you have
seen up to this point into practice.

16.5   Recommendations to work with files and folders

- Avoid working with hardcode paths; use relative paths instead. Hardcode paths
  are different from one computer to another or between different operative
  systems.
- If the program performs Highs-Speed digital acquisition, consider using binary
  files or TDMS Files; otherwise, use text files. Text files are easy to read and
  allow sharing information with other programs.

Use the function Check if File or Folder Exists before creating or replacing a
file or moving a file from one location to another.

Chapter 17

Real-time programming

Several applications require dedicated systems for their implementation. Some examples are aerospace systems, specialized laboratories, or acquisition and processing systems for medical applications [28]. In this sense, a nondedicated system is not the best option to solve these tasks. In this sense, industrial systems such as CompactRIO^{TM} allow solutions completely dedicated to the specific function. This chapter introduces the use of these systems, which, together with the previously studied tools, will help the developer implement sophisticated solutions.

17.1 CompactRIO^{TM} for industrial systems

The real-time module needs to be installed to create real-time applications using the CompactRIO^{TM} systems. This module helps with the creation of VIs that are executed in embedded hardware such as CompactRIO^{TM}. The difference between using the real-time module with embedded hardware and a normal VI on a computer using hardware like myDAQ^{TM} is that systems like CompactRIO^{TM} take advantage of the real-time operating system to guarantee reliability and precise temporization, which is something that cannot be ensured on a VI running on a computer which is also executing multiple tasks at the same time as the VI is being executed [29].

In order to create a real-time application on embedded hardware as the CompactRIO^{TM}, other modules need to be installed on the computer before connecting the CompactRIO^{TM}. All the necessary software are LabVIEW^{TM}, LabVIEW^{TM} Real-Time, LabVIEW^{TM} FPGA, and the CompactRIO^{TM} device drivers. It is recommended to install the software in the mentioned order to avoid communication problems.

For the rest of the chapter, the CompactRIO^{TM} NI cRIO-9063 (see Figure 17.1(A)) and the modules NI 9263, NI 9201, and NI 9403 (see Figure 17.1 (B)) will be used. The CompactRIO^{TM} NI cRIO-9063 controller has a CPU Dual-core at 667 MHz, 256 MB of DRAM, 512 MB of storage, a FPGA Zynq-7020, and four module slots. It works with a power supply between 9 and 30 V and can communicate through the USB device port or the RJ-45 Gigabit Ethernet port. The module NI 9263 (the first slot from left to right) is a voltage output module with ±10 V analog output voltage range. The module NI 9201 (the module on the second slot) is an analog voltage input module that supports ±10 V input voltage range. The module NI 9403 (the module on the third slot) is a bidirectional digital input/output module with 32 channels that work at 7 microseconds.

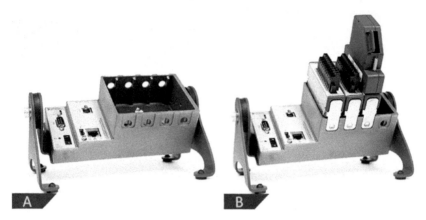

Figure 17.1   (A) CompactRIO^{TM} NI cRIO-9063 and (B) CompactRIO^{TM} NI cRIO-9063 with modules NI 9263, NI 9201, and NI 9403

17.1.1   Installing software on CompactRIO^{TM} system

After installing the necessary software on the computer, it is also necessary to install software on the CompactRIO^{TM}. This is done using the NI MAX^{TM} software installed on the computer with the LabVIEW^{TM} package. After opening the NI MAX^{TM}, open the remote systems tab. This will load the NI cRIO-9063 (make sure that the system is powered and connected to the computer), open the NI cRIO-9063 tab, select software, and click on the Add/Remove Software button at the top of the window, as shown in Figure 17.2.

Figure 17.2   NI cRIO-9063 on NI MAX^{TM}

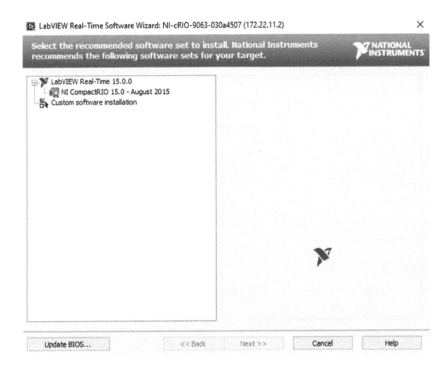

Figure 17.3   LabVIEW^{TM} Real-Time Software Wizard

After clicking the Add/Remove Software button, the LabVIEW^{TM} Real-Time Software Wizard window will open, as shown in Figure 17.3. On this window select the recommended software set, which in this case is the NI CompactRIO^{TM} 15.0 – August 2015, then click the next button, and a list with the recommended features selected will appear, click next again, and a list of the features to be installed will appear, click next again, and the installation of the software on the NI cRIO-9063 will start, once the installation finishes the message "Your LabVIEW Real-Time" target has been updated successfully will appear and the CompactRIO^{TM} NI cRIO-9063 is ready to use with LabVIEW^{TM}.

17.1.2   Creating a real-time project on the CompactRIO^{TM}

To work with the CompactRIO^{TM}, a new LabVIEW^{TM} project must be created, from this project, the VIs will be uploaded to the CompactRIO^{TM}, and the computer can be used as a Human Machine Interface to control the VIs, which are executing on the CompactRIO^{TM}. Once a new project is created, right click on the Project tab and select New>Targets and Devices... this will open the window as shown in Figure 17.4(A), this window is used to indicate which target or device is going to be used. In this case, the selected folder is the Real-Time CompactRIO^{TM} which will find any CompactRIO^{TM} target connected. After selecting the NI-cRIO-9063 a new window to select the RIO programming mode

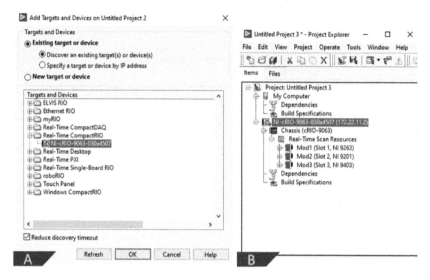

Figure 17.4   (A) Add target to project window and (B) project with NI cRIO-9063

will appear, for this case Scan Interface will be selected (LabVIEW^{TM} FPGA Interface will be used later in this chapter). After clicking continue, the NI-cRIO-9063 target will appear on the project explorer, as shown in Figure 17.4(B). This new tab includes the Chassis, where the modules can be found under the Real-time Scan Resources. Each module tab contains a variable for each of its channels.

17.1.3   Real-time programming on CompactRIO^{TM}

The first step to start programming with the CompactRIO^{TM} is to start the connection between the computer and the target on the project by right clicking on the NI-cRIO-9063 tab and selecting Connect. After doing this, a deployment progress window will appear, and the message "Deployment completed successfully" will be shown on the deployment status. Once the deployment is completed, the dark green led on the NI-cRIO-9063 icon tab will turn light green.

The next step is to create the VI on the target. This is done by right clicking on the NI-cRIO-9063 tab and selecting New>VI. This will create a new VI under the target tab. This VI can be programmed as a normal VI, with the difference that this VI will be executed on the CompactRIO^{TM}, and it can use the channels of each module as variables. Figure 17.5(A) shows the project explorer with a VI called Analog Read on the NI-cRIO-9063 tab, and this VI is an example of how the CompactRIO^{TM} can be used to perform analog voltage measurements. Figure 17.5 (B) shows the front panel of this VI, where the waveform chart is used to display the voltage measurement, and the Count(uSec) controller is used to control the measurement sampling in microseconds. Figure 17.5(C) shows the block diagram of the VI, where the orange rectangle with the AI1 text is the variable for channel 1 of the NI 9201 module, this variable is added to the block diagram by dragging it

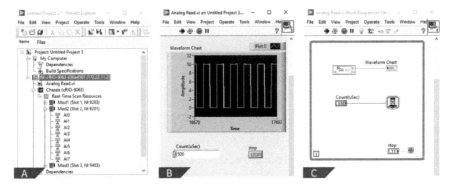

Figure 17.5   Analog read on real-time target. (A) Project explorer, (B) front panel, and (C) block diagram

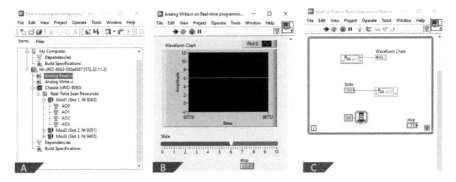

Figure 17.6   Analog write on real-time target. (A) Project explorer, (B) front panel, and (C) block diagram

from the project explorer on the Mod2 tab selecting AI1. The function on the blue square in the middle to the right is the wait function for real-time targets; it is found on Functions palette>Real-Time>RT Timing. This function works similar to the Wait(ms) function but with three different counter units (Ticks, microseconds, and milliseconds). Note that the VI from Figure 17.5 is running on the CompacRIO 9063 and it is running at faster run-time that a computer would and with better timing precision. The signal being measured is a squared signal with 50% of duty cycle ranging from 0 to 10 volts generated with a function generator connected to channel 1 of the NI 9201 module.

The use of the other modules on the CompactRIO™ is pretty similar; for example, Figure 17.6 shows an example of the use of the module NI 9263 for analog write. The slide on the front panel is used to modify the output voltage from 0 to 10 volts and this voltage is read using the analog input and shown on the waveform chart. The block diagram shows the AO0 variable from module 1, which sets the output voltage depending on the value of the slide. The AI1 variable reads the voltage value and displays it on the waveform chart. Physically, the channel output 0 of the NI 9263 module is connected to channel input 1 of the NI 9201 module.

The previous examples show how an input or output from the NI 9263 and NI 9201 modules can be dragged from the project into the block diagram to read or write voltage values on the respective modules. The module NI 9403, a digital input/output module, works similarly, with the difference that the inputs and outputs of each channel must be defined from the module properties. This is done by right clicking on the Mod3 tab (which is the NI 9403 module) and selecting properties, this will open the module configuration (see Figure 17.7), where all the channels from the NI 9403 module can be defined as input or output.

Once the NI 9403 module channels are defined, it is ready to be used on the block diagram. Figure 17.8 shows an example where channel 1 is used as an output and channel 0 as an input. A Switch is connected to DIO1 to control the output value of channel 1 and a LED is connected to DIO0 to read the value of channel 0. Physically, channel 0 and channel 1 are connected, so when the switch is turned on the LED is also turned on.

The previous VIs are simple examples of how real-time programming is performed on the CompactRIO^{TM}. Real-time systems can be used to create applications for different areas like testing, monitoring, control, etc. Real-time systems are capable of faster run-times, more reliability, and more precise temporization than a VI being executed on a computer. But, although real-time systems are faster than computers, there is another option for programming at faster execution times and

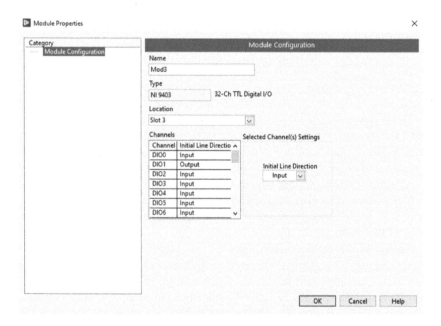

Figure 17.7   NI 9403 module properties

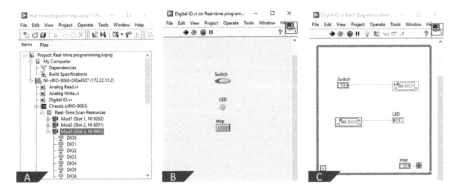

Figure 17.8 Digital input/output on real-time target. (A) Project explorer, (B) front panel, and (C) block diagram

other advantages. This other programming mode is called LabVIEW™ FPGA interface mode.

17.1.4 FPGA programming on CompactRIO™

FPGA stands for field programmable gate array, which basically are programmable logic blocks interconnected to perform complex combinational functions or simple logic functions such as AND, OR, NOT, XOR, etc. [30]. The CompactRIO™ 9063 has an FPGA embedded, and it is programmed using the LabVIEW™ FPGA Module. This is done by compiling the VI code into the instructions to program the FPGA embedded in the CompactRIO™.

Before starting to program on FPGA, it is important to know the differences between creating a program on FPGA mode and a VI running on real-time or the computer. The main difference can be explained using the example of Figure 17.9, this VI has four while loops that perform simple operations, normally can be said that these while loops are executed in parallel, but this is not 100% true, internally the processor is performing one task at a time for each while loop to simulate parallel execution. On the other hand, The FPGA would truly perform a parallel execution between loops running in parallel since each loop is compiled into a separated logic circuit. Parallel execution is one of the main advantages of the FPGAs. Another advantage is the execution speed, since the VI is compiled into a logic circuit, it can run at high speeds. For example, comparing them with micro-controllers which can achieve speeds of 10 MHz, the FPGAs can reach speeds of 100 MHz.

To use the FPGA of the CompactRIO™, the LabVIEW™ FPGA Interface programming mode must be selected when adding the CompactRIO™ 9063 to the project. Once this programming mode is selected, the NI-cRIO-9063 tab will appear on the project with a few differences from the Scan Interface mode, as shown in Figure 17.10. The main difference is the FPGA Target tab, which is where the VIs that will be compiled into the FPGA mode will be placed.

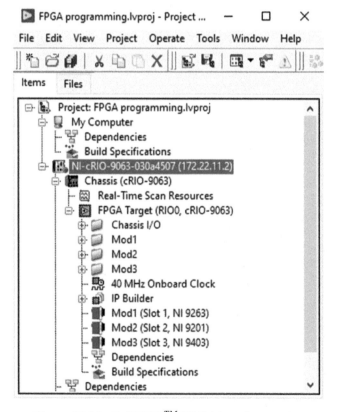

Figure 17.9   *While loops running in parallel*

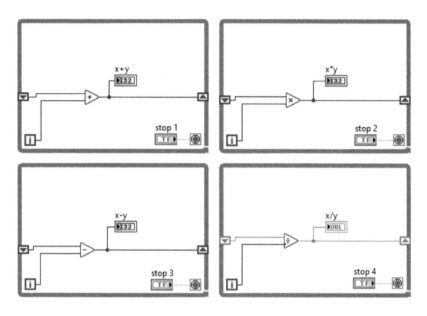

Figure 17.10   *LabVIEW^{TM} FPGA interface project*

Figure 17.11 shows an example of analog write and read similar to the one shown in Figure 17.6, but programmed in the FPGA interface mode. Figure 17.11 (A) shows the LabVIEW^{TM} project where the FPGA target contains the Analog Read-Write FPGA VI, which is the VI created to read and write analog signals into the corresponding modules at the FPGA level. The NI-cRIO-9063 tab contains the RT user interface VI, a VI on the real-time level used to monitor the controls and indicators on the Analog Read-Write FPGA VI. Figure 17.11(B) shows the front panel of the RT user interface VI, which contains a waveform chart to display the analog signal read, a slide to send the output voltage value to the VI on the FPGA level and a stop button which is used to stop this VI and stop the VI on the FPGA level.

Figure 17.11(C) shows the RT user interface block diagram, this VI is on the real-time level and communicates with the VI on the FPGA level. This VI contains three functions used to communicate with the VI on the FPGA level, these

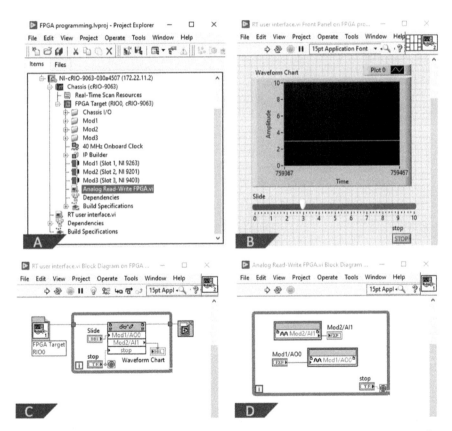

Figure 17.11   Analog Read-Write. (A) FPGA project, (B) real-time user interface front panel, (C) real-time user interface block diagram, and (D) analog read-write VI on FPGA

functions are found on **Functions palette>FPGA interface**. The first function to the left is the **Open FPGA VI Reference**, which opens a reference to the **FPGA VI** specified, to select the **FPGA VI** right-click on the function, then on **Configure Open FPGA VI Reference …** and on the new window select the **FPGA VI**. The next function inside the while loop is the **Read/Write Control**, which is used to write values from the slide to the **Mod1/AO0 control**, which is a control on the **FPGA VI**, it also reads the values from the **Mod2/A1 indicator** from the **FPGA VI** and shows them on the **Waveform Chart**. Finally, the **stop control** stops the **RT user interface VI** and sends the signal to the stop control on **the FPGA level VI** to stop this VI too. At the right of the block diagram, there is the **Close FPGA VI Reference** function that closes the reference to the **FPGA VI** and resets it. Figure 17.11(D) shows the **Analog Read-Write FPGA VI**, a simple VI that writes the voltage output on the **Mod1/AO0** and reads the voltage input on the **Mod2/AI1**. In order to load this VI into the **CompactRIO^{TM}**, it must be compiled,

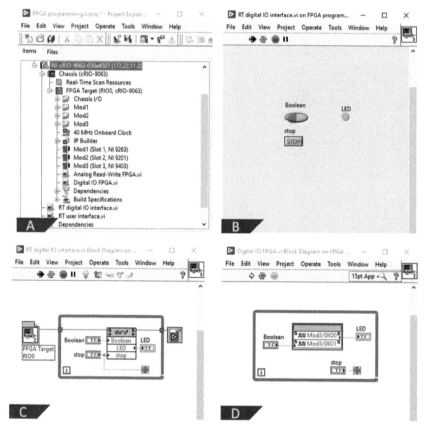

Figure 17.12   Digital input-output. (A) FPGA project, (B) real-time user interface front panel, (C) real-time user interface block diagram, and (D) digital input-output VI on FPGA

this is done by pressing the run button on the front panel or block diagram of the FPGA VI, then a new window will appear, select "Use the local compile server", this will open a window that will generate intermediate files, once it finishes loading a new window the compilation status will appear, this process may take a while depending on the computer used to compile the VI, once the compilation process finishes, the VI will start running. It can be stopped, and it will start running again when called by the VI on the real-time level. Note: The channel AO0 and AI1 are physically connected through a wire on the CompactRIO™.

The use of the digital inputs and outputs is similar to the example in Figure 17.11, the digital channels can be dragged into the block diagram of the VI at the FPGA level in order to be used as inputs or outputs. Figure 17.12 shows an example of digital write and digital read on the FPGA level using the module NI 9403. Figure 17.12(A) shows the project explorer with the Digital IO FPGA VI on the FPGA level and the RT digital IO interface VI on the real-time level. Figure 17.12(B) shows the front panel of the RT digital IO interface VI, which is the VI on the real-time level used to communicate with the VI on the FPGA level. Figure 17.12(C) shows the block diagram of the RT digital IO interface VI, which includes the Open FPGA VI Reference for the Digital IO FPGA VI, the Read/Write Control for the Boolean control, the LED indicator, and the Close FPGA VI Reference. Figure 17.12(D) shows the block diagram of the Digital IO FPGA VI.

The shown projects in Figures 17.11 and 17.12 are simple examples of how the CompactRIO™ is used at real-time and FPGA levels, respectively, and how VIs on each level can share information between them. The next section shows a more complex example of how to take advantage of the FPGA to measure signals at higher frequencies.

17.2   An application example with CompactRIO™

This section presents an example of how the CompacRIO can be used at the real-time and FPGA levels to read signals at high frequency, process the signals, and send the information between VIs. This project consists of a program to determine a motor's angular position while it is rotating at ten revolutions per second. The motor has a sensor that generates a pulse for each motor rotation. The angular position is determined by generating a pulse train with a VI on the FPGA level using the digital IO module, the number of pulses generated by the pulse train on a motor rotation is used in relation to the number of pulses generated at the moment of calculating the angular position. Suppose the pulse train generated 100 pulses in a rotation, and at the angle calculation instant, the pulse count was at 55. In that case, the angular position of the motor at that exact moment is 198 degrees. Figure 17.13 represents the pulse train signal and the motor pulse.

Figure 17.14 shows the project explorer. Here can be seen the User Interface VI at the real-time level, the Data acquisition FPGA VI at the FPGA level, a Data control, a FIFO called Data to store the data acquired, and the modules of the CompactRIO™.

Figure 17.13   Pulse train generated by the CompactRIO^{TM} at FPGA level and motor pulse signal generated by a sensor for each motor rotation

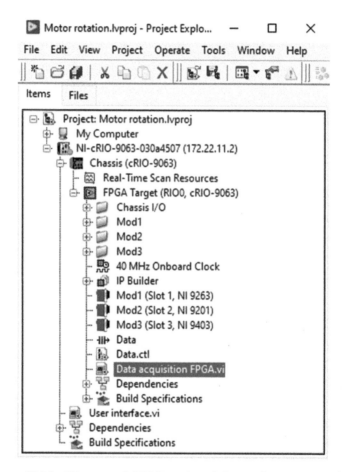

Figure 17.14   VIs, control, FIFO, and modules on the project explorer

Figure 17.15 shows the User Interface VI, which is the VI at a real-time level. The front panel contains the Pulse train (Hz) control to modify the frequency of the pulse train, the Pulses indicator displays the number of pulses counted at that exact moment, the Motor angle (degrees) indicator displays the angular position calculated at that exact moment, the Pulses per rotation indicator displays the number of

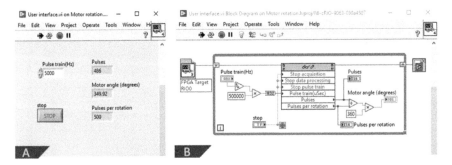

Figure 17.15   *User interface VI to communicate with the VI at the FPGA level. (A)*
Front panel and (B) block diagram

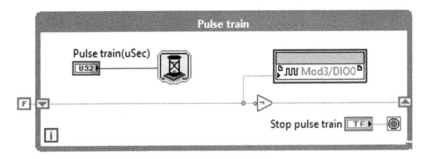

Figure 17.16   *Pulse train while loop from the Data acquisition FPGA VI, this*
while loop generate a squared signal through the Mod3/
DIO0 channel

pulses counted, and the Stop control stops the current VI and sends the signal to the
VI on the FPGA level to stop. The block diagram makes the communication with the
VI on the FPGA level using the Open FPGA VI Reference, then inside the while
loop, the value of the Pulse train (Hz) control is converted to microseconds which is
the unit used on FPGA level VI to generate the pulse train, the value in microseconds
is sent to the Data acquisition FPGA VI through the Read/Write Control function.
The stop control stops the while loop and sends its value to the Read/Write Control
function on the terminals Stop acquisition, Stop data processing and Stop pulse
train, which are the stop controls inside different while loops running in parallel on
the FPGA level. Also, the Read/Write Control has two output terminals: one of
them is Pulses, which is the value of the counted pulses at the moment, this value is
converted to degrees and shown on the Motor angle (degrees) indicator; and the
other output terminal is the Pulses per rotation, which is shown on the indicator and
it is also used to calculate the angular position. Finally, there is the Close FPGA VI
Reference outside the while loop to close the VI at the FPGA level.

   The Data acquisition FPGA VI is the VI at the FPGA level, and it contains
three while loops running in parallel, the Pulse train while loop (Figure 17.16),

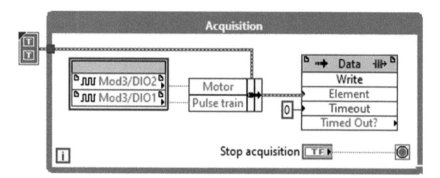

Figure 17.17   Acquisition while loop from the Data acquisition FPGA VI, this
while loop stores the data read from Mod3/DIO2 and Mod3/
DIO1 channels into the Data FIFO

Acquisition while loop (Figure 17.17), and Data processing while loop
(Figure 17.19). The Pulse train while loop generates a squared signal through the
Mod3/DIO0, this signal is generated by inverting a Boolean value each iteration
using a shift register and the Not function. The frequency of this signal is controlled by the Pulse train (uSec) control connected to the Wait function, which
receives the wait time value in microseconds.

The advantage of generating the pulse train on the FPGA level is that the
timing of the pulse generator will not be affected by other operations across the
project since this part of the code is being executed separately. The output on
Mod3/DIO0 is physically connected to Mod3/DIO1, which is read on the
Acquisition while loop as shown in Figure 17.17. The task of the Acquisition while
loop is to bundle the signals from Mod3/DIO2 (Motor rotation signal) and Mod3/
DIO1 (Pulse train signal) into a cluster to be stored into the Data FIFO.

FIFO stands for First In First Out, and it is a data structure that holds the
elements in the order they are received. When the elements are extracted from a
FIFO, the first element extracted is the first element that was stored. The FIFO
used in this project is called Data, and it was created on the project explorer window by right clicking the FPGA Target tab and selecting New>FIFO, this will
open the FIFO properties window on the general category where the Name, type,
requested number of elements, implementation, and control logic can be modified.
For the Data FIFO on this project only the name was modified to Data on the
general category. The other modification is on the data type category where the
data type is changed to a custom control. When the custom control option is
selected, a new window will appear to select the custom control. In this case, the
custom control selected was the Data.ctl control, which is a custom control that
contains a cluster with two Boolean values (Motor and Pulse train), one for the
Motor signal and one for the Pulse train signal. This custom control is also placed
outside the Acquisition while loop to be connected to the Bundle By Name
function, then the cluster is connected to the Element terminal of the Data FIFO,
which is the terminal where the data is stored. Figure 17.18 represents how the data

Motor	0	0	1	1	0	0	0	0	0	0	0	0	0	0	0	0	0	0	0	0	0	0	0	1	1	0
Pulse train	0	0	1	1	0	0	1	1	0	0	1	1	0	0	1	1	0	0	1	1	0	0	1	1	1	0

Figure 17.18   Example of the data stored on the Data FIFO

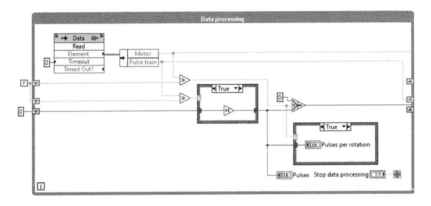

Figure 17.19   Data processing while loop from the Data acquisition FPGA VI, this while loop process the data stored on the Data FIFO counting the number of pulses for each rotation

is stored in the Data FIFO, it is a collection of ones and zeros that represent True and False, respectively, for each signal. As can be seen, this representation shows True values for each pulse. This is because the FIFO stores the value that the signals had each loop iteration, and to count the pulses correctly, only the first True value of each pulse must be counted, the other values for the same pulse have to be ignored.

Figure 17.19 shows the Data processing while loop, this is where the elements on the Data FIFO are extracted to count the pulses of the pulse train for every motor rotation. The Data FIFO inside the while loop is using the read method, when a FIFO is dragged into the block diagram, it appears on the write method, this can be changed by right clicking on it and selecting Method>Read. The Element terminal of the FIFO is connected to the unbundle by name function to extract the signals separately, then each signal is connected to a shift register and to a Grater? Function to count the detect the pulses. See how the x input terminal of the Grater? Function is connected to the actual value of Motor or Pulse train signal, and the y input terminal is connected to the shift register which is the past value of the corresponding signal. This is done to take into account only the first time the signal changes from False to True, which counts as a pulse and ignore the rest of the True values until another change from False to True occurs. Now that the pulse train can be detected, they are counted using the case structure and the Increment function. When a pulse is detected, the value on the Pulses indicator is incremented by one and when no pulses are detected the value stays the same since the tunnels of the case structure on the False case are directly connected. When a Motor signal pulse is detected, the value of the Pulses indicator is also displayed on the Pulses per rotation indicator, and a zero value is sent to the shift register of the Pulses indicator to reset its value on the next while loop iteration.

As you can see, programming in FPGA interface mode can be really useful when used properly. In the example of this project, three while loops are running in parallel to take advantage of the FPGA properties since they are being executed separately on the hardware. But this does not mean that they cannot share information between them, this is done using the FIFO data structure which is used to store the information acquired in one while loop, and then it is extracted in another while loop.

References

[1] Kodosky, J. (2020). LabVIEW. *Proceedings of the ACM on Programming Languages*, 4(HOPL).

[2] Bress, T. J. (2013). *Effective LabVIEW Programming*. Noida: NTS Press.

[3] Essick, J. (2013). *Hands-on Introduction to LabVIEW for Scientists and Engineers*. Oxford: Oxford University Press.

[4] Jennings, R., and Cueva, F. D. L. (2020). *LabVIEW Graphical Programming*. New York, NY: McGraw-Hill Education.

[5] Hubbard, J. R. (1994). *Programming with C++*. New York, NY: McGraw Hill.

[6] Cukic, I. (2018). *Functional Programming in C++*. New York, NY: Simon and Schuster.

[7] Jerome, J. (2010). *Virtual Instrumentation using LabVIEW*. New Delhi: PHI Learning Pvt. Ltd.

[8] Vizcaíno, J. R. L., and Sebastiá, J. P. (2011). *LabView: entorno gráfico de programación*. Barcelona: Marcombo.

[9] Hahn, S., Reineke, J., and Wilhelm, R. (2015). Towards compositionality in execution time analysis: definition and challenges. *ACM SIGBED Review*, 12(1), 28–36.

[10] Ambardar, A. (1995). *Analog and Digital Signal Processing* (p. 700). Boston: PWS.

[11] Scavuzzo, C. M., Lamfri, M. A., Teitelbaum, H., and Lott, F. (1998). A study of the low-frequency inertio-gravity waves observed during the Pyrénées Experiment. *Journal of Geophysical Research: Atmospheres*, 103(D2), 1747–1758.

[12] Liu, H. H. (2011). *Software Performance and Scalability: A Quantitative Approach*. New York, NY: John Wiley & Sons.

[13] Blume, P. A. (2007). *The LabVIEW Style Book* (Vol. 3). Upper Saddle River, NJ: Prentice-Hall.

[14] Harris, C. R., Millman, K. J., Van Der Walt, S. J., et al. (2020). Array programming with NumPy. *Nature*, 585(7825), 357–362.

[15] Aggarwal, C. C. (2018). An introduction to cluster analysis. In *Data Clustering* (pp. 1–28). London: Chapman and Hall/CRC.

[16] Ehsani, B. (2016). *Data Acquisition using LabVIEW*. Birmingham: Packt Publishing Ltd.

[17] Machacek, J., and Drapela, J. (2008). "Control of serial port (RS-232) communication in LabVIEW". In 2008 International Conference-Modern Technique and Technologies (pp. 36–40). IEEE.

[18] McRoberts, M. (2011). *Beginning Arduino*. New York, NY: Apress.

[19] Prakash, A., Gupta, L. R., Singh, R., Gehlot, A., and Beri, R. (2020). *Biomedical Sensors Data Acquisition with LabVIEW*. New Delhi: BPB Publications.

[20] Bitter, R., Mohiuddin, T., and Nawrocki, M. (2017). *LabVIEW^{TM} Advanced Programming Techniques*. London: CRC Press.

[21] Joo, H. (2017). A study on understanding of UI and UX, and understanding of design according to user interface change. *International Journal of Applied Engineering Research*, 12(20), 9931–9935.

[22] Gupta, S., and Jhon, J. (2005). *Virtual Instrumentation Using LabVIEW*. Uttar Pradesh: McGraw Hill India.

[23] Luo, J. (ed.). (2012). *Soft Computing in Information Communication Technology*: Volume 1. Berlin, Heidelberg: Springer Berlin Heidelberg.

[24] Stevens, W. R., Fener, B., and Rudoff, A. M. (1998). *Unix Network Programming, Networking API's: Sockets and XTI*. 3rd edn., vol. 1. Upper Saddle River, NJ: Prentice-Hall.

[25] Dick, S., Riddle, A., and Stein, D. (1997). *Mathematica® in the Laboratory*. Cambridge: Cambridge University Press.

[26] Kalicharan, N. (1994). *C by Example*. Cambridge; New York: Cambridge University Press

[27] Toro, C., Wang, W., and Akhtar, H. (2021). *Implementing Industry 4.0*. New York, NY: Springer International Publishing.

[28] Estrada, L., Vázquez, N., Vaquero, J., de Castro, Á., and Arau, J. (2020). Real-time hardware in the loop simulation methodology for power converters using labview FPGA. *Energies*, 13(2), 373.

[29] Levine, W. S. (2005). Handbook of networked and embedded control systems (No. TK7895. E42. H29 2005.). D. Hristu-Varsakelis (Ed.). Boston: Birkhäuser.

[30] Stratoudakis, T. (2021). *Introduction to LabVIEW FPGA for RF, Radar, and Electronic Warfare Applications*. London: Artech House.

Index